TO THE GOOD LONG LIFE

TO THE GOOD LONG LIFE

WHAT WE KNOW ABOUT GROWING OLD

MORTON PUNER

UNIVERSE•BOOKS
New York

Published in the United States of America in 1974
by Universe Books
381 Park Avenue South, New York, N.Y. 10016
© 1974 by Universe Books

Library of Congress Catalog Card Number: 73-80054
ISBN 0-87663-191-X

Printed in the United States of America

CONTENTS

INTRODUCTION

> It is as though walking down Shaftesbury Avenue as a
> fairly young man, I was suddenly kidnapped, rushed
> into a theater and made to don the gray hair, the wrinkles
> and the other attributes of age, then wheeled on-stage.
> Behind the appearance of age I am the same person, with
> the same thoughts, as when I was younger.
> —J. B. Priestley
> *(at age 79, on being asked—on the
> occasion of publication of his 99th
> work—what it's like being old)*

In word and study, the data are consistent: Most people over 70
are secretly young, disguised in old skin. The aging and the old
don't think of themselves as aging and old and don't see themselves as others do. It may take an aging woman much longer to
make up in the morning and come away with a result that satisfies
her. An aging man may find, among other things, that his clothes
no longer fit as well. Both sexes would rather not have too many
mirrors around. But underneath that aging skin and body, both may
feel as alive as ever, and with a strong need to celebrate life. Unfortunately, custom and tradition say they're not supposed to. When
they do show the feeling, they're likely to get startled, strange, or
outright hostile looks from younger people. So they usually hide it,

retreat behind their skins, and go into the limbo of "being old." With many good years wasted.

It is a tragedy of life in Western society that we force this despondent role upon aging men and women. Growing old starts early—soon after conception, if you look at it biologically—but the growing-up part is considered healthy and a cause for satisfaction and some joy. Definitions of middle age vary (sometimes according to the age of the definer), but from 40 or 50 years on, life is supposed to be all downhill and deterioration—up to the time when you're written off as a fellow-human, no matter how you may feel about yourself, no matter how many years of life may still be ahead.

This comes close to the crux of this book. It can be fairly said that there is no real or unalterable reason why the last half of life should not be as good, fresh, exciting, and productive as the first. No reason at all, *except* for (*a*) prejudice, (*b*) poverty, (*c*) poor health, and (*d*) much ignorance. Ancient and formidable enemies all, these are yielding daily to the onslaughts of reason, the needs of society, progress generally, and that mustering of disciplines called the science of gerontology. The breakthrough point is close or at hand. Some of the old are shyly coming out from behind their skins and showing that they can enjoy a good time and Lord-knows-what-else. And each child born today has an infinitely better chance of living a longer and more fulfilled life than did his grandparents.

Almost the same may be said for today's young adults under 30, but they, having been born earlier, are not natural heirs to quite as much improvement and progress; they must work somewhat harder for the same result. In a sense, this book is particularly suited to their needs, although, at this moment in their lives, they may not agree: A person under 30 just doesn't think too much about growing old. The concern usually starts later, at whatever age he or she starts worrying seriously about losing the bloom or powers of youth, and its desirability. It gets much more urgent with first intimations of mortality—graying or falling hair, becoming short-winded or arthritic, most of all suffering a heart attack. These are coupled with a sense of outrage and injustice when the idea sinks in: Inevitably you must wither and die.

This book tries to explain many of the things we have recently discovered about growing old. The reader should find its insights personally helpful, but no effort is made—or could be made in this context—to solve all specific problems. (There are a number of self-help books, usually on narrower fields of aging, on the market.) In saying that the book is meant for anyone, of any age, who finds it interesting and useful, I am trying to broaden the book's appeal—but attempting to avoid a common trap. One problem afflicting the aging is our tendency to be "age-oriented"—to think of people solely in terms of their chronological ages and to classify, discriminate, and sometimes destroy accordingly. (Any man or woman over 45 who has recently looked for a job will instantly understand.) The truly old, whatever their years, may read it with profit because it will give them confirmation and reassurance about things they know or have felt or wondered about. But it is primarily for people between the ages of 30 and 60, for the most natural of reasons: those are the years when we are interested in aging and can still do a great deal about it.

There is some emphasis here on psychological and social aspects of aging, but a highly clinical example from the third type— physical aging—will make the point. It comes from the chapter on "Nursing Care" in *The Care of the Geriatric Patient,* edited by E. V. Cowdry and Franz U. Steinberg:

"Bladder sphincter tone can be strengthened by teaching the individual to deliberately interrupt and restart the urinary stream. This exercise should begin at the first sign of decreasing control, whether this occurs when the person is 30 years of age or 60 years of age."

Sixty, 30—or at any age, of course. Growing old is a lifelong process, and the disabilities of age—physical, psychological, or social—are products of all that has come before. So are the advantages. A man cannot, say, step down from his job at 65 and assume that his hard-won leisure years will automatically be rich and enjoyable—not unless he has prepared for them, as he earlier trained for his job, as he earlier trained to become husband and father. We may do the proper exercise to improve "sphincter tone"; the problem is graphic and tangible enough. It is all the other problems of aging—the nonphysical ones—that we ignore until it is, in the most literal sense, too late. Consistently, we are least prepared for growing old, for being old, than we are for any other phase or activity of life.

A skillful scientist can make a fair prediction, on the birth of a baby, of how long that baby will live by examining it carefully, analyzing cells and tissue, finding out about its heredity, the longevity of its parents and other ancestors, their circumstances and environment. (He can do even better if he makes use of a computer.) By the time the child is 15, its life span can be predicted with far greater accuracy; now the scientist will know how it is developing physiologically and emotionally, how it will respond to stress and wear of time, even how susceptible it will be to the degenerative diseases that come with age. Almost all the predictors are in the young; finding one's way to the good long life is a matter of encouraging the tendencies, in all areas of life, that will assure it.

With full appreciation that the research findings reported here are not my own, I can also say that this is, in its way, a personal book. I am now 52 years old—middle aged by anyone's definition —and along with most of my contemporaries I don't quite know how it happened, where all the years went. But working on this book has reassured me: I can't complain. I'm living at a good time, with knowledge and opportunities that never before existed. By the charts, I've got about 22 years ahead of me—a longer life expectancy than my father or his father had. With everything I've learned while researching this book, I think I have a better chance of making those years good ones. I hope the reader will find the same pleasure in discovery.

1 THE PROMISE OF AGE

We are in the midst of one of the quietest, least-heralded, most fruitful revolutions in history: the conquest of age as we have known and feared it. All the evidence is that we—science and modern society—are on the verge of massive changes in our views of the old and in the state of being old itself. Spurred on by the discoveries and recommendations of the relatively youthful science of gerontology, man is learning enough and becoming concerned enough, for the most selfish of reasons, to improve the quality of life after 60, 70, and beyond. We are fast coming close to the promise inherent in the idea of *"la troisième age"* (the third age), the French term for the later years, which suggests a renewal of life, or, at least, a new plateau of life—which is as it should be when one thinks of the pleasures deferred in the striving years of youth and middle age.

Growing old, being old, have long been among the most dismal experiences known to mankind. We have often extolled the old in words and damned them in deeds, shunned them and cast them aside to die. It is death that haunts and frightens us. The aging and the old have appeared to be its visible symbols and our enemies, so we have shrouded age in myths and stereotypes to hide our fears and prejudices.

Overall we have imposed the idea that youth is beautiful and that age is ugly and tragic. To take one stereotype about growing old, the idea seems to be accepted that life must be dull in old age, that senses are blunted, that colors and tastes and enjoyment of life are

11

no longer keen. (This is reinforced by perfectly fine writers who accept the idea uncritically: "The young voice pulled him up and reminded him of the bright, sharp world of his teens in which all the colors were vivid and pain was always acute." Another writer, referring to a child's perceptions: "He sees the intensity of colors and textures in a world still new.") The idea is so pervasive that even the old—particularly the old—accept it.

Age and sex are the two primary characteristics by which we identify people. When we first meet someone, we normally think of that person as "a young woman," "an old man," "a boy," and then go on to fill in with other details—looks, dress, mannerisms, social and economic class. We are labeled and judged by our age and, if we appear to be old or growing old, quickly dispatched beyond some personal pale.

The negative view of old age runs all through the life cycle. Children do little more than tolerate old people outside their family unit. (They may be indifferent to, or, if pressed, show their exasperation with grandparents, too.) Young adults are immersed in newly discovered drives and opportunities and, if they think about the old at all, may regard them as being vaguely responsible for whatever is wrong in their lives.

Growing old begins to concern men and women in their thirties, as they approach middle age—or even earlier, if they have to contend with problems of aging parents. Middle age, perhaps the worst of times, is often the time of greatest stress and anxiety. It is then that there is the rising sense of frustration, fear, and defeat, the awareness that fame and fortune will never come, that the best of life is past. Middle-aged people have fearsome double burdens—paying for the support of both younger and older generations, juggling the values of one against the other, feeling ambivalent or guilty toward both—all the while that the prospect of their own old age stares them in the face.

It is in middle age that the fear of death is often strongest, that we play a numbers game addressed to the question, "How much more time do I have?" A middle-aged man notices the ages given in newspaper obituaries, recalls his father's age at death as an omen for himself, reads each new report about life expectancy anywhere in the world and calculates it in terms of himself.* (It may be easier for the middle-aged woman, who, freed from the tensions and striving of her maiden years, often blooms with new self-confidence, becomes a matriarch, and acts as her husband's "body monitor"—concerned about his health, heart, diet, and waning energy.) Growing old becomes acutely felt and sometimes obsessive to people in their middle years with each new, shattering sign of advancing age, apparent or real. After that, staying alive, living as well and as comfortably as possible, is the sum of life.

It is true that there is sensory loss as one grows older, often considerable and affecting most or all of the physical senses. But anyone who has ever seen a *troisième age* group of French tourists on their first Mediterranean cruise, or Golden Wedding couples on an outing in Wisconsin, or their counterparts in England, Scandinavia, or anywhere in the world, will know how keenly the old can enjoy life. Bifocals, hearing aids, canes and all—when away from the drabness of "normal" old age, they will be as excited and lively, and as noisy, as teen-agers on a spree. Always there are the adjustments and compensations. An older pleasure seeker makes up for sensory loss by greater emotional response, his appreciation heightened by maturity and the fact that he knows his time is short and that there is so much beauty and novelty still to be shared.

This was clearly expressed by psychologist-philosopher Abraham H. Maslow, who, in his early sixties, suffered a serious heart attack but survived long enough to express his joy at being alive although aging and ill. He said, in a tape sent to his publisher just before his death in 1970:

"My attitude toward life has changed. The word I use for it now is the post-mortem life. I could just as easily have died so that my

---

* And probably falls into the trap of adding up hardwrought facts, taken from different contexts, to make senseless points. *Fact:* The life expectancy at birth for a Swedish female is 76.42 years, the highest for either sex in any country. *Fact:* Professional workers tend to live longer than manual workers; so do their wives. *Fact:* Physical activity, weight control, and avoiding cigarettes contribute to longevity. *Conclusion:* A lawyer's wife in Stockholm, who exercises and diets regularly and never smokes, should live much longer than an Albanian female (life expectancy at birth 67.0) who has let herself go, is sedentary, chain-smokes, and is married to a tractor driver. On the other hand, she might not.

living constitutes a kind of an extra, a bonus. It's all gravy. Therefore, I might just as well live as if I had already died. One very
important aspect of the post-mortem life is that everything gets
doubly precious, gets piercingly important. You get stabbed by
things, by flowers, and by babies, and by beautiful things—just
the very act of living, of walking and breathing and eating and
having friends and chatting. Everything seems to look more beautiful rather than less, and one gets the much-intensified sense of
miracles."

The wonder of "the very act of living" is not at all rare among
the aging and the old; they can feel pain and pleasure as well as the
young. Many, in fact, do not think of themselves as being old. "A
man is as old as he feels," and if he feels unwell one day he keeps
hoping that he'll be in shape again the next. A 70-year-old man will
refer to a 75-year-old next door as an "old man" but he would be
stunned to hear himself put in the same category.

A Duke University study of "Factors in Age Awareness" shows
clearly how people put off identifying themselves with the old.
Some 135 men and women—all over 60—were asked: "Do you feel
that you are now . . . (a young adult person), (a middle-aged
person), (an elderly person), (an old person), (an aged person)?"
More than half of the 60-to-64 and 65-to-69 age groups felt they
were young or middle aged. So did almost a quarter of those
over 75. Both men and women followed the same pattern in deciding
where they belonged—or, more to the point, where they didn't
belong—in the category of the old.

The study found that chronological age, race, and feeling of
health are "significantly related" to a person's awareness of his age.*
There are other more purely psychological reasons why people do
not—or do not want to—think of themselves as old. If they grew
up and grew old sharing the bleak, negative view of old age, they
cannot now believe that horror has descended upon them. But at all
points in life, few people think of themselves in the same age terms

---

* Blacks tended to think of themselves as being older than did whites
of the same age. The authors attribute this to three "basic threats":
They have lower longevity and a greater feeling of financial insecurity
generally and, in this study, older black subjects were actually in poorer
health than white ones.

as others see them. A girl of 18 may think that she has matured greatly and become wonderfully sophisticated since she was 16, and is now a woman of the world. A boy of 18 may feel that he has now accrued enough wisdom and judgment to dispute all authority, particularly that of his parents. For an adult to tell them, "You're still in your teens and have much to learn," would be considered unfair and irrelevant. Few 19-year-olds think they are still teen-agers no matter how young they appear to the 40- or 50-year-old.

The process soon goes into reverse as we get older and keeping young—not maturity—becomes the goal. A woman who gives her age as 29 or 39 because she can't face the idea of slipping over into the next decade is not exactly lying; she may really believe that she is no older than she says and that it's just a quirk of the calendar that makes her appear to be 32 or 45 on her driver's license. Age awareness, and the cruelty of seeing ourselves as others see us, strikes everyone at one time or another. It was a decade ago that a doctor, after examining me, concluded with the words: "You're in pretty good shape for your age," which was then 42. For my age! The doctor was looking at me and judging me as a man in his forties— one of *them*. That was a decade ago and, obviously, the memory lingers.

We don't categorize ourselves by age for another simple reason: each individual life is a continual process, and we age second-by-second, not decade-by-decade or by brackets—young, early middle age, late middle age, etc. This idea is expressed by Wilma T. Donahue, retired co-director of the institute of gerontology of University of Michigan-Wayne State University. (Since her "retirement," Dr. Donahue has served as technical coordinator of the 1971 White House Conference on Aging and as a director of the International Center of Social Gerontology.) She recently talked about the experience of seeing people again whom she had not seen since her youth:

"I have never thought of them as older people and suddenly I see them as old and I gather a sense of their being different. . . . To them, just like I am to myself, there is a consistent personality. I don't recognize that I was 20, 30, 40, 50, 60 and so forth. I just seem to be a consistent personality that's lived a whole life. I realize I look the same to them as they look to me. As far as my feeling is concerned, I don't have that sense. I have the same sense of being a whole person with spirit and interests that are consistent with my life."

The self concept of the old—as not being old—is not shared by the rest of our age-oriented society. We tend to see them plain, every wrinkle and artifice exposed. Our comments—"You're 75? I never would have guessed it"—are usually gentle lies. We really mean: "If I'm 40 you must be 80—and I never want to look like you." Our dislike of old age is strong; we show it, at best, by being heedless. For example, although I have spent more than two decades working in the field and learning about the ways of prejudice and the evils of discrimination against racial, religious, and ethnic minority groups, not until recently did I give the old a thought, except to share in every stereotype about them.

To adapt a famous line, "Imprisoned in every old man a young man is wildly signaling to be let out." Given the opportunity he does—and then the man in his third age is accused of reverting to second childhood, of not "acting his age." I was on a cruise boat with *troisième age* Frenchmen and women; I joined in the general feeling of condescension, tinged with disgust, toward those rickety old people, dancing, drinking, singing, and generally living it up. "Old fools" was the attitude, even when an old man explained, "You don't understand. There never was a *belle époque* for us. Our youths were poor and joyless. These, now, are our good old days."

In researching this book, I came across an article about a 90-year-old woman, daughter of a missionary, who has taken up the guitar in New York and now goes around, professionally, playing and singing her own songs: "How to charm the bald" and "No old age for me." One paragraph said: "In spite of her 90 years she is agile and trim. Her cheeks are firm as a result of facial exercise, her pink wool dress falls modishly to her knees, while her blue eyes sparkle behind contact lenses." It was the contact lenses, most of all, that set me to hooting.

I know a 60-year-old Englishwoman who has just married a 45-year-old man. My reaction was: He needs a mother; God only knows what she needs. I would not have given the matter a thought had the woman been 45, the man 60.

I would not have given *any* of these people a second thought had they been young. In each case, my interest and reaction were based on prejudice. My standards of taste and convention were being abused, as though my standards were all that mattered. These older people were trying to fill out their lives. Each was doing the best he or she could to give some freshness and novelty to life, actively fighting disengagement—the living death—we expect of the old.

The story of growing old, as we read about it or relate it to ourselves, appears to be a grim one: the plot is strewn with horrors and indignities and the dénouement is always death. Maurice Chevalier is supposed to have said, when asked on his 80th birthday how it felt to be old, "Great—when you consider the alternative." That, too often, seems to be about the best of it. A major effort of this book, however, is to show that it is *not,* that in our society old age is becoming a better and happier stage of life. In the past there was tragic irony to the words of Robert Browning in his "Rabbi Ben Ezra": "Grow old along with me! / The best is yet to be, / The last of life, for which the first was made . . ." In our time, or certainly our children's, the quality of the last half of life will be so vastly improved that the irony will be lost.

Not only the old avoid thinking of themselves as old; the middle aged don't think of themselves as middle aged, either. Even the definitions of age groups wander considerably; the onset of middle age may be put as low as 30 or as high as 45, its close at 59 or 64, depending on the purpose of the statistician defining it.* This book follows the general and somewhat arbitrary practice of declaring that old age starts at 65, mainly because that is the customary age for retirement for men in the United States, Great Britain, both Germanies, France, Belgium, Holland, Luxembourg, Spain, Portugal, Finland, Israel, Poland, Australia, and many other countries. (There

* A better system of classification was suggested at a World Health Organization conference held in Kiev in 1963: people 45 to 59 to be called middle aged; 60 to 74, elderly, and 75 and over, aged. This system would focus attention on the 60-to-74-year-old group—"the young-old" —many of whom have been retired compulsorily, are very fit, but, with all their skills and understanding, are somehow debarred from active roles in society.

are variations within this, constant pressures to lower the ages, and women usually retire from three to five years earlier.) In the USSR, Czechoslovakia, Hungary, Italy, and Japan, however, retirement comes for men at 60 and for women at 55, also with variations. Greece has it as 62; Sweden and Denmark at 67. Canada, Ireland, and Norway have the highest retirement age, 70; Yugoslavia the lowest, 55 for men and 50 for women.

There is nothing scientific about using retirement age to mark the beginning of old age; it may have little to do with a person's physical or mental condition. But retirement is one of the two momentous (and often cataclysmic) events of later life. (The other is the death of a mate.) It affects a man's sense of worth, alters his role in life, and changes his standard of living, usually for the worse. It clearly signals to him the advent of old age, or the type of life he will be leading until the end of his days. In a sense, retirement—as a type of disengagement—makes a man old; unless he is wonderfully sustained with built-in resources and serious interests, he tends to think of himself as being considerably older the day after retirement than he was the day before.

Gerontologists concerned with problems of industry and labor often call for a practical and consistent definition of middle and old age. "Aging" describes a process, so there is no point, they say, in referring to "an aging worker" in statistics or legislation. "Aged" implies very old; "elderly" has no precise meaning at all; the euphemisms of "senior citizen" or "mature adult" have even less precision. Since 65 is still a standard age for retirement, they suggest that it be incorporated in the definitions—age 45–64 to be called "middle age"; 65 and over to be called "old"; if middle aged and attached to the labor force, "middle-aged worker"; if 65 or over and retired, "retiree"; if 65 and still working, "old worker."

Scientists, of course, look at growing old in a different way. Different species of life are born, programmed, as it were, with the capacity to live different life spans. The maximum known life span for a giant tortoise in captivity, for example, is 177 years, for an elephant 57 years, for an ox 30 years, for a cat 21 years, for a gray squirrel 15 years. Exceptional life spans among humans are difficult to verify; the highest figure is about 150. These are *maximum* life spans, which, in mammals, are usually about twice the average life span or age of adult death. Within each species, heredity seems to be most important in determining the length of life. Some studies suggest that a mother's genes are more important than a father's in contributing to the length of life. No matter which, a gerontologist's cliché is "To live a long time, pick your parents carefully." Another cliché is "Nobody dies of old age"—we die of diseases or organic weakness due to progressive loss of vital cells before we reach our maximum potential life span. A few daring scientists predict that in the next few decades we may be able to reset a cell's genetic program to prolong life, perhaps double the average span, by overcoming organic failures. It is an idea that keeps breaking into Sunday supplements, to the annoyance of other gerontologists who are more concerned with prolonging the good years with greater quality, not with the maximum span itself.

James E. Birren, head of the University of Southern California's gerontology center, breaks down age and aging into three types:

• *Biological age* is closely related to chronological age, age since birth, but is based on different concepts and sets of measurements. It refers to how far along in his own potential life span a man has traveled. A scientist studying biological aging will look into the processes that limit the life spans of species and individuals and try to find why they have determinate lengths of life.

• *Psychological age* is determined by a man's behavior—as it develops over the life span—relative to the people about him. A study of psychological aging includes the study of "capacities, perception, learning, problem solving, feeling, emotions, skills, and social behavior as they emerge and change."

• *Social age* is set by a study of a man's acquired social habits and status, and how he fills the social roles and expectancies for a person of his cultural or social group.

How these three concepts of age overlap and interact sets the real life span of each individual. There are a tempo and rhythm to the life cycle—growing up, working, establishing a family, fitting into a community, worrying about status, aging, sex, death, the future of one's children, striving, striving, and finally disengaging. If a man feels that the years have taken a toll of his physical energy (as a result of biological aging) and he can no longer handle old problems or adjust to new ones (psychological aging) and withdraws from his usual roles in society (social aging), he is old, whether he is 65, 75, 85—or only 50.

What is happening now promises just the opposite effect.* In each of the three types of aging we are making progress, of a type and at a speed without precedent, that permits gerontologists to have this optimistic view: The likelihood is that in the next generation the man of 65, 75, or even older will feel and behave as young as the 50-year-old of the past generation.

This is one premise of *To the Good Long Life.* Others are that aging is inevitable but to be neither feared nor shunned; that all life is good but can be better. If there is some emphasis on the non-biological aspects of aging in this book, it is because the subject is often ignored but of critical importance. *Joie de vivre* and long life go together; a person's attitude toward being alive is actually one good predictor of his longevity.

There is, if one can transcend the ache of it, some humor in growing old. I am indebted to psychologist Dennis B. Bromley of the University of Liverpool for confirming some of my own observations: You suddenly realize you are growing old, the first time a young woman gets up to offer you a seat on the bus; or the first time a girl you had your eye on comes to you for fatherly, plain fatherly, advice about her boy friend. There are innumerable such signs: if you are a man, the first time you realize you're much too old to have an older woman as a mistress; the first time you bump into another car and your adversary calls you "Pop" instead of cursing; the first time you go to a reunion of your fellow-veterans

---

* The promise now holds true only for Western industrial society. We know the physiological, psychological, and social predictors of longevity. But the nomadic Ik of Uganda live their good years between the ages of 15 and 19 and are "well on their way out" by 25. Life expectancy at birth for the African population of Chad is 29 for a man, 35 for a woman. In South Africa, for the white population, it is 65 and 72; for the "Asiatic" population, 58 and 59; for the "coloured" population, 49 and 54. (Latest figures and terminology from the 1970 *U.N. Demographic Yearbook.*) In Syria, it is under 53 for both sexes; in adjacent Israel—with about the same climate but a different, more "western" culture—it is almost 70 for men and 73 for women. These discrepant figures tell much about man and his diverse ways, but there is little the gerontologist can do about them.

of World War II and feel that surely you're at the wrong meeting—
they must all be survivors of World War I. Women undoubtedly have
their share and more: the first time a truck driver doesn't whistle;
the first time that same young woman gives you a seat on the bus; the
first time you're called "Mom" and you don't have a single one of
your children in tow—an endless list, quite independent of gray
hairs, wrinkles, freckles on the forearms, and your strange appearance in photographs and mirrors.

The injunction, "Act your age," is meaningless. If followed literally, it would mean that each individual must fit into set patterns of
psychological aging, often joyless and destructive. It would mean
dressing and behaving somberly, becoming an accomplice in "disengagement," in assuming proper appearance, nothing more. "Be
yourself" is a considerably more worthwhile cliché, even when it
means that behavior will be considered tasteless or unbecoming to
one's years. George Santayana was offering life-giving advice to all
generations when he said: "The young man who has not wept is a
savage, and the old man who will not laugh is a fool."

2 THE WORLD GROWS OLDER

Growing old is no longer a solitary matter. True, many of the aging are lonely. But they are less and less alone in intimate concern with their destinies. Growing old has achieved the status of a major international and public issue, and governments of industrialized countries, if not trembling over it, are at least busy talking about the problem. It is not a matter of compassion for "senior citizens," "members of the third age," or whatever the local euphemism.* It is hard reality based upon demography and, increasingly, good politics. Until recently, the old were relatively negligible in numbers among the population of "developed" countries—as a group, they were remnants of the past, out of the picture. What accounts for the great new wave of interest on the part of governments, business and industry, science and medicine, and people generally, is that the aging and the old are no longer "they" but—more so each passing year—"we."

In 1940, 14.8% of the U.S. population was 55 or older; by 1970, 19%. In the 1960s, the number of children under the age of 5 *decreased* by 11%, while persons 64 or older increased by 17%—a situation paralleled in much of the Western world. And a new breed of elder is arising.

Gerontologist Ethel Shanas says, "I think we now have a population of older people who are better educated than they were 25

* Perhaps only the British persist in calling them "old people."

22

years ago, more sophisticated, and these people [will] have to organize . . . I was one of those who do not want to see a hardening of the lines between age groups but I feel that older people have to do it in self-defense." Another gerontologist, Bernice L. Neugarten, says, "I don't think old people are going to be as passive a group in society as they have been in the past." Marguerite L. Buser, an 81-year-old retired British schoolteacher, writes eloquently of the need for an "old age liberation movement," a movement made up of the old, for "one cannot be familiar with the terrain of a country which one has not yet visited." And 69-year-old Margaret Kuhn of Philadelphia, in organizing a movement of "Gray Panthers" —named after its members' hair color—declares, "Our oppressive, paternalistic society wants to keep the elderly out of the way, playing bingo and shuffleboard . . . We are not mellowed, sweet old people. We're outraged, but we're doing something about it."

These statements of the 1970s are addressed to an interim problem. Bingo and shuffleboard aside, many of today's old do suffer from indignities, deprivation, and inequities beyond imagination. Six out of every ten aged American women living alone have incomes below the poverty level. The bustling, enlightened city of Sheffield is, also, in the words of its spokesman for the British Medical Association, a "geriatric slum." One reason why we see so few old people in the streets of large cities is because they dare not leave their homes—they are immobilized by the pace, crowds, perils, and lack of transportation facilities suitable for the slow-moving. But two other facts are paramount: In a variety of ways, the old —men and women of 65 or more—are far better off than at any time in history. And, in the future, the bumper crop of the old will, if not inherit the earth, populate it in great numbers with considerable power and much greater well-being.

The "earth" in this case is limited to Western industrial society, which is where, proportionately, the old are. The rest of the world still has "young" populations, with indexes of aging at about the level of Europe's a century ago. The aging of the populations of Western society represents a demographic revolution; it is due to the unprecedented declines in both mortality and fertility in the 19th and 20th centuries. Demographers do not agree about why the process has taken place—whether death rates declined before birth rates, or whether the Industrial Revolution and rising standards of living initiated the changes, but the trends will clearly alter the future.

At the present rate, the earth's population will grow fourfold during the next century, the World Bank reported in 1972. Growth will be greatest in the developing countries, which will have 87% of the world's population in a hundred years. (They now have 56%.) A recent United Nations study confirms that the annual rate of growth will continue to be lower, by far, in the developed nations. The rate is now estimated at 2% globally, but it is, for example, only 0.6% in Scandinavia, four to six times less than in Asia, North Africa, or Central America.

For life expectancy, the situation is just about reversed. People living in countries with the smallest population growth can expect to live longest. A man in Denmark, Norway, or Sweden has a life expectancy at birth of 70 or more, a Moroccan 50, a Guatemalan 48, an Indian under 43.

The U.S. population has been aging during the entire period for which statistics have been recorded. The median age for white males was 15.9 in 1790, 23.8 by 1900, and 30.4 by 1970. More to the point, in the century from 1850 to 1950 the percentage of persons 65 or older rose from 2.6 to 8.7 (while the proportion of persons between 45 and 64 doubled); in 1960, it was 9.2; in 1970, 10—about three times the percentages of people over 65 in India or Brazil.

The trend will accelerate; the elders will account for a growing percentage of the U.S. population in the years to come. Right now, and until 1975, the fastest growing segment of the population is the 65-to-69 year-old group. From 1976 to 1985, it will be the 70-to-74 year-old group, growing at the rate of more than 20%, barely beating out their seniors—those 75 and over—who will increase at the astonishing rate of 18%.

It is the same in Western Europe. Between 1930 and 1962, the proportion of people over 65 had risen from 7.6% to 10.6% in the "inner six" Common Market countries; and from 7.8% to 11.5% in a bloc formed by Great Britain, Ireland, and Scandinavia. In France, in October 1969, more than 12% of the population was over 65, about 60% of them women. The projection is that France's over-65 population will rise to 14% by 1980.

Always, the reason is the same. It is not that life spans have markedly increased; a middle-aged adult today can expect to live barely a few more years than did an adult 200 years ago.* It is the sharp lowering of infant mortality and the lowering of the birth rate in developed countries that make the difference. The "aging" of the population does not mean that old people are living much longer—not yet, in any event. It means that the proportion of elderly people is now much greater than ever before, that in the total populations of the developed world, the young are being replaced in numbers by the old.

Among other things, this suggests that the world of tomorrow,

---

* In 1900, a 50-year-old American man could expect to live another 20.7 years; in 1950, another 22.6 years. Since then, life expectancy at 50 has barely increased, hovering at about 23 years in the 1950s and 1960s. (American women do somewhat better. For the more recent period, at age 50, their life expectancy increased by more than two years.) In Denmark, Norway, and the Netherlands, life expectancy for men of 65 actually decreased in the years between 1951 and 1965 and was almost stationary in the rest of the developed countries. The fact that life expectancy for adults has barely increased in recent years seems surprising in view of the great strides made in medicine and in standards of living. The facts are that most gains relate to life expectancy *at birth* and they were made between 1900 and 1950 as medical advances defeated the great killers of the young. (Before then, 20% to 40% of all infants born alive died during their first year, a figure since reduced by at least 90%.) Since then, antibiotics have helped most age groups, but the same dramatic progress has not been made to date against principal killers of men and women over 65 in the United States, Canada, and Western Europe—arteriosclerotic and degenerative heart disease, cerebral vascular diseases and malignant neoplasms. And a high standard of living is not, in itself, an assurance of longevity; it depends how "high" is defined. In the United States, where personal incomes and production are highest—men live an average of 67.1 years, women 74.6 years, ranking only 24th for men and 9th for women among the nations of the world. The pace of American life, and calories and cholesterol, are among the culprits, perhaps, and the death rate for men from cardiovascular disease is 50% higher in the United States than in Western Europe. It is true that American nonwhites, with lower incomes and lower standards of living, have a much lower expectation of life at birth—only 60.5 years. But this is due in large part to infant mortality—almost double that of whites—and, with all the dents of life on body and soul, a nonwhite reaching the age of 74 has surpassed the white on a life expectancy table and can expect to live longer than he.

despite the common assumption, will not be dominated by young people, least of all in government. There has, in fact, always been a tendency toward gerontocracy—rule by elders—in both primitive and highly developed societies. In the vast majority of tribal societies, older men serve as chieftains, or in judicial roles, or as counselors. In developed countries, the skills and conditions going into governmental leadership are particularly complicated ones, requiring long years to develop. Not only do the skills mature slowly; it takes a long time to become familiar to and trusted by a constituency. While gerontocracy as a form of government seldom exists, there is a disproportionate number of older men in higher levels of government. The peak years of service for prime ministers of England and presidents of the United States and the republics of Europe are between 55 and 59 years, not old but in the higher range of middle age.

We tend to believe otherwise, that governments are increasingly in the hands of younger men.* This is because age is so relative a matter: when we are young, government officials all seem so old. As we get older, they become our contemporaries—hence seemingly younger. (There are exceptions, as in the case of John F. Kennedy, who became president of the United States at 43, and among some of the newer African nations.) Most likely we *want* to believe that leadership is in the hands of the young, on the stereotyped grounds that young is "fresh and pure," old is "stale and evil." The stereotypes are meaningless, however: The noblest moments of history have been presided over by the middle aged and elderly (as have many of its worst moments, too). To quote Ramsey Clark, former U.S. Attorney General, "I wouldn't trade fifteen Alexanders at 21 or William Pitts at 23 for one Oliver Wendell Holmes at 80, in terms of human values." Or in terms of understanding the processes of law and government, and the minds and needs of men.

Aging or old themselves, political leaders paid little attention

* The average age of U.S. senators on first taking office was 45 years in the period 1789 to 1860, the earlier years of the republic. From 1931 to 1966, the average age was 52, seven years older, with much of the real power, held by reason of seniority, in the hands of men considerably older.

in times past to people over 65 or in retirement. They didn't have to: there were far fewer people over 65 and those who were didn't retire.

Two hundred years ago a man worked until he was physically decrepit or, in rare cases, had amassed enough money or goods to live without working. Pension plans for old-age retirement or disability have been in force in one form or another in a few countries for barely a hundred years. Germany, under Bismarck, was the first country to introduce a modern form of social security in 1883—an accident insurance program—with old-age pensions following a few years later. Austria and Hungary soon followed and, in 1908, Great Britain set up a system of noncontributory pensions to needy persons who had reached 70. The United States was still slower. Its agricultural economy set the general pattern of life in the 19th century, there was little unemployment, and family groups assumed responsibility for their members in need. The work ethic was so strong that indigence and need were associated with laziness and incompetence. Not until Franklin Roosevelt's New Deal and the Social Security Act of 1935 was there a national program of assistance to the needy aged. Today, all Western nations have a variety of pension, social security, and health benefits available to their old. They are sometimes inadequate —perhaps more inadequate relative to general income in the United States than elsewhere—but the economic position of the old cannot be compared to what it was in past centuries.

The change is clearly visible to people living today who knew the condition of the old in their youths. Baroness Stocks—better known as the British broadcaster, author, and educator Mary Stocks—was born in 1892 and remembers her childhood visits with an aunt, a Poor Law Guardian, to the old people's quarters in the St. Pancras workhouse. "They were there because they were destitute. There were more old women than old men because women, being the tougher sex, die less readily and live longer. At night they slept in dormitories; by day they sat round tables in enormous wards, killing time as best they could," she writes. "For the old men, smoking was some comfort but not one easily come by. For the old women there was knitting or sewing. . . .

"Even then, in the early years of Edward VII's reign, inquiries

were being made into how many of these old people could be
rescued from the dreary routine of these workhouse wards and
enabled to live independently, if a modicum of cash could be
made available. . . . Now today much has changed and all for the
better . . . old people are no longer herded into a workhouse by
sheer destitution and there are no more workhouses to herd them
into. If they can look after themselves, a pension helped out by
supplementary benefits will enable them to do so. In fact, things
are not nearly so bad as they were . . ."

This, and far worse, has been reality for *most* of the old throughout history. Our nominal attitudes of respect and honor for the
old have been set by the Bible, and particularly by the Old Testa-
ment. Our literature gives the impression that the old have
profited by these attitudes through the centuries. They may have,
within stable and prosperous family units, but for most people
throughout history—other than a small élite—life has been unstable
and beset by grinding poverty and toil. Ulysses, in the *Odyssey,*
tells his father: "Warm baths, good food, soft sleep, generous wine.
These are the rights of age and should be thine." It is problematic
how many old people have been able to avail themselves of those
rights, in Homer's time or up to the recent past. George Cheyne,
in *An Essay of Health and Long Life,* first published in London
in 1742, gives nicely contradictory advice, quoting such lines as
"You must eat less, or use more Exercise, or take Physick, or
be sick," and summarizing: "Nothing conduces more to *Health* and
Long Life than *Abstinence* and *plain* Food with due *Labour.*" The
advice may be applicable to masses of people—perhaps most people—
in Western society today. But in his time, Dr. Cheyne was primarily
speaking to his social and economic peers and to himself. (He
weighed 448 pounds at the age of 51, reduced drastically, and
lived to 72.) In the 17th and 18th centuries, a little more food
and a little less *Labour* might have strengthened the bodies and
lengthened the lives of a majority of ordinary people.

Higher income, shorter hours of work, better nutrition and
medical care, and access to the bounties of life are the lot of most
people in the Western world today. In a variety of ways, the old
share in these advances as society generally, not just the family
unit, increasingly accepts responsibility for their welfare. To say

this is not to deny that the old have grave problems and frustrations today, or even to say that they are being treated fairly—they are often victims of prejudice, pure and simple. But many of their problems are, indeed, the problems of progress. Retirement age is getting lower all the time: In 1900, a man at 65 had 6.5 years of work ahead of him and 2.8 years of retirement. Today at 65, a retiring male has no more years of work and a life expectancy of ten to fifteen years to fill up somehow. The average man a century ago had to work until he dropped; today he has a new set of problems: how to get along on a reduced income, how to fill his time creatively (or at least productively), how to maintain the self-esteem and self-concept he had as a producer and wage-earner—and how to stay out of his wife's way. A Duke University study showed that a good two-thirds of all early retiring men had wives who dreaded it. Overall, 55% of wives are sorry when their husbands retire. It is not just the lowered income; for a wife, too, it means a change of habits, a sign of age, and more work with her husband around the house all day.

Mandatory retirement at a set age is now one of the hottest issues among those with professional concern. Futurologist Herman Kahn says right off: "Certain reforms would seem to be obvious —first and foremost people should be allowed to work without penalty." And then, in explanation of the value of people normally considered too old to work, he says: "The most successful economy in the world is the Japanese, run by people in their late sixties and early seventies. You're just not anybody in Japan until you are in your mid-fifties; mid-forties is young." Dr. Nathan W. Shock, chief of the Gerontology Center of the National Institute of Child Health and Human Development in Baltimore, says that Americans "have not yet really adopted the importance of voluntary work [for people in retirement]. With the male we've still got a culture that says, basically, unless you get a paycheck, what you're doing isn't worth doing." The Soviet Institute of Gerontology reports that "man could live longer if he were allowed to work longer." The International Center of Social Gerontology, based in Paris, devoted an entire conference, held in Dubrovnik in 1972, to the subject of "Leisure and the Third Age." One report noted that 20% to

30% of all retired people live alone, making essential their participation "in clubs, and organized vacations and travel." Another said that 56% of retired Americans pass at least two hours a day doing absolutely nothing and that gratifying and productive use of leisure time comes close to being the single greatest problem for the old in industrial countries.

We've come a long way.

Against this setting, the passivity of the elders may be a thing of the past. Their role of dependence for favors on family and friends is pretty much behind them and, as Gray Panther Lady Margaret Kuhn says, shuffleboard is not enough. It is likely that today's middle aged will see the day when the position and strength of the old will change society as we have known it. Based upon current trends and the realities of gerontology, this will come about by a confluence of forces:

• Their rise in population in proportion to the rest of society, combined with free time and their will and need to do something with it.

• The sustained improvement of their condition, with more passion and freedom to take action on their own behalf. More and more they are being freed of the indigence of the old, and laying claim to a role in consumer societies. As they meet in their organizations, clubs, "senior citizen centers"—all recent developments—they are gaining a measure of group identity, something the old never had before. Often the interest of the old in political affairs is keen, but they have always voted as individuals, not as a bloc. Perhaps the only movement of the old that ever achieved some political significance was the Townsend Clubs of the 1930s in the United States, but that movement was somewhat eccentric, its program was based upon unreal economics, and it died a natural death. The numbers of the old, their attitudes and level of sophistication are different today.

• Perhaps most important, the old will no longer be the old—not as we have known them in the past. Even today, because of social, economic, and scientific changes, the old neither look, dress, feel, nor act like the old of yesterday. This tendency may be sharply accelerated within the next twenty-five or thirty years, as the process of aging is slowed down.

So eminent a gerontologist as Alex Comfort of University College, London, has joined colleagues who believe that the time is close when this will be achieved, and the biological clock reset or changed. The aim is not to increase the years of senescence but to add additional years to the prime of life—to make middle age last forty years or more. There are at least half a dozen major theories for slowing down aging, and one or more of them will unquestionably work out. Biochemist and Nobel Laureate John H. Northrop notes that fifty years ago scientists felt that discovery of the philosopher's stone—to transmute the elements—was impossible and that finding an elixir of life was simply improbable. The first is now in everyday use; an elixir of life has been more elusive but, he says, "there is plenty of evidence that the difficulties of the search are more practical than theoretical."

Some fear that physical science may again outstrip common wisdom. Almost twenty years ago, physicist and Nobel Laureate Sir George Thomson called for the major scientific effort to slow down the aging process. "There does not seem to be anything in the nature of the reproduction of tissue which demands its death," he said. "I believe medical research should spend increasing effort on the prevention, which at first will be postponement, of old age." But he also warned that "permanent youth will bring its problems, and the politicians and the preachers of the future may well curse the physiologists as heartily as they do now the inventors of the atomic bombs."

"Permanent youth," however, is not the issue. The scientist's effort is something else: to slow down the aging process, to extend middle age, and to lessen the disabilities of old age—in effect, to prolong the good years. Still, there is confusion over the aims of gerontology, and the fear that the human race may have to face "the unspeakable disaster" of immortality. This is the view of economist Kenneth Boulding of the University of Colorado: "I may not be being academic," he says, "but who wants to be an assistant professor for five hundred years? The only thing that makes life tolerable is death at a reasonable age."

The prospect of immortality—or being an assistant professor for five hundred years—is hardly imminent. Somewhat more realistic —but equally beside the point—is the recent utterance of Professor Sir Richard Doll of Oxford University. "I am not convinced that we should spend more time in trying to reduce mortality rates in people over 65," he told a meeting of the Medical Journalists' Association in London. "It is much more important to keep them happy and relieve their disabilities . . . It would be irresponsible at the moment to mount a program to make everyone live to 140."

Professor Doll, who is 60, said that people over 65 should be prepared to accept death and live to the full and enjoy it, rather than merely trying to live a little longer in fear and boredom. In fact, he went on, it is the "social responsibility" of the old to "live dangerously" and not expect the Health Service to spend time and money on research into prolonging their lives.

Both professors—one an economist, the other a medical doctor— seem to have a limited view of the overall aims of gerontology. A somewhat more considerate note comes from biochemist Harry Sobel of Colorado State University. It would not be "too difficult to achieve" a program for controlling longevity by limiting life spans to 65 years, he warns. After all, the children of a man over 65 are no longer reliant upon him; he no longer contributes to the national product; his existence requires long-range planning, costs more in taxes, and affects the national economy.

"From the point of view of certain political economies, his continued presence—if there are many like him—may very well interfere with national growth," Dr. Sobel says. "This could be a serious matter for emerging nations."

But Dr. Sobel makes clear that he is being facetious in even considering a program for limiting life spans at age 65, that the idea is nonsense. His point is that any system for the control of longevity must take into account—must indeed be derived from— the objective to be achieved. Professor Doll seems to believe that keeping the old alive is a drain on the economy and unwarranted; Dr. Sobel implicitly believes that each man's "creative potential . . . must be permitted to be developed, expressed, and manifested from birth until the last breath he takes," according to the democratic principle of "individual dignity"—that each man ought to retain his intrinsic worth throughout his whole lifetime.

"If society will permit this change to take place within the grand scope of things to come, it will represent the greatest achieve-ment of man and the greatest gift of man to man," he concludes. It is rarely said quite this grandiloquently but this is as good

a statement as any of the philosophic aims of gerontology. Because
he is a biochemist above all, Dr. Sobel then goes on to remind
his audience of two "biological principles" with "enormous
implications":
  • Human potential for creativeness may exist despite extremely
    advanced physical debilitation.
  • Stimulation maintains mind and body and disuse accelerates
    their deterioration.

A most realistic view of an older world—and the warning that
we are not yet ready for it—comes from Edwin Kaskowitz, executive
director of the Gerontological Society. Noting that two-thirds of
all hospital beds are now filled by people over 65, he says that
"we're bleeding now because we cannot properly take care of the
old. If there is a real biological breakthrough, watch out—the
implications are staggering. The problems industrial societies face
now, in shortages and in environmental crises, may seem minor if
we have a dramatic change in the demographic picture."

"We don't know enough and haven't made as much progress
as we must," he says. "What will it be like if most people live
ten or more years longer? What happens to the brain, how much
more senile dementia will there be? Now less than 5% of the old
are in institutions. Suppose in the future it is 25%."

One person who has looked at the prospect for longer life
and found it, on the whole, exciting and good is Harvey Wheeler
of the Center for the Study of Democratic Institutions, Santa
Barbara, California. Pointing out that even the "conservatives"
among molecular biologists were persuaded that within ten to
twenty-five years man's internal clocks would be alterable, Wheeler
said that the stretching out of longevity—so that forty years or
more of life "would be experienced with the vigor of a forty-year-old
—comes to us at just the right time in history. . . . Increased
longevity will bring many startling changes: Time for contempla-
tion, time for the painstaking acquisition of wisdom to catch up
with the breathless pace of science, time for truth to expose error."
Wheeler saw an entirely new situation in a society where the elderly
outnumber all others and in which power, wealth, authority and
prestige change hands:

"The terms of exploitation will be reversed. The elderly will no longer be second-class citizens; that role will be visited upon the young . . . Youth-centered styles will give way to age-centered styles . . . The only function of the young will be to become elderly; they will have no role to play in society. The motto of the elderly will be: Slow down, there is no rush, there is time for everything. And as this becomes a reality, society itself will slow down—slow down so much that history itself will disappear. Indeed, the individual will take the place of history . . . Institutions were once immortal because man was transient. The reverse will be true: Institutions will be transient, disposable. Men will be immortal. For the first time in human experience we will be able to visualize men without institutions, without history, and without traditions. New vistas of freedom hitherto unimagined will exist."

Wheeler's picture of the future went beyond that. The values inculcated in younger years never really leave the old, he said, and "1995 will witness the rise of a dominant class of elders preserving into their nineties, and many decades beyond, the life-styles, the protest movements, the arts and crafts, the communes, and the diseases of the present . . . Today's elders drink Gerito!, sing 'Shine on Harvest Moon,' and play shuffleboard; the vigorous hundred-year-olds of the future will turn to pot, 'Lucy in the Sky with Diamonds,' and group nude-ins."

There is a considerable element of speculation in this (including some doubt about the number of old people who sing "Shine on Harvest Moon"). What is certain is that the old forty and fifty years from now will have life styles markedly different from today's. They will be products of a more affluent society and the age of the mass media. They will come out of a culture of mobility and wide social interaction, people who are accustomed to more choices in planning where they will live and travel, whom they should visit. They will have been developed in a time when more attention was paid to the "whole personality," less to the work ethic and the idea that the purpose of life was to work for a living.

Robert J. Havighurst, professor of education and human development, emeritus, University of Chicago, and past president of the Gerontological Society, is a man of measured words. He sees the outlines for the immediate future this way: "The evidence is building up that the social environment of people over 60 years of age is becoming richer with possibilities of life satisfaction . . . [With their greater freedom] we are likely to see people searching actively for ego-involvement and disengaging rather slowly. The self, or the personality, is likely to make use of the opportunities provided by society, in spite of the limitations set by the body."

Even some of these limitations will be set aside as our world grows older but man becomes a little less mortal.

3 THE COURSE OF LIFE

All of us are born, mature, and die. As we live out our life span, we age in a complex interaction of mind, body, society, and environment—an interaction of unlimited permutations—and none of us ages in exactly the same way. Our bodies more than our minds age in common patterns; it is more our appearance than ourselves that has led to the stereotypes of the steps along the way—how it's *supposed* to be as we grow older.

The best known, most memorable, most appalling view of the life cycle is probably Shakespeare's seven ages of man in *As You Like It*:

> . . . At first, the infant,
> Mewling and puking in the nurse's arms:
> Then the whining schoolboy, with his satchel,
> And shining morning face, creeping like snail
> Unwillingly to school: and then, the lover,
> Sighing like furnace, with a woeful ballad
> Made to his mistress' eyebrow: Then, a soldier;
> Full of strange oaths, and bearded like the pard,
> Jealous in honor, sudden and quick in quarrel,
> Seeking the bubble reputation
> Even in the cannon's mouth: and then, the justice;
> In fair round belly, with good capon lin'd,
> With eyes severe, and beard of formal cut,

Full of wise saws and modern instances,
And so he plays his part: The sixth age shifts
Into the lean and slipper'd pantaloon;
With spectacles on nose, and pouch on side;
His youthful hose well sav'd, a world too wide
For his shrunk shank; and his big manly voice,
Turning again toward childish treble, pipes
And whistles in his sound: Last scene of all,
That ends this strange eventful history,
Is second childishness, and mere oblivion;
Sans teeth, sans eyes, sans taste, sans everything.

Other views of the later part of life are not much happier. Titian, in the 16th century, symbolized the traditional three ages of man as an infant in a cradle, a shepherd playing the flute, and an old man meditating on a skull. In Greek mythology, the riddle of the sphinx was also based on three ages—

What goes on four feet, on two feet, and three,
But the more feet it goes on, the weaker it be?

—The answer being man: as an infant crawling on all fours, in manhood erect on his two feet, in old age on tottering legs aided by a staff. (Before Oedipus solved it, all who had failed to answer the riddle were promptly devoured by the Sphinx.)

Shakespeare's sixth and seventh ages together make up the conventional idea of old age, which, it is commonly believed, has its own three components—the state of being elderly, then of being senescent (and marked by degenerative changes), and finally of being senile, including Shakespeare's "second childishness," a term which libels old age.*

* This is not to denigrate Shakespeare, whose psychological insights were remarkable and are often analyzed and related to scientific discussion today. Hamlet, for his Oedipus complex, is a staple for psychoanalysts. For gerontologists, it is King Lear. Most old people need stable environments to feel secure and, the older they get, the more they need calm and familiar patterns. The play proves the point: In the jargon of a scientific text, octogenarian Lear—despite some errors of judgment—functioned reasonably well until rejected by his two older daughters

In fact, gerontologists—and particularly the psychologists among them—dislike talking of any such clearly demarked ages of man (and, particularly, of senility and second childhood). Their grounds are that all such terms are either misunderstood, or misused, or meaningless as generalizations. Each of us is the same person throughout life, more different from anyone else as we get older. Wilma T. Donahue talks of "the consistent personality" at 20, 40, or 60. Perhaps the personality is not so consistent as it is unfolding, influenced by all that has come before or surrounds us, and influenced by the state of our bodies. All are the unique products of personal history, experience, nutrition, accidents, and streams of life. "A man is responsible for his face after fifty" is not a fully valid axiom—he has had little control over many things that have happened to him. But his face does reflect his past, and faces after 50 are all much more different from each other than are faces at 10 or 20.

There are more immediate hazards in stereotyping people as belonging to any of the "ages of man." Pigeonholing people makes them subject to standards, patterns, and ways of behavior that are often neither real nor desirable for them. A man of 70 may be younger, in most ways, than a man of 50—and happier for it—until caught up by other people's notions that he is an old man. Call a man old or middle aged often enough and he becomes old or middle aged, by Shakespeare's definition or whatever definitions are current; he may even, because it is expected of him, give in to weakness he never felt before and assume the shuffling gait of an old man. An exuberant young woman of 35, on reading that the middle years of life (as arbitrarily defined by some industrial gerontologists) are 35 to 54, may go into a tailspin. Suddenly she feels as old as her mother who *is* properly middle aged by the standards of another time and culture, and matronly and prissy. The 35-year-old woman may really have another 35 or more exuberant years ahead of her—if she doesn't bow to what is expected of her years.

---

and displaced. In a strange and turbulent environment, he became hostile and disorganized and showed symptoms of senile dementia. But when his faithful youngest daughter, Cordelia, expressed her affection and sheltered him, Lear responded and again became fairly well integrated.

Study after study shows that many middle-aged people still regard themselves as "young," and many elderly people think of themselves, at worst, as being "middle aged." Conceptions of "ages of man" being what they are, this is fortunate; they are managing to have better self-concepts and to lead fuller lives. They are also serving to prove that there are no rigid "ages of man"—only ages of individual people, some younger or older in different ways.

If it is misleading and harmful to fit people into three or seven stereotyped "ages of man," how can we best understand the components of the life cycle—what happens to us as we grow older? After all, there *are* common characteristics to the aging process, far more complex and profound than those drawn in caricature by Shakespeare.

In fact, life span developmental psychology is concerned with just this subject. The study of man's age-related behavior—from birth to death—is now one of the fastest growing of academic disciplines. More than forty years ago, Charlotte Bühler, of the Psychological Institute of the University of Vienna, became one of the pioneers in this field and her influence continues to shape the science to this day.

There have been many studies of personality development in childhood and adolescence, almost none in the later years. In 1950, Erik H. Erikson, professor of human development at Harvard University, published one of the few theories of personality development to range from infancy to old age. His theory now occupies a place in most texts on the subject:

The development of the ego—an individual's experience of himself and his conception of himself—is what determines his behavior throughout his life; all of us, according to Erikson, go through eight stages of ego development by the time we reach old age. Each stage represents a choice or crisis for us. How we make that choice or meet that crisis affects all subsequent stages, the development of future personality, and our success in adapting to the world.

These are Erikson's "eight stages of man" (with the desirable or life-giving choices in italics):

• In early infancy, development of a sense of basic *trust* versus a sense of distrust. A newborn baby is sensitive to pain, pressure, temperature, touch, taste, and smell. How he is treated—the warmth, sustenance, gentleness given him—may influence his personality through all other stages.

• In later infancy, when bowel control has been established, a growing sense of *autonomy* versus a sense of shame and doubt.

• In early childhood, a time of great locomotor development and much independent moving about, a developing sense of *initiative* vesus a sense of guilt.

• In the middle years of childhood, a period of taking up school, games, hobbies, a sense of *industry* versus a sense of inferiority.

• In adolescence, a sense of *ego identity* versus role confusion. Here ego identity means a certainty of self, and a sense of continuity and belonging, the awareness that life includes a career, sex role, and a system of values.

• In early adulthood, the development of *intimacy* versus a sense of ego isolation. Intimacy means a relationship with a loved and mutually dependent partner of the opposite sex; together they may regulate the cycles of work, procreation, and recreation.

• In middle adulthood, the development of *generativity* versus a sense of ego stagnation. Generativity is the expansion of ego interests, and a sense of having contributed to the future; the concept includes productivity and creativity, and a concern with establishing and guiding the next generation.

• In late adulthood, a sense of *ego integrity*—a basic acceptance that our life has been inevitable, right, and meaningful—versus a sense of despair and fear of death.

A different psychological crisis becomes basic at each stage of development, but the same issue exists in earlier and later stages, in different degree of form, Erikson says. The problem of ego identity is paramount in adolescence but it also exists in later life, modified by the way it was coped with in adolescence and by a person's life history. And, unless he has successfully resolved his earlier crises, in his later years a man cannot solve his problem of ego integrity, believe that his life has been meaningful, and be unafraid of death.

There is no "correct" number of stages of life, writes Robert J. Havighurst, and there are no scientifically established age limits for the various stages. Through the life cycle, behavior is determined by three forces that operate differently at different times. At first —up to about age 25—the major force is the unfolding of genetic possibilities, physical and mental, as modified by the social environment. After that, two other forces predominate—the ego and the situation in which the ego operates: the physical body and, again, the social environment.

Havighurst also describes the life cycle in eight stages, but in a different manner from Erikson. He does it by decades. In each of eight decades of life there are "dominant concerns" that govern behavior. A person grows from one dominant concern to the next, on through the eight decades or as long as he lives. The dominant concerns are seen more clearly in the adult decades of Havighurst's eight stages than in childhood or adolescence; this is because the young have so much to accomplish, so much developing to do, that no single term quite includes all their major concerns.

These are Havighurst's dominant concerns in the life cycle:

Age 0–10: Coming into independent existence
The child's body becomes physically independent, through maturation of bones, muscles, and nerves, and through learning of physical skills such as jumping or swimming. His mind develops and he becomes able to communicate and cooperate with other people. He becomes an autonomous person, in body and conceptual equipment, and morally autonomous too, as his conscience develops. Although growing up biologically is the dominant force, the ego also develops, largely out of the child's experience with his family and in school. If the family gives adequate emotional support and mental stimulation, the child will be able to make the most of his inherited biological potentials.

Age 10–20: Becoming a person in one's own mind
Now there is a fairly even balance between the forces of maturation, the developing ego, and the situation in which the ego operates. (Erikson has integrated everything arising out of this into one overriding psycho-social task—that of achieving identity.) During this period, the adolescent becomes a young man or woman

biologically and learns an appropriate sex role. He makes a choice of occupation and develops an ideology, social and political. He chooses his own clothing and friends. At the start of this decade a boy would answer the question "What kind of person would you like to be when you grow up?" by saying he would like to be like his father—a girl like her mother—or like some glamorous or romantic figure. By its end, both would answer differently; they would want to be like an imaginary person created as their ego ideal, composed of qualities they have chosen as most desirable.

Age 20–30: Focusing one's life

Now that he has psychological identity, he must make the choices that give him a social identity. Out of a variety of possibilities he selects a combination that marks him as a unique person. He takes a job and starts to grow with it. He accepts a marriage partner. He lives in one community and forms a consistent ideology. This is a period of maximum concern with oneself and one's immediate, personal life. (It is also the age period in which one votes least frequently.)

Many young people take the whole decade to accomplish the task of focusing their lives. They may try several occupations, several love affairs, several religious variants and political ideologies. (An upper-middle-class youth is likely to spend much time and energy on this concern; other young people with simpler identities achieve a stable focus earlier, even before their twenties.)

A young woman who does not marry in this period is likely to spend time and energy trying other possible elements of social identity, and to have a challenging and complicated—and sometimes anxious—life in her twenties.

Adult education is consistent with the idea of focusing one's life —it is largely a practical, up-grading type of education, to help a person get a better job or help a young married woman become a better housewife or mother.

Age 30–40: Collecting one's energies

This is the period of least introspection or self-awareness. Self-doubts have been put to rest. The ego is in command, maturation introduces no new factors, and the situation is generally stable.

The worker grows in skill and experience, and is promoted accordingly; the skilled worker reaches the height of his skill and earning power. The young scientist starts to produce research papers. The mother is more experienced, too, and can rear her children with relative ease and pleasure. Home-making also is done more skillfully.

It is a time of relatively great stability, freedom from anxiety, and general psychological well-being. Older women, especially, are likely to look back upon this decade as the best of their lives. But for some young business or professional men with ego-involving work, the period is not this smooth; they may be fiercely competing for promotion, with much anxiety and striving.

Adult education now may be for the same purpose as it was in the decade before—to improve occupational or home-making skills—or it may be made up of things that add to a person's social life, such as bridge-playing, dancing, or learning a craft or a foreign language.

Age 40–50: Exerting and asserting oneself

Now a person is generally at the peak of his life cycle (although he may have more actual power later on). He exerts his maximum energy, in ways of his own choice. A woman is no longer tied down to her children and can be active in clubs, or take a job, or spend more time with her husband (if he has the time). The activities of "citizenship" become more important than ever before. A person with leadership potential begins to assert his leadership now—or he never does at all. Home-making becomes more important in a different sense, that of creating and maintaining the most pleasant place possible in which to live. The parent-child relationship is as important as ever, but, in this period, parents have to learn how to set their adolescent children free.

There is a negative side to this decade, too. The body starts giving intimation of problems to come. The menopause may result in changes in a woman's ego, although these changes are not, necessarily, at all negative. A woman may become more free to exert and assert herself after the menopause; her sex life may become more satisfactory; she may be able to assume more roles outside of the home, as worker or in community action. But women and men start to lose their physical attractiveness in this decade (unless they strenuously fight to maintain a youthful appearance) and health problems appear increasingly. Toward the end of this decade, heart attacks begin to take a toll among men. Ulcers also increase in frequency.

Age 50–60: Creating a new life style

This is the most interesting and challenging decade of adult life. For some, it is a period of creativity and new life; for others, a time to hang on almost desperately to what has been achieved before. Now the ego changes and turns inward toward the self, and thought begins to replace action as a mode of dealing with the world. The attitude toward the future changes radically: In the forties the future seemed indefinitely long and there was time for everything; in the fifties a person starts ordering his priorities—he knows he may not have time for everything he would like to do.

Physical power is diminishing, and men and women begin to have doubts about their occupational, social, and intellectual power. The symbols of influence accepted or rejected casually or carelessly in the forties are looked at jealously in the fifties. Proof is constantly needed: is the power still there? A woman may have an affair with a younger man to reassure herself that she is still attractive. A man may react the same way, or, if he is having doubts about his mental skills, learn a new language just to prove a point.

Many people still have the energy and curiosity about life to create a new life-style, one that gives more satisfaction. A man may deliberately widen the scope of his activity through travel, or take on a new responsibility in his business. A woman's central concerns as a mother no longer fill her life and she may seek a new career, either in employment or social-civic activity. This is a new period for many women, sharply different from previous ones; they may respond with ambivalence, regretting the disappearance of the old but savoring the new.

The body becomes a problem. The decline of physical strength and skill has started in the early fifties and the body is less and less favorable for the operation of the ego. People are sick more of the time, and they discover limits to what their bodies can do. Most women are spending more time on the care and nurture of their husbands whose health and sense of well-being may become precarious. A woman may achieve a kind of maturity in which she accepts and enjoys what life has to offer. By the end of the fifties, the libidinal fires begin to die down in men, one of several threats to the ego characteristic of this decade.

A man seldom gets promotion on his job—his colleagues are beginning to expect him to slow down. Although power, influence, and productivity are pretty much at a plateau, it does not seem that way to the individual: he feels that he must exert himself more if he is to avoid losing ground.

The experiences with the body and social situation are accompanied by subtle, far-reaching changes in the ego. The world no longer seems simple and easy to master just by working at it. It is now more complex, and the ego has its doubts.

Age 60–70: Deciding whether to disengage and how

With some physical and mental effort, people in their sixties are as good as they ever were. Their wisdom and prestige give them ample power to make up for waning biological resources. But as the sixties wear on, there are visible changes both in ego and social effectiveness.

The situation in which the ego operates tends to deteriorate for most people. Body and health are sources of weakness for many. Most men lose their jobs during their sixties, some by choice but most because of the workings of an arbitrary retirement policy. Most women lose their husbands before the end of this decade. (Becoming a widow is not always a misfortune for the woman, but it does force a reorganization of her life and her ego.)

The crisis of the sixties for most people is the process of disengagement—the decreasing interaction between themselves and their society. When a person stops working or loses a spouse or becomes less active as a parent, citizen, club or church member, he is experiencing one kind of disengagement—behavioral disengagement. There is an interaction between this and the ego, which may be in conflict with the process. Many people resist disengagement as long as possible: a man may refuse to retire or, if forced to, seek other jobs. A person may resist gentle hints that he or she is too old to continue as president of a club or fraternal group. Some people become jealous of their younger colleagues, and are bitter and critical. There are studies of aging which show that people have stable attitudes for the twenty years leading up to 60; then they again develop a new and stable set of attitudes by 70. But at about 65 they are often ambivalent and inconsistent in their attitudes. It is a period of inner conflict.

People who have been passive and dependent most of their lives disengage most easily. Others fight bitterly against it. Their self-respect depends on maintaining activity and influence. At the beginning of the sixties, people feel and resist the pressures to disengage imposed upon them by their bodies and social environment. But by the end of their sixties, the question becomes: how to disengage comfortably? What roles must be given up or reduced, what satisfactions may be retained or gained?

Age 70–80: Making the most of disengagement

Half the population of modern society reach the age of 70 and beyond. For them, there may be a new outlook on life that is as satisfactory to the ego—or more so—than the two previous decades. Erikson calls this the achievement of "integrity." Charlotte Bühler calls it a sense of "self-fulfilment" when the life work is completed and one can live in the past and present without worrying about the future.

By now, a person has achieved or accepted a state of disengagement from the active social roles of middle age and has formed a new and final pattern of engagement in less demanding roles. If he is in reasonable health, and his social and economic situation is stable enough, his ego operates freely and with considerable satisfaction. At this age, a person usually needs family or friends as his link to the social world. He spends much time and energy in routines of home and personal life that would have seemed unimportant twenty years earlier.

There seems to be much difference in the way men and women manage their lives in this period. Men seem to be more introverted and to rely more on "thinking" to cope with the situations of later life. Educators and counselors still have relatively little experience with programs to improve life satisfaction in this decade, but both knowledge and opportunities are steadily increasing. In any event, this decade (and, indeed, whatever time follows) can be thoroughly

satisfying to the person living through it—far more than is supposed
by most younger people.

This matter-of-fact analysis of major elements of the life cycle
looks illuminating, local, and simple. It *is* logical and illuminating,
but hardly simple: It is hard-wrought, and comes out of the
hundreds of studies and new perceptions made by Havighurst,
his colleagues and associates, and their relatively few predecessors.
Havighurst started to work in the field of aging in 1945—a long
time ago in the short history of gerontology—as a psychologist;
now, he writes, he tends to operate more as a sociologist. A few
years ago, he began an address at a Gerontological Society meeting
as follows: "One of the principal unanswered questions about the
human life cycle is: How do people structure their lives after about
age 65? Under what conditions do they achieve satisfaction?"
He stopped himself, suddenly struck by the realization of how far
gerontology had traveled. When he first started out, he explained,
he would not have thought, in talking about people over 65,
of using so active a term as "structure their lives." The idea that
a person growing old could be taking any such initiative would
simply not occur. The widespread, and according to Havighurst,
superficial view of aging held in the 1940s saw it as a period of
declines, losses, and stresses, with society outside the family doing
little to help an older person make a satisfactory adjustment.
Havighurst did not say it but this dramatic change of roles in
thirty years—for society and for the old themselves—is one clear
sign that what he and his colleagues arc taking part in is *the* quiet
revolution of our times.

It is also a recent idea to study the processes of aging in the life
cycle, not just the end product. There have been philosophical
studies of aging throughout history, but research on the psychology
of aging began with the work of Lambert Adolphe Jacques
Quetelet, who today would be considered a sociologist and psychologist as well as a mathematician. His *Sur l'homme et le dévelop-
pement de ses facultés,* published in 1835, influenced many scholars,
including Francis Galton, a gentleman-scientist-hobbyist, whose
Inquiries into Human Faculty and its Development (1883) explored

individual differences in relation to age and development. Both Quetelet and Galton documented some of the changes that occur with age and made clear that there is a considerable degree of difference in the aging process from person to person.

The study of age-related behavior from birth to death grew from such interests as these and from the "baby biographies"—biographical studies of children and their day-to-day changes in structure and functioning—first done in Europe in the late 19th century. In the United States, G. Stanley Hall, a student of William James, published a major study, *The Contents of Children's Minds,* in 1883. Twenty years later, Hall was still writing about children with a genetic philosophy that had much appeal to educators. His language, if fresh then, is incredibly quaint today: "The guardians of the young . . . should feel profoundly that childhood is not corrupt . . . there is nothing else so worthy of love, reverence, and service as the body and soul of the growing child" is a typical turn of phrase. Still, the idea of fitting the school to the child instead of the child to the school was a reasonably fresh one at the time, and his work did influence many educators.

Twenty years later, Hall had turned 78 and was writing about the other end of the life span. His *Senescence: The Last Half of Life,* published in 1922, looks idiosyncratic today. He was to die within two years of its appearance and, in his book, he did some of his own life review and reminiscence. It also contains bits of poetry, "sayings," philosophizing, and a discussion of medical and physiological aspects of aging, including a lengthy treatment of the problems of constipation. But his chapter reporting results of a questionnaire given to old people on their self-perceptions and attitudes was novel and important in its day, and *Senescence* is a milestone of sorts in gerontological writing and still useful as a source of ideas and reference.

Hall started with children and wound up writing about the old. He did not make the mistake, as others have, of equating the two in the life cycle. James Birren, commenting on Hall's contribution, says that "despite his specialization in child psychology, [he] struck an independent note, suggesting that older people . . . have unique psychological processes, which probably exhibit a higher degree of variability than do the functions of youth." Shakespeare did much damage to the image of the old with his definition of "second childishness"—"sans teeth, sans eyes, sans taste, sans everything." No matter what the sensory loss suffered by the old, Hall recognized the superficiality of thinking of aging as the inverse of childhood. The course of life does not flow backward; it is physical weakness, dependence, and reduced "ego energy" that give the impression of "childishness." When an old person must depend on others for food and shelter, he is placed in the position of a child with its parents. They become the source of strength and belonging, and the old person looks to them for affection and for rules of obedience —as does a child. There are other reasons, too, but there is no such thing as "second childhood." "Many of the impairments of the aged cause them to act in very childish ways," notes Professor John G. Taylor of the University of London. "However, aging is certainly not a reversal of the developments of childhood, but rather a process of increased error in the programs formulated in earlier years."

The fact that middle age is called *middle* age somehow suggests that it is surrounded by equal parts. The context is really quite different. "If we think of life as a play, middle age is the period leading up to and away from the climax of the story," writes psychologist Theodore Lidz. "The characters have all been on stage, the theme and countertheme introduced, and as the third act ends, the play reaches its denouement and the fourth act moves on toward an inevitable conclusion."

As the drama intensifies, Dr. Lidz says, these are the questions that are asked: "Can the themes draw together, goals be achieved, and satisfaction attained? Will the relationships that have been established provide fulfillment and happiness? Or must one come to terms with getting by, or with disappointment and disillusionment?"

At the start of middle age, there still seems time to start anew and to salvage the years that are left. As the years pass, the questions are resolved and the course fixed, for better or worse. Arthur Miller's play *Death of a Salesman* is a powerful telling of this phase as it struck Willy Loman, haunted by knowledge of his failure and doom. Many observers have noted that it is not women or the young but middle-aged men who sob on seeing the play, seeing their own crises and fears—and failures—acted out before them.

The approach to middle life from young adulthood is more of a psychological matter—a state of mind—than are other changes in the life cycle. The onset of adolescence or adulthood is marked by more specific body changes, often dramatic ones, from year to year. In childhood and youth, to become older also means to become more attractive or bigger or stronger and thus more important. A boy or girl of 5 or 10 or 15 is very conscious of chronological age and is worlds apart from a boy or girl just a few years older. In middle age, chronological age is no longer the same decisive point of reference; the 40-year-old and the 45-year-old work and play together without giving much thought to the age difference (unless they are obsessed with age). In the middle years it is the qualitative differences that matter—problems of career, family, and body—and a person does not rely primarily on chronological age for clocking himself. (Chronological age becomes important again in old age; an old person tends to become acutely conscious and—if in good health—even boastful of his years; they have become a source of pride and achievement.)

The middle-aged person often sees himself as the bridge between generations. He must understand, or try to understand, both his children and his parents. Economically, he is taxpayer and provider for both young and old. He is now center stage and his responsibilities are enormous; sometimes he is both shocked and overwhelmed by his role. Dr. Bernice L. Neugarten of the University of Chicago cites examples of how the awareness of middle age comes to people:

"I used to think that all of us in the office were contemporaries, for we all had similar career interests. But one day we were talking about old movies and we realized that the younger ones had never seen a Shirley Temple film or an Our Gang comedy . . . it struck me with a blow that I am older than they. I had never been so conscious of it before."

And: "When I see a pretty girl on the stage or in the movies— we used to say 'a cute chick'—and when I realize, 'My God, she's about the age of my son,' it's a real shock."

This is, of course, concomitant with that other awareness of middle age discussed elsewhere in this book: that the body is slowing down. It creaks and groans. A father pretends to enjoy playing ball with his teen-age son and only barely hides the puffs and wheezes—and his concern over getting a heart attack. An office worker notices that his old overcoat seems a little heavier this year—heavier to put on, that is. A woman sees the menopause looming—and is not sure until it happens how much suffering it entails and what it will mean to her.

Middle-aged people seem to feel less distant from their parents than they do from their children. "I sympathize with the old now, in a way that is new," said one person in Dr. Neugarten's study. "I watch my parents, for instance, and I wonder if I will age in the same way."

They feel closer to their parents because they believe an older generation can better understand and appreciate their responsibilities. And the middle aged usually keep better control of their annoyance with the idiosyncracies of the old. There is "greater projection of the self in one's behavior with older people," Dr. Neugarten writes, "sometimes to the extent of blurring the differences between generations." She tells how one woman showed her own lack of awareness (or her denial) of her mother's aging:

"I was shopping with mother. She had left something behind on the counter and the clerk called out to tell me that the 'old lady' had forgotten her package. I was amazed. Of course, the clerk was a young man and she must have seemed old to him. [But] I myself don't think of her as old . . ."

Most of us are shaken by the experience at some point of finding out how a mother, father, or other intimate—judged solely by appearance—looks to the outsider. Yet we all approach strangers in about the same way. Unless they are marked by the unusual, our first reaction is to judge and respond to them by their sex and age. In a day of clever cosmetics, wigs or long hair for men and women, and unisex clothes for the young, it is possible for sex or age or both to be indeterminate. In such cases we are confused until we figure out how to behave.

Dr. Neugarten also analyzed how middle-aged men and women perceive age. She found that they generally divided adults into four periods—young adulthood, maturity, middle age, and old age. But perceptions of age differ according to backgrounds. The typical upper-middle-class man—a business executive or professional—tended to divide the lifelines differently—later—than did an unskilled worker. The upper-middle-class man found that 30 was the dividing line between young adulthood and maturity, 40 the dividing line between maturity and middle age, and 65 the line between middle and old age. Asked to respond in a somewhat different way, he would say that a man is "mature," "in the prime of his life," and with "the greatest confidence in himself" at the age of 40. He would not really consider him "middle aged" until almost 50, or "old" until 70. The unskilled worker saw the lifeline moving more rapidly. For him the dividing points were 25, 35, and 50, with a man being "middle aged" by 40 and "old" by 60.

Throughout all strata of society, we do a good deal of labeling by position in the life cycle—judging by age, segregating by age, rejecting or approving by age. The harm of doing so is sharply evident in cases of forced retirement, but it takes its toll in countless other ways, including the isolation and loneliness of many of the old. It is, above all, a form of discrimination, like evaluating people by their sex, color, ethnic origin, economic or social class.

Dr. William R. Looft of Pennsylvania State University believes we should reverse the age-old tendency and try to achieve some degree of age integration—much as we have sought integration of peoples of different races and backgrounds. "The elderly would benefit from this change toward age integration," he says, "for they are the ones who currently suffer most from age stratification." To show how segregation by age group can damage, he cites an example from the other end of the life cycle: In 1966, a specialist in child development reported that children removed from a gloomy, debilitating orphanage and placed in normal situations showed enormous gains in intelligence and social competence—gains that were maintained throughout adult life.

There is, he says, the "exciting possibility" that the same could happen to the old, or some of the old, if they were removed from institutional life and brought back into their homes.* (He also

* Some of the problems—and hazards—of attempting this are discussed in Chapter 11, "The Old in Their Institutions."

suggests that greater efforts be made to keep them at home in the first place.) But he concedes that many old people will continue to live in institutions and hospitals. This being so, he asks, why not try to integrate all ages within the institutional setting? To bolster his case, he cites a study made by two psychiatrists who found that the most typical activities in age-segregated wards are "sleeping and doing nothing." However, in an age-integrated ward, there was much social interaction and "a sense of community." Other studies support this, including the finding that the old themselves report being happier in apartments—usually on the ground floor—in age-integrated housing developments than they are in purely "senior citizen" communities. The sight and sound of youth about them (assuming they can also shut both out when they wish) help keep an old person alive, too.

Life-span education is another approach to age integration, Dr. Looft says. In any case, education should be considered as a life-long process, one that provides intellectual and emotional satisfactions as well as fostering vocational and personal skills. But the life-span educational approach—all generations going to school together—would also reintroduce the young to the old. This, he believes, "might dispel much of the distaste and fear that young people have for the aging process and for old people."

Dr. Looft recently asked a group of people, ranging in age from early adolescence to advanced old age, who they believed were "the important sources and transmitters of information to children and adolescents growing up today." The "wisdom of the old" made no showing at all in this study; not one of several hundred persons interviewed mentioned that their grandparents had an important role in passing on information. Even old people interviewed denied that they mattered much as sources of information or wisdom.

Education and the mass media now fulfill the function that once belonged to the old and experienced. Progress is so fast, with so much information being produced, that many old cannot keep up with the young. A good percentage of the jobs and interests which now appeal to young people did not exist forty or fifty years ago; on the most practical levels the old cannot advise the young. But Dr. Looft sees remedy for the situation in the creation of centers for life-span education, in contrast to schools for children and youth.

These "might just be the catalyst to reverse the situation," he says. "Young people might develop a respect for the experience and wisdom of the aged, and the aged might come to see the value of the ambitions—and the complaints—of the young."

People at the far end of the life cycle—no matter how improved their situation in recent years—cannot, by themselves, do much about age integration. They have less control than most adults over where they will live, and with whom, and over the nature of their society. There are many reasons why the old, as a group, have as little power as they do, but a leading one is this: the old have little group identity, little ideology in common, and consequently have been almost unable to organize in their own behalf. This may change in the future when there are even more old and active people, as some gerontologists suggest, but until now the exceptions to the rule are usually eccentric ones.

"Senior power," a term few people take seriously, once threatened to sweep the United States, or, at least, alter the course of its politics. In the first year of Franklin Roosevelt's New Deal—on January 1, 1934—Francis E. Townsend, an elderly physician from Long Beach, California, announced his plan for a government allowance of $200 a month to every citizen 60 years old or more. (A dollar then had more than three times its value today.) The pension was to be financed by a sales tax; each allowance was to be spent by its recipient within thirty days, thus assuring, the hope went, a wave of spending and booming business that could take the sales tax in its stride. The Townsend Old Age Revolving Pension plan had enormous appeal in those depression-ridden days. Dr. Townsend and his aide, Robert L. Clements, welded Townsend clubs in a hierarchic national organization, complete with a *Townsend National Weekly,* Townsend stickers, buttons, and speakers' manuals.

Within a year, the Townsend forces were said to hold the balance of political power in eleven states west of the Mississippi and to be solidly based in Massachusetts, Indiana, Illinois, and Ohio. Men and women, aged warriors all, rose up at their annual convention to sing: "Onward Townsend soldiers, / Marching as to war, / With the Townsend banner / Going on before." By the end of 1935, it appeared that the Townsend plan had gained ten million supporters.

Its strength distressed Democratic Party leaders, who feared that Townsend members might swing the elections to the Republicans in 1936. They didn't. The Democrats scored a memorable victory in 1936. New Deal measures had taken some of the bite out of popular discontent. This, combined with the more implausible aspects of the Townsend Plan (Democratic leaders sought to relegate the organization to the lunatic fringe), eventually led it to wither away.

There have since been other appeals to the old to act as a cohesive pressure group. The "McClain movement"—the California Institute of Social Welfare—was probably the most effective in organizing the elderly. Its most radical aim was to eliminate the means test in California's Old Age Assistance Law. Its greatest success came in 1948, when California voters passed a proposition changing the law's administration and raising the benefits. But this victory came by the smallest of majorities, 1% of the vote, and a year later the proposition was repealed. At the peak of its activity, the Institute membership was made up of only 7% of the California population over 65.

Margaret Kuhn and her Gray Panthers are trying to do better. In 1973, she announced that she and other Gray Panthers were planning protests and picket lines or whatever it might take to win improvement for the old. Testifying before the Senate's Special Committee on the Aging, she proposed a national health service "to provide help to all of us in a coordinated manner, taking over diverse and splintered health services which public and private agencies now attempt to provide." Her cause is reasonable, but Gray Panther membership throughout the United States is a scant 1,500—not enough to make a dent, but 1,500 more than it was two years earlier. One great trouble with America, she says, is the "Detroit syndrome—we want only the latest models in our society . . . the old models are undesirable and scrapped." Miss Kuhn, who had considerable experience in church action programs before retiring to become a founder of the Gray Panthers, says her group "is muscling in on society. We'll do it with militancy, demonstrations, badges, anything to get a place at the table."

Maybe. But all such movements, of the old, for the old, suffer the common disability. "The Gray Panthers can be a universalizing force in the social revolution," she says. "We're all growing old, every one of us. We all share this." We all *do* share it, but not many of us own up to it. Within every old person is a young one, or at least a middle-aged one, trying to escape the idea of old age. Bernard Baruch, in his eighties, said, "Old age is fifteen years older than I am" (a revealing remark about Baruch, since people in their early seventies usually believe that their old age will start in five, not fifteen, years). A volunteer worker in a large New York home for the aged proudly announces her years: "79 next April. And when I'm old, I hope to become a resident here." A 72-year-old small-town merchant hoots at the mention of William O. Douglas, calls him an old goat, because the Supreme Court justice was born in 1898, is still on the bench, and has a considerably younger wife. Still, the merchant has given no thought at all to his own retirement, believes he is still in his prime in all ways, and can't keep his eyes off the grocer's daughter.

Because each person sees himself in continuum in the life cycle —as the same person always—he does not think of himself as being old, not in the same sense that others do. Nor does he view himself as part of a separate and distinct group with its own sociological identity. Thus the old are not prone to organize as a pressure or political group. Cornell Universiy studies, conducted over a period of years, found that a majority of persons interviewed, all over 60 and some in their higher seventies, consider themselves middle aged. Another study, of 115 applicants for apartments, also found that most considered themselves middle aged—although their average age was 72 and the public housing facility they sought to enter was designed solely for the aged and included the county senior center. A Purdue University report suggests that people in all age categories identify middle age and old age by relative, not by absolute criteria. "It all depends upon the individual," most respondents said.

The lack of group identification among old people shows in many ways. Sociologist Frank A. Pinner and his associates analyzed attitudes of elderly pensioners and found that they hesitated to identify themselves as aged, much preferring to be called "citizens." Interviews with a subgroup showed no evidence at all of a "we feeling."

We may wish the Gray Panthers all success in dramatizing the issue—but we may also be thankful that there is no great burst of "senior power." The problems of the old are properly the interest of all generations; an old-age bloc makes as much sense as a middle-aged bloc or a junior citizens bloc. The old *do* vote: a study made of three U.S. presidential elections, 1960 to 1968, showed that 68% of all persons over 65 voted, compared to only 58% of those in the 21-to-29-year-old age group. But bloc voting, in narrow self-interest, can be as deadly if done by the old as by any other group. If the Townsend Plan had succeeded, it easily might have set back an American economy barely risen from the depression.

There is a myth that youth is radical or revolutionary, that the old are conservative or reactionary in their politics. The course of life produces many changes, but this is not at all one of the inevitable ones. It happens, often enough, that new school-tax propositions are beaten back in suburban areas where many old people live, al-though the schools badly need improvement. But this is not be-cause the old vote as a bloc opposed to better schools. Nor do they vote against improvement just because they are old. They vote as individuals living on fixed incomes who feel that they can not afford to pay more for other people's children.

Most likely in all cases, what the old show is a form of social, not political, conservatism. Gerontologists increasingly question the myth of the conservative old (as others are now questioning the myth of the radical young). One example of the fallacy of the "conservative old": In the 1968 presidential election, Candidate George Wallace's greatest appeal was to "law and order" and the maintenance of the racial status quo—an obvious appeal to "con-servatives." But he drew a larger proportion of votes from the under-35 generation than he did from among the old; people over 65 were least responsive to him.

What the old tend to do, according to political scientist John Schmidhauser, is retain their affiliation with the party they first voted for. Does this brand the old as "conservative," assuming the word means rigid adherence to outdated ideas? Schmidhauser says not at all: "The contents of party programs change, sometimes radically, over the passage of years," and as far as we know, "the aged may accept such changes along with other age groups." Age alone is not what makes a political attitude.

Many studies challenge the assumption that conservatism and old age go together; older people can and do make broad social adjust-ment. It is true, however, that from 55 years on, people tend to be steadfast in their voting preferences and do less ticket-splitting or independent voting than other age groups, Dr. Schmidhauser says. Older people also more consistently vote for the candidate they say they're going to vote for. This is not a mark of inflexibility but something else: the old are more careful and deliberate than the young. The "conservatism" of the old may be more a sign of that tendency than anything else.

When and where a man was born is more important than his age in influencing his views. Each generation takes off from a different starting point, with a different context and culture, Angus Campbell, of the University of Michigan's Survey Research Center, reminds us. Someone raised in the pattern of race relations in the United States in the 1920s starts out with a different view of civil rights issues from someone raised in the 1960s.* "In this sense there is always likely to be a certain lag in the attitudes of older people," he says. "Some of this difference persists and contributes to the generational differences we see at any particular time."

There is no real evidence of substantial political change, left or right, over the life cycle.** A recent longitudinal study found that college students kept "a considerable constancy" as they reached

* And, for the prejudiced older white person, one of the views hardest to get rid of. A Nashville, Tennessee, study found that the older the white person, the less willing he is to interact with Negroes. As Negroes grow older, however, their prejudice does not expand in the same way: The study found that older blacks are as willing as younger ones to interact with whites, with a wide variety of interracial attitudes.

** There is no evidence of any great change in religious attitudes either over the life style or, at least, between middle and old ages. In many countries, it is expected that older people will attend church more often and take a role in church affairs, and they often do, but this is cultural conformity more than an expression of a return to religion. In the United States and Great Britain, people are less apt to attend church regularly in their thirties (because of family and career pressures), but otherwise there is no significant change in pattern throughout the life cycle. If older people seem more devout—as they do in France—it is probably because they were born in a time when most people were more devout. One point made in a number of studies that is conclusive: People over 90 tend to have a strong belief in an afterlife.

middle age; some became more conservative, some more liberal, but without consistent drift in either direction. Far more important than position in the life cycle is the position in life. A young parent will gladly pay school tax, while an old person, barely getting by on his fixed income, will balk and—as an afterthought—bolster his point by complaining about socialism in the schools. But that same old person may ardently support a federal program for paying medical expenses for people over 65 even though "such programs are considered rampant communism in some sections of the population," Dr. Campbell says. People generally are far less ideological than we suppose; at any age, a man reacts to a situation as he sees it at the moment, and he may be led to support conservative or liberal policies or—with little sense of conflict—both at the same time.

Generational conflicts may be overstated or due to reasons other than age itself: Differences in attitude between age groups "are far less impressive" than those *within* the same age groups, Dr. Campbell says. No matter where we stand in the life cycle, we are too heterogeneous to make common cause solely on the basis of age. Dr. Campbell's conclusion is probably a happy one: "There is no instance in modern history in which a major political movement has grown out of the interests of a particular age group and it seems improbable that any such development will occur soon."

Thus the old are not the ones to be expected to fight, collectively, against age discrimination. The target group to make reforms is among the majority, not the minority—as it is when we try to end segregation of racial or ethnic minorities, or to implement equality among the sexes.

"In the case of the aged, this should be equally true," declares psychologist K. Warner Schaie of West Virginia University. "As in any other revolution, it is not the oppressed masses (in this case the elderly) who successfully change the system, but rather a small group of members of the establishment (here the young adult and middle aged) who through enlightened self-interest . . . take the necessary first steps to question and reform."

Abandonment of the age-graded society would serve two fundamental aims, he says. It would contribute to "an improved quality of life" for the elderly, and "it would have a general impact on the quality and dignity of all human existence."

This is perfectly sound revolutionary rhetoric, and missionary zeal is as welcome in gerontology as it is in any good crusade. On the face of it, an age-integrated society—or, at least, a society without age stratification—sounds as Utopian as a classless or prejudice-free society. It also sounds as difficult to achieve. Yet there are two reasons why this particular effort might succeed where others falter. One is universal appeal: there is no question of anyone's special interest in working toward integration of the old— if we survive, we will *all* be part of that group some day. The other is historical precedent: until recently, when a family sat down to supper, just about the whole of the life cycle was apt to be represented at the age-integrated table.

4 WHY WE MUST GROW OLD

Harry Linder, an old friend from New York, came to visit me last summer. I live in St. Tropez in the south of France and Harry wanted to see our foremost attraction—the topless girls sunbathing at Tahiti Beach. Harry spent a fine afternoon walking up and down the beach by himself—it was too hot for the rest of us—and came back proclaiming "First class" and "Never saw better." He didn't have the right clothes for beach ogling, and the next day his wife, much younger than he and wonderfully solicitous, bought him shorts and a T-shirt emblazoned with last year's slogan, DIRTY OLD MEN NEED LOVE. Harry may fall asleep from time to time at dinner parties, but on the beach, in full August sun, he was completely alive.

Harry is, of course, neither dirty nor old. Or, rather, he is old, but in one sense only—biologically. He still oversees a business in New York although he has some trouble with his hearing and had to give up his five cigars a day last year because his heart occasionally skipped a beat. His joy in being on the Riviera was dampened only because he could no longer watch his favorite television commentators discussing national politics, a subject he is an authority on—that and the prospects for the next presidential election. He does not think of himself as "old," but many of his contemporaries have long since died, and he is wont to say before going to bed, "Good night. I'll see you in the morning—God willing." He says it in good humor; his wife believes he is expressing about as much concern as a child who recites: "If I die before I wake, I pray the Lord my soul to take." He jokes about himself: "My new passport photo. They mixed it up with some repulsive old man's." On this visit, Harry drove to St. Paul-de-Vence to have lunch at the Colombe d'Or and to tour the Maeght Foundation and other nearby museums. His taste is refined and his mind as clear as a bell, a statement that would annoy him—"Why shouldn't it be?" By the calendar, Harry Linder is 86 years old.

Harry Linder must soon die, no matter how young his psychological or social age. As an American white male of 86, he has a life expectancy of a little more than four years.* He may live a few years longer than that; both his parents had long lives, and his genes are probably programmed to give him an exceptionally long life, too. He does not yet have, at least not in critical form, any of the degenerative diseases that kill the old. In any event, aging and disease are not the same thing, a distinction often overlooked. "In fact," says Carl Eisdorfer, former director of Duke University's Center for the Study of Aging and Human Development, "no one dies of old age [but from] some defined disease or pathologic entity which leads to the inability of a vital organ to do its job and this, almost by definition, leads to the cessation of life."

Exactly why Harry Linder must die is one of the questions scientists from many disciplines are now trying to answer. They are exploring the biological processes of aging itself—not just the diseases that accompany age—and when they have satisfactory answers they will also know how to slow down the aging process. There are several major theories about why we age, and even an effort to develop a composite or "unified" theory of aging. But there is not yet general agreement as to which, if any, of the present theories are valid.** All that is certain is that the process of aging

---

* American blacks start out with lower life expectancy at birth— seven years less—but if they reach their mid-seventies, overtake whites. By the age of 86, an American black can expect to live about seven more years.
** The fact that there is, as of the moment, no completely satisfactory answer to the questions of why we age and how to retard aging can be a cause for embarrassment to scientists who are asked the questions all the time. In giving an award lecture to a group of gerontologists,

involves the death of cells, often because the cells fail to reproduce themselves accurately. Most of the body's cells must be reproduced at a regular rate, except for brain cells which die off at a rate of about 100,000 a day after we reach maturity. (We start out with a total of 10,000 million, probably more than we need to begin with, fortunately.) These are never replaced, nor are some other cells such as those of the heart muscle.

The body's cells replace themselves by dividing whenever necessary, but with some loss or error as we get older. As the total population of cells decreases, or as the rate of reproduction goes down, our body ages. That much is reasonably certain; *why* the loss and error is another story, subject to a variety of theories.

We all must age biologically, although at different rates of speed (there is even the phenomenon of prematurely aged children).* Biological aging is universal—men and women, dogs, cats, horses all grow old in similar ways; a dog's hair will turn gray, he will have a decline in nervous functions and muscular reaction, he may develop eye cataracts. Although Harry Linder is doing better than most men, he has all these biological characteristics of aging:

• He is less sensitive to touch and pain, to light and even to intense pressure than when he was younger. (Although glare bothers him.) His sense of smell has long been reduced; his sense of taste is no longer what it was, either. His hearing first decreased for high-pitched tones, later for the lower ones. He has so far escaped senile cataracts, but has needed reading glasses since his forties and they no longer serve him as well.

• His body temperature is lower than before; rectal temperature in very old people may fall as low as 90 degrees Fahrenheit, instead

---

Charles H. Barrows, Jr., expressed this frustration by reporting a current sad and somewhat sick joke:
  Patient: "How can I keep from growing old?"
  Doctor: "Run across the expressway at night."
  * Caused by progeria, a rare disease. The young victim will run through his life cycle in a few years and have the physical appearance and internal changes of premature senility, including wrinkled skin, loss of hair and teeth, wasting of muscle, the shuffling gait of an old man by the time he is 12. Victims of progeria usually die of heart disease before they reach 30.

of the normal 98.6. He doesn't perspire as much as he used to, a mixed blessing but a sign of biological aging.

• He has problems in digestion and intestinal upset. The inability to chew well is one cause—he has problems with his dentures—as well as reduced activity of stomach and intestine which have brought about constipation, a common ailment of the old.

• He's had to give up drinking alcohol. His liver and kidneys are less efficient; after 80, the kidney filters only half as well as it did at 20. He urinates a lot, with nighttime urination being a particular problem, because of prostatic enlargement, which occurs in three-quarters of all men over 55.

• Harry was just looking at the beach. It is possible, however, for him to have intercourse (although much less frequently than in middle life). Males have a form of menopause, too, considerably later than in women, but usually with less atrophy of the reproductive organs.

• His heart doesn't pump as much blood (about 30% less than when he was 30), and some hardening of the arteries increases the resistance to blood flow. His lungs no longer have the same total capacity, and lungs and lung fiber are less flexible and elastic; Harry no longer breathes in and out as much air in a single breath. He has mild shortness of breath but has not been diagnosed as having emphysema, common to old people and particularly to heavy smokers. In sum, his lungs are about 40% as effective as they were in young manhood.

• His voluntary movements are slow, probably because of the reduction of the total mass of his muscle fibers as well as the aging of his central nervous system, which is now about 15% less effective. (Muscle fibers are replaced by nonmuscular scar tissues in the very old.) His loss of brain cells is not apparent; his mind is clear, but he is now probably slower and more deliberate—and perhaps wiser—in thinking things through than when he was younger. His brain weighs less than it did in his youth; because its vessels have not yet hardened enough or occluded, he has thus far escaped a stroke, which can happen to some of the very old.

• His skin is not what it used to be. It is less elastic, dry, and wrinkled. He has freckles—ephelides—on hands and face because of an uneven distribution of pigment and small bruises—black-and-blue spots—caused by eruption of the now fragile small blood vessels. What hair he has is white. (Older women suffer from thinning hair, too, but rarely from total baldness.)

• He has, but not to an advanced degree, the stooped and shuffling gait that comes with old age. This is caused by a stiffening of joints, the partial bending of the limbs at hip and knee joints, and the decalcification of the bones—they are now more porous. There is also a tendency for ligaments to calcify.

• His muscles now are generally flabbier and weaker. Harry is actually shorter than he used to be: shrinkage, mainly in the trunk, takes place in the seventh and eighth decades of life. He is also lighter than he used to be because of loss of tissue; he remembers fondly when eating and a tendency to overweight were problems in his middle years. (Proper nutrition—eating to stay alive—is one of the basic problems of the old, as we shall see.) He does not understand why he seems more portly than he used to be although his weight is down. The answer is that abdominal depth and circumference increase in old age as the muscles weaken and fat is redistributed from peripheral to central and internal parts of the body.

A Boston study of more than 2,000 healthy war veterans, aged from 22 to 82, shows other striking changes in physique as we age. The greatest single loss was in grip strength—a reduction of 29% between the third and eighth decades. Next was the loss in the triceps skinfold, a measure of limb fat, which went down by 22%. Calf circumference was reduced by 6%, the circumference of the upper arm almost as much. The 70-year-olds in the study were 3.5% shorter and almost 6% lighter than the 20-year-olds, which is only partly accounted for by the fact that the younger men were born when people tended to be somewhat taller and weigh more.

The greatest increases in the bodies of the old were in abdominal depth (13.3%) and circumference (6.5%) and chest depth (8%) —this last so well-known a pattern that it is called "senile chest." If an old person suspects that his nose and ear lengths and breadths have increased, he is quite right; the increases range from 6% (for the tip of the nose) to 10.5% (ear length). "Head, face, hand, and foot measurements were similar at all ages," concludes the study.

Small consolation to Harry. His nose is longer and thicker, his skin wrinkled. His biceps and thighs are thinner, his abdomen sags, and he is shorter and stooped. With the changes in his nervous system, his reflexes and gait are slower. He is a mess in shorts and T-shirt, and none of the girls look back at him the way they once did. Being young in heart and mind and old in body is a bore, nuisance, and frustration—and he knows it can only get worse. However, he accepts the inevitable, as most healthy people do, with much equanimity; he no longer feels cosmically cheated and outraged by his age, as he did at 40.

In his daily life back home, he has all these problems and more, and has to make adjustments or find compensations for them. Because his senses are not what they once were, he is less alert and often caught short; he sometimes gives wrong answers because he couldn't hear the questions; sometimes he just ignores people. He is too proud to wear a hearing aid (which may, or may not, help him—getting properly fitted is not easy for the old). He can't read timetables and prefers books with larger type. He has trouble boarding buses and even more trouble hearing the rapid snarls of a bus driver announcing where the bus is going. He still drives a car but drives so slowly that he exasperates other drivers, is somewhat of a traffic hazard, and probably shouldn't be driving at all. He has trouble crossing streets before the lights change. He is deathly afraid of being hit by a car, and his fear is well grounded—in one year 25% of all traffic accidents involved people over 65 (who make up 10% of the population).

He dislikes going outside his usual routine—home to nearby office, to lunch at his club, to office, back home. Out of orbit, he cannot readily find a place to relax when tired, or a urinal which he often needs. He suffers little pain, just aches. He is not immediately imperiled by major diseases, is just old. By his own definition, he is a physical wreck. When his newsdealer asks each morning, "How are you today, Mr. Linder?" he hardly knows what to say. He knows the line of Seneca, "Old age is an incurable disease," and once almost answered: "I'm fine but I've got an incurable disease" but thought better of it.

Dr. Eisdorfer is technically correct—"Nobody dies of old age." But as they reach advanced age and lose more and more healthy cells, or the cells become sluggish or turn into connective tissue, the very old dry up, become stringy, and somehow fade away, with one or another of the degenerative diseases—heart disease, cancer, atheriosclerosis, hypertension, and others—doing the final job. Somehow, the older a person gets, the less specific his problems become. They all flow into one another. "Pathological processes are no longer separately difficulties of the stomach, of the kidneys, or of the heart," says Dr. Alfred H. Lawton. "Nor are they any longer distinctly complications from deterioration of the physical, behavioral, or the spiritual facets of life."

Without disputing Dr. Eisdorfer, other gerontologists suggest that it be looked at another way: that old age be thought of as another degenerative disease—not as man's inevitable fate—so that it can be classified as a scientific problem and handled accordingly.

The ultimate goal of all research on aging is to increase the length of the good years and "improve the performance and well-being of older people," says Dr. Nathan W. Shock, chief of the Gerontology Center of the National Institute of Child Health and Human Development. His center has been testing and keeping records of some 700 aging male subjects since 1958, analyzing their loss of function and the effects of that loss. The effort is to develop fundamental information on the nature of the aging process itself. "The more we know about the underlying causes of aging," says Dr. Shock, "the more we are apt to devise and introduce a drug, or pill, or experimental condition that can have an impact."

Aging does not happen only in the old. If biological aging is to be considered deterioration, then it begins at conception. "We see the effects of aging in the developmental part of life," Dr. Shock says. "There are certain structures, even in the fetus and embryo, that deteriorate and must disappear before the next stage can appear."

Biochemist and science writer Isaac Asimov relates aging to the natural process of evolution. One-celled organisms divide, and each of the two daughter cells has the same genes as the original cell. "If the genes were passed on as perfect copies from division to division forever, the nature of the original cell would never change no matter how often it divided and redivided," he says. But this doesn't happen, the copy is not always perfect. "There are random changes ('mutations') every once in a while and, gradually, from one parent cell, different strains, varieties, and, eventually, species arise," he adds. Dr. Asimov believes that "for the good of the species it seems best for the old to die that the young might live." Behind all the theories of the aging process is one basic idea: As we get older, there is information loss in the basic genetic material of the cell, DNA (deoxyribonucleic acid). DNA is the key molecule of life. It transmits heredity and enables living things to reproduce. The abundance of theories arises from the doubts as to how and why DNA loses its information. It may be lost through mutation or by somehow "blurring." Or the cell may undergo molecular change when its molecules link with other molecules—"cross-linkage." This may be due to a number of factors, certainly because of the radiation present in the environment, or because of X-ray or atomic radiation—all radiation hastens the breakdown of DNA molecules.

Cells have characteristics that limit their function. For one thing, normal healthy cells do not reproduce forever as scientists once thought. This discovery was made accidentally by Dr. Leonard Hayflick of Stanford University's School of Medicine in 1961; he found that cells cultured from lung tissue of an embryo doubled about fifty times, then stopped; cells cultured from adult lung tissue had only about twenty more doublings left in them, and the assumption is that the older the person the cells are taken from, the fewer times they will be able to divide. Cells also suffer from intracellular sludge (especially lipofuscin), a product of normal cell activity, which may accumulate over time and eventually impair cell function.

The various theories of aging are still unproven and debated by gerontologists. A listing of major ones includes:

• *The wear-and-tear theory:* One of the older theories, this holds that constant use over time wears out all complex systems, the human body included. The theory is the easiest one for the laymen to embrace. It sounds right—"So-and-so died because he was just worn out." It seems reasonable for other reasons, too: If a kidney, say, is severely damaged, it cannot completely recover from the stress and is more vulnerable to disease. But as a general theory of aging it has serious gaps: it does not explain the life-span differences between various species of mammals, or why—even in the same species—different strains have different life spans. (A beagle may live twelve to fifteen years compared to only eight or nine years for a mastiff. What makes the mastiff wear out first?)

• *The waste product theory:* According to this theory damaging substances accumulate in the cell and interfere with its function. Autopsies on some old people have found that an insoluble substance —an age pigment called lipofuscin—may make up as much as 30% of the weight of the tissue. But there is no evidence that this accumulation interferes with cell function or speeds up aging. This theory has its counterpart in an older one: that each cell is endowed from conception with a definite amount of a vital substance; when it is used up, the cell dies; when enough cells die, the organism dies. "The trouble is," says Dr. Charles H. Barrows, Jr., of the Johns Hopkins School of Hygiene and Public Health, "no such 'vital substance' has ever been identified."

• *The cross-linking theory:* As we age, blood vessels, tendons, and skin lose their elasticity. This is because of cross-links between or within the large molecules in connective tissue—specifically collagen and elastin (fibrous protein molecules), which give these tissues their elasticity. The theory assumes that when these molecules get tangled, they result in larger aggregations of molecules which prevent essential chemical reactions from taking place. The trouble with the theory is that it rests entirely on experiments made with collagen and elastin, which happen to be *extra*-cellular proteins; many or most facets of aging are thus not covered, and the theory is considered to be of limited application.

• *The free radical theory:* Free radicals are unstable molecular fragments that readily react with nearby molecules to form chemically stable bonds. They are also strong cross-linking agents and may also upset the information content of important molecules—this is probably how they do their damage. This theory is also considered of limited application.

• *The auto-immune theory:* Immune reactions that are normally directed against "foreign" proteins or tissues somehow act up and begin to attack body cells because, in effect, they can no longer tell friend from foe; either information is blurred or the other cells are somehow changing and look "foreign." There is increased incidence of the "immune diseases" in old age, but many biologists, like Howard J. Curtis of Brookhaven National Laboratory, believe this theory should be classed along with other degenerative diseases— such as cancer—and is in no way all-inclusive.

• *The somatic mutation theory:* One of the genetic theories of aging, this has much support among scientists. The genetic structure of the cell—the chromosomes—dictates the cell's function. (All the cells in the body are somatic except the reproductive ones of sperm and ova.) Chromosomes are very delicate structures—the DNA in human chromosomes contains the code for over 100,000 kinds of protein—and may be damaged spontaneously or by other agents. They recover slowly, or not at all, and fail to synthesize the right protein. The damage—the mutation—will be handed down to all daughter nuclei as the cells divide. The mutations accumulate until many cells are functioning poorly and eventually die—and so does the organism. Despite the support given this theory, many scientists believe that it cannot be the only biological mechanism responsible for aging. This theory is similar—and in some respects identical—to

• *The error theory:* Alterations or errors occur in the cell's DNA molecule and these bring the cell's functions to a halt.

Now rising above these theories and encompassing some of them is that of the *genetic program:* the idea that from conception to death our total life span is programmed in the genes, that after a while the program spelled out in the DNA or genetic material simply runs out, like a tape recording, and cell function stops. The idea of programmed biological obsolescence is a favorite of many, including Dr. Charles H. Barrows, Jr., of Johns Hopkins, who also serves on Dr. Shock's team. The theory holds that, in effect, the fertilized egg has a timetable stamped into it for embryonic development, birth, the baby's first teeth, first step—up to all the later developments of the aging process, including wrinkles, body changes, and susceptibility to degenerative disease and death. Dr. Barrows believes that some of the other theories may be correct to a point—but that the genetic program is the underlying reason for the changes they note and try to explain.

The genetic program theory now has considerable acceptance. It does not, of course, run its course in a vacuum, and there is much evidence that environment—particularly nutrition and temperature—influences the way it works. Dr. Clive McCay of Cornell University published the results of his breakthrough study as long ago as 1932; he showed that the life span of rats could be extended by as much as a third by restricting the calories in their diet. In his experiment, control rats were given essential protein, minerals, vitamins, and an unlimited supply of calories; the "underfed" rats had the same diet—but without enough calories to develop normally. They were thus kept in a juvenile state for up to 1,000 days. When their caloric intake was increased, they rapidly grew to normal size—and lived longer (up to 1,465 days) than the control rats, none of whom lived longer than 969 days. Dr. Barrows has made related experiments with rotifers—minuscule, many-celled acquatic animals. When their nutritional intake was cut in half, their life span increased from 34 to 55 days.

Reducing temperatures had a similar effect. Rotifers grown in an environment of 35 degrees centigrade lived only 18 days; at 25 degrees, they lived to 34 days. Other scientists have experimented with fruit flies: at 30 degrees, they lived only 13 days; at 10 degrees, up to 120 days. The rate of chemical reaction increases with rising temperatures; these experiments are interpreted to mean that the life span is also related to "the rate of living."

Dr. Bernard L. Strehler of the University of Southern California sees the possibility that temperature-reducing drugs might add twenty or more years to average life expectancy. If the human organism reacts about the same as laboratory specimens have responded to tests, a very minor reduction in temperature, about three degrees Fahrenheit, could do the job, he says. Dr. Strehler has raised the possibility that the longer-lived people may actually have slightly lower than average temperatures.

Control of nutrition and temperature offers real possibilities for slowing down aging although they are crude techniques—undoubtedly, more refined ones will soon be found. There have also been successful experiments with parabiosis—a surgical technique in which connections have been made between the blood vessels of old and young rats. The old ones were "rejuvenated," quickly reached a reduced cholesterol level, and survived beyond their anticipated life spans. This technique is a crude one, too, for prolonging life; the eventual quest is for a "youth factor" circulating in the blood. This remains to be isolated, if it exists.

Nothing resembling an elixir of life has yet been found. But the rate of discovery increases each year; each new discovery brightens the prospects for finding the diet, the drugs, pills, genetic manipulation, or other conditions which will hold back age and extend the good years, with their vitality. In 1973 Dr. Alex Comfort of University College, London, said that he hoped science would find a technique for "interfering" with aging within the next three or four years. The hope is that in the future people of 50 will look and feel like today's 40-year-olds, that men and women in their eighties will have a biological age of 60.

There are many people who can't wait. In Europe, particularly, cell therapy is a large, still growing business. The therapists use injections—usually tissue extracts from fetal lambs—to "revitalize" the body. Despite the cost of such treatment—as much as $2,000 for a series of eight injections—and the number of famous and rich people who seem to have taken them, there is not yet, and may never be, scientific evidence that they work. Nor do many scientists support the claims made for such drugs as Gerovital, which is made up mainly of the anesthetic procaine.* Gerovital does have its value—as an antidepressant—and it is this fact that probably helps people *think* they feel better or younger.

Which is very much to the point. Gerovital may serve to prolong life, but for other reasons. Depression—dreading and dwelling upon old age and its infirmities and fearing death—is as good a way of hastening the end of life as intracellular sludge. The last chapter in this book is about the "longevity syndrome," the complex of factors that help people live long lives successfully. Good health is one of them; so, too, are happiness, concern for others, involvement with people, and many interests—a celebration of life. Or, in the scientific language of Duke University's Erdman Palmore reporting on an investigation: "Remaining active in some meaningful social role affected people's longevity on all three major levels —physical, psychological, and social."

---

* Gerovital is apparently *the* thing to take at the moment. A typical advertisement for a rejuvenation center—this one in Spain and appearing, inexplicably, in the "Holidays and Travel" section of the International *Herald Tribune* in Paris—reads:
REVITALISATION—"El Bosque" Health Center. Extensive range of treatments for Obesity, Rheumatism, Bronchitis, Coronary sufferers, etc., including Underwater massage, Finnish Sauna, Mud bath, Inhalation, etc. Rejuvenation cures (Gerovital H3), Plastic Surgery (Nasal remodeling, face-lifting, etc.) English speaking physicians. Be always young and fit. Write for brochure to "El Bosque" . . .

At 86, Harry Linder's genetic program may be running out, but he pays very little attention to the matter. He loves his wife and his work. He has a passion for animals and takes his dog out every night although he is constantly being warned about the dangers of walking on New York City streets after dark. ("I'll go down fighting," he says—meaning only that he loves his dog and will take his chances.) He loves other things too. On his return home, he wrote me a bread-and-butter note, taking particular note of the state of my garden. He added a postscript:

"About that walk along Tahiti Beach. I don't know if girls looked as good when I was younger. I could never see enough of them to know. I love the way they look and flirt (although not, alas, with me). Wasn't it Oliver Wendell Holmes—about my age and in my situation—who said, 'Ah, to be seventy again'?"

5 AGE AND NUTRITION

A food-and-health expert of a generation ago bombarded his public, via radio and printed page, with the slogan, "You are what you eat." Those are unnerving words, summoning up as they do the picture of people walking about made up—depending upon their origins and taste—of semidigested bits of plum pudding, *schnitz un knepp, tripes, chapatti, cholent, chlodnik,* or chili. Among things wrong with the slogan is that it may be turned around to "You eat what you are" to make equal sense. We eat those dishes if we are, respectively, British, Pennsylvania Dutch, French, Indian, Jewish, Polish, or Texan. Not only do we eat our regional or ethnic specialties on our own home ground; we are all, to a degree, culture and habit bound, and food tastes and customs acquired in childhood linger, sometimes all our lives, and no matter where we are.

We also eat what our social and economic status tells us to eat and what is necessary for prestige. We eat things that have symbolic value, we eat what we think is good for us, what doctors and others tell us to eat. And we eat what we believe to be appropriate to our years. For these and other reasons, as we grow old we become more and more vulnerable to food fads and fancies and a host of problems and conflicts unknown to younger generations.

Nutrition throughout the life cycle is one of the factors that determine how long we will live. A good diet will help a person live out his "normal" life span—whatever it may be. A poor diet will shorten his life. Diet is directly related to such common ailments —and eventual killers—of the old as atherosclerosis ("hardening of the arteries" and its complications are the immediate cause of death of 50% of the people in advanced industrial societies), hypertension (which may be more influenced by early diet but takes its greater toll among the old), and diabetes (suffered by 5 to 6% of all people over 65). A look at the old around us will quickly show the importance of diet and diet control: There are few people over 80, virtually none over 90, who are fat simply because the fat don't live that long.

Good nutrition for the old is not really different from good nutrition for the young; the rules of balance are basically the same except that the old tend to need fewer calories and more, perhaps, of certain vitamins and trace elements. This is not to say that the old do not have special food problems. They do—they are more likely to suffer a range of digestive disturbances and other abnormalities. And almost all old people have at least one nutrition-based degenerative disease that will contribute somehow to a shortened life span.

Some of the old are obsessed with problems of diet. The signs of aging make them dwell upon their body and its needs. They reject or select certain foods because of their effect upon aging and the degenerative processes. There are, indeed, things they can do, but not as much as they would like and others, vendors of a thousand products, claim. It is lifetime habits that really matter, not the rigid—or quirky—diets that the old sometimes suffer through.

Eating became one of man's greatest pleasures a long time ago. There is no reason why the old should not enjoy their food, too. Physiologist Henry A. Schroeder of Dartmouth Medical School offers this advice to his fellow-doctors: Don't make dietary rules so strict that food becomes distasteful and the pleasure of eating turns into a chore for the old. If a doctor does this, he says, he has deprived the old of some of the joy of living and turned a therapeutic measure into a harmful one.

Dr. Schroeder says that first consideration should be given to "what people like to eat, not necessarily what they should eat. The physician should adapt his thinking to include social, religious, racial, ethnic, and psychologic factors."

These account for some of the vulnerability of the old in matters of diet. Because "we've always had them," a middle-class widow will seek out higher-priced groceries and processed foods than she can afford—although for nutrition's sake she can do better for less money. Other old people have almost the opposite habit but are equally penalized: Each culture of the world has its own type of "good" nutrition with an indigenous balance, so sensitive that even the condiments used play a nutritional role. The balance can be easily upset in times of crop or distribution failure, wars or depressions. People who grew up in such times may never know what a balanced diet is; many of the old maintain the poor diets of their deprived years simply because they have never learned better.

To some people in rural areas, store-bought bread has more prestige than home-baked bread even though it costs more and is not as good—and the older members of the family are deprived of one of their staple joys. If an urban neighborhood changes, an Orthodox Jewish woman living alone may be in distress because her kosher butcher has moved and the nearest one is now ten blocks away, out of her range. The grandfather of a black family moving into the same neighborhood may have a related problem; the shops there don't carry quite the same food he's been accustomed to, and his children, now that they've moved, are more interested in Julia Child recipes than in soul food. The problem is even worse for an elderly parent who was born and raised abroad and who lives with his children. The children or grandchildren have thoroughly assimilated eating habits and rarely prepare old-country dishes. In this case, an old man may increasingly refuse to eat the "new" dishes, partly because he really doesn't like them, partly to show his defiance and independence. His nutritional intake may thus be lessened, which is bad enough, He may also silently brood at mealtimes, withdrawn from his family, and actually age faster psychologically because of the conflict over food.

Other aging and old people sit at *their* tables barricaded behind jars, tubes, and boxes of medicines, vitamins and other nutritional supplements, and eating high-priced organic or health foods. The joys of eating are no longer the issue; foremost in their minds are their everyday problems—undiagnosed aches and pains, blood and muscle tone, fatigue, constipation, indigestion, "rejuvenation." They are naturally vulnerable to food fads and diet idiosyncracies.

Books, magazines, and advertisements in all the media spread gospels of wild ideas about nutrition. "Quackery in nutrition and health food stores thrive in areas in which retired people with average incomes live," says Dr. Schroeder. Noting that in every widespread fad, there is "usually a grain of truth and an enormous amount of chaff," he goes through a list of health food specialties: curing vegetable juices (no benefit), single so-called vitamins such as rutin and lecithin (unnecessary), unsaturated fatty acids (better in oils), bioflavonoids (unnecessary), rose hips (value undetermined), and "a variety of curious, irrational, and wonderful concoctions guaranteed to cure what ails you." He has a wry and clinical view: "Probably all these preparations are harmless, except to people's pocketbooks."

Millions of people have been swallowing large doses of vitamin E or smearing it on their skins to help their problems and delay the ravages of age. They may have been dismayed when the National Research Council of the U.S. National Academy of Sciences announced late in 1973 that there is no clinical evidence that vitamin E cures the diseases people think it will and that most claims made for it are based upon misinterpretations of the results of animal research. It does seem to prevent and cure atherosclerosis in rabbits, but there is no evidence at all that it helps in treating cardiovascular disease in humans.* The aging and old also buy huge quantities of iron additives, in the belief that a high concentration of iron in the blood reduces "fatigue." Public health specialist Sandra C. Howell warns that "the 'fatigue' may mask (or be generated by) depression, cumulative social loss, or real disease, none of which are affected by iron supplements . . ."

* A recent international scientific symposium was concerned solely with vitamin E and its value. Most reports made the point that it is still very much of a medical and scientific enigma and of little proven therapeutic value to humans. However, vitamin E has no known adverse side-effects although some people have been taking fifty times the recommended daily allowance. In answer to an interviewer, Dr. M. K. Horwitt, the "father" of human vitamin E research, is reported to have said: "If you take away their vitamin E, some patients get very depressed and uncomfortable. It's their security blanket. So I let them have it." Some fifty scientists were invited by Dr. Horwitt to the symposium, sponsored by General Mills Chemicals, Inc., which makes hundreds of tons of vitamin E each year.

The "natural" or "organic" vitamin preparations come in for particular criticism by nutritionist Jean Mayer of the Harvard University School of Public Health. He says they're nonsense. "A molecule is a molecule is a molecule—there's absolutely no way for the body to distinguish between thiamine extracted from rice bran and thiamine made elsewhere. *All* vitamins are natural vitamins in that they're made with natural atoms and put together in a certain way, and that's it . . ."

Dr. Mayer's concern here is the "fantastic amounts of money" people waste on the so-called organic or natural vitamins; he is not at all saying that the aging may not need vitamins and other supplements. Most people get all the vitamins, minerals, and protein they need from a good regular diet. With age and less physical activity, however, there is less overall need for food and less intake—but just as much need for mineral, vitamin, and protein nutrients. Thus the density of nutrients in what the old do eat should be greater—if it is not, they may, indeed, need supplements. (There is *never* any reason to take more than 100% of a recommended dietary allowance, he says—all the rest is waste.)

Dr. Mayer stresses that it is most important that the old preserve the quality of their diet, and, along with everyone else, be educated to the value of primary foods: fruit, vegetables, meat, fish, eggs, milk, and whole grain cereals (in particular). Vitamin E, for example, is widespread in all of these. So are the trace minerals: iron, zinc, fluorine, chromium, and others.* Unless any of them are proscribed by a doctor, he says, the primary foods will adequately nourish most everyone. Others are not that sanguine about people eating the right foods; Dr. Schroeder says that, all things considered, "daily supplements of vitamins for the old are safe, logical, and desirable as insurance against possible deficiencies" and to help keep the old in as good health as possible.

All this is academic to many other old people—the ones who

* Dr. Mayer favors fluoridation of water for a reason other than the protection of children's teeth: It serves the old, too. A higher level of fluoride in water helps fix the calcium in bones so that the elderly don't develop osteoporosis—a common condition that leads to repeated bone fractures and fragility.

don't eat the right foods and don't take vitamins either. Eating badly and malnutrition are endemic among the old, particularly if they are poor, and those with the greatest need for nutritional supplements are usually the last ones to get them: They don't know about their value, don't go to doctors, don't want to go to the bother or expense.

Malnutrition is often a "subclinical" disease with symptoms that are neither evident nor clear-cut. Doctors rarely get to see patients with malnutrition only; they are usually called in when a person gets a more dominant disease such as pneumonia, although it may have been malnutrition that allowed the patient to get the disease and contributed to its severity. This is a regrettable fact; a number of recent surveys conclude that the detection of malnutrition in the old is well worthwhile—their response to treatment is "nearly always satisfactory."

The old have two other special reasons for being badly nourished. Some don't feel hunger and become indifferent to food because, particularly after 75, their senses of taste and smell have been reduced and the stomach is less active. And many of the aging and old live in isolation.

The social life of the adult is built around the pleasures of food and drink; when the social life is gone, the pleasures seem to evaporate, too. Old people, men and women, frequently complain that they have little incentive to prepare food for themselves if they live alone. This is not only a statement of fact, says psychiatrist Jack Weinberg of the College of Medicine, University of Illinois. It is also a rebuke to those who fail to perceive the "isolation and aloneness" of the old, he says. Dr. Weinberg explains why solitary eating may be so dreary: Food eaten by itself "lacks the condiment of another's presence which can transform the simplest fare to the ceremonial act, with all its shaded meanings."

The "ceremonial act" of mealtime usually takes place three times a day, at set hours, in our society. The frequency and timing of meals, however, is much more a matter of custom than of any great physiological need. An Englishman may feel that he can't go to his office without a substantial breakfast; a French manual worker may eat no breakfast at all, except for coffee, but take a ten o'clock break for a sandwich, before eating again at noon. A Spaniard may not understand how anyone can eat supper as early as 7 or 8 p.m. An American may change his eating hours completely one day of the week—for Sunday brunch—and suffer no upset, unless he drinks too much. Even the feeling of hunger is learned or conditioned by where we live and what we do, by what culture or family establishes as the "right" time to eat.

There is no need for the old to stick to conventional mealtimes and eating and drinking habits if their systems suffer because of them. The old often do experiment with mealtimes (usually to the annoyance of their families). Some try avoiding liquids at night, to avoid bladder pressure while they sleep; some try eating their "heavy" meal at noon (although the rest of the family eat it at night, when they are reunited) in order to digest things while awake. They may eat scant or no supper, and then suffer stomach contractions from hunger while trying to sleep.

These systems are hardly ideal. Bladder permitting, it is probably best for the old to have a nutritious drink before bedtime; they tend not to drink enough liquids during the day, and everyone needs enough to produce a quart or more of urine a day. And the old should eat enjoyably but never heavily; a heavy meal does more violence to their systems than it does to those of younger people who are more active and have better digestion. Most scientists concerned with nutrition and aging believe that numerous small meals—four or more a day—are best, provided that the nutritional values are kept up. Among their advantages for the old: The system is never taxed, the small meals are more digestible, and they help the old to manage and control obesity.

Being fat is murderous. Dr. Nathan W. Shock says that if we could "suddenly wave a wand and eliminate all the obesity in the population" we would be more likely to increase the life span than by any other means. As we grow old—and when it is too late—we see most clearly the damage done by overeating. If a man is aging and fat, the odds are that he won't live much longer unless he can do something about it—and he is probably too habit-bound to make the change. If the aging and obese wish to slow down the progress of degenerative diseases, Dr. Schroeder says, "it is mandatory that they regain the body weight of their youth." But the doctor can only point the way. "The will of the patient is the all-important factor," he adds. The will is usually too weak unless the person has reached the point of becoming indifferent to food. Not many fat people live that long.

A quick crash-diet is never recommended for the old. A sudden reduction in calories leads to the breakdown of irreplaceable muscle tissue. A crash-diet also carries with it the danger of depriving the old of the vitamins, protein, and elements they vitally need. Still, calories *do* count, and any sensible diet depends upon the reduction of calories. At 65, a person needs about 20% fewer calories than at 25. Many nutritionists warn the old about sugar, even if they do not have diabetes: Refined sugar gives them calories and little else. Among other foods with empty calories are white flour, alcohol, rich desserts and candies, and refined fats.

It is possible to subsist on a diet containing almost no carbohydrates, as Eskimos do. Given enough protein, a sustained low-carbohydrate diet makes most sense for the old (although it would have been easier and better had they started long before growing old).

Physical activity is necessary, too, for good health and a reasonable weight. However, exercise by itself—without diet—cannot be taken seriously as a weight-reducing means for the obese old. Perhaps a professional football player can eat gargantuan meals and then go out on the field and work them off. The kind of physical activity that burns up calories would tax the heart, lungs, and spirit of an old, fat person and probably kill him—particularly if he is a city dweller and has never been especially concerned with physical fitness. There are always such examples as that of King Gustaf V of Sweden who played tennis actively until he was in his late eighties.* However, he had kept fit all his life; unlike most others, he had the means, opportunity, and will to do so, and his case is memorable mainly because it is so rare. Books and articles on exercises for the old inevitably say, "Consult your physician before

---

* A more extraordinary case is that of William J. Moore, who received great attention in August 1972, when he celebrated his 100th birthday in a hospital, recovering from injuries suffered during a tennis game. Mr. Moore, an educator and son of a slave, had been a professional tennis player and felt no reason to abandon the game just because it no longer gave him his living. He died in June 1973, of ailments presumably unrelated to tennis.

starting." These usually involve gentle exercises to improve circulation, limber up the body, and keep the old in social contact with others. And some of them are to be done in bed, on awakening, just to get the body used to a change of position.

Regular exercise of the right type can postpone deterioration and help the level of physical capacity, says Henry Montoye, head of the Sports Physiology Laboratory at Michigan State University. It should also help the old to pick up "interest in other people and the world about them, their energy for doing mental work and, in general, their . . . vigor for carrying out everyday activities," he declares. But for burning up calories, only diet really helps most old people. Walking is heartily recommended as exercise for the fit old but, calculates nutritionist A. B. Peyton, a person has to walk a mile to burn up a cola drink, 4.5 miles to burn up a piece of mince pie, and 5.3 miles to burn up a slice of chocolate layer cake.

Exercises, even strenuous exercises, can be of benefit to *some* of the old. Dr. Herbert A. de Vries of the University of Southern California, testing men between the ages of 52 and 88, found that jogging, swimming, and calisthenics brought about improvement in arm strength, blood vessel and heart function, and oxygen-carrying capacity. There was also some reduction in body fat, blood pressure, and nervous tension. These were laboratory experiments and, Dr. de Vries makes clear, any physician prescribing exercises for the old should pick his regimen with the same care he uses in choosing drugs. A doctor must have deep insight into an old man or woman's physical condition—and considerable courage—before he can tell his patient to jog home from his office. *Walking* home to a low-carbohydrate diet and gentle exercises is considerably safer.

This is not exactly to dispute Dr. de Vries, who says there seems to be no danger to the cardiovascular system in healthy old men with normal blood pressure if exercise is done systematically and in moderation. And he has proven that old people have a capacity to adapt to physical training. But people are faddish, and exercises for the old are now coming into vogue. There is always the prospect of 70- or 80-year-old men and women, caught up in it all and feeling no pain, going out and doing exercises on their own. They should be warned; the following study has to do with rats, not with people, but the principle may be the same:

Three scientists at the University of Massachusetts, Amherst, put rats of four different ages—120, 300, 450, and 600 days—on a treadmill, running twenty minutes a day, five days a week, for a year and more. They also kept a control group of sedentary rats that didn't get the exercise, just ate somewhat less food.

The youngest group of exercising rats did fine; 80% of them survived compared to only 64% of the sedentary group. But only 33% of the oldest group of rats on the treadmill survived, compared to 80% of the sedentary old ones. Overall, those that started running before they were 400 days old—probably middle age for a rat—lived longer than sedentary rats of the same age; the exercise helped bring them closer to their maximum life span. Those that started after 400 days had a much lower survival rate (54% to 83%) than those that didn't do a thing except eat moderately. The authors of this study suggest that there probably is a "threshold age" for starting an exercise program, after which it is more likely to kill than prolong life.

There are, it must be said, more mysteries to nutrition and aging than have been suggested here. There are changes and complications through the years, many of them not understood, and no two old people are alike; each is more different from the other than when they were young.

• As they age, some old people outgrow allergic reactions to certain foods. But they may also develop new allergies to other foods or additives. A process of sensitization and desensitization occurs as we age, and it goes far beyond allergic reaction. A man may dislike liver most of his life, mainly because its texture bothers him, or feel that skim milk tastes like chalk. Suddenly, in his old age, because of changed sensitivity, he may develop a strong preference for both.

• Old people may usually drink alcohol in "moderate" quantities. If there is no disease, age alone does not predispose a person to damaging effects from alcohol. Doctors sometimes advise old patients to drink, say, wine; it dilates small blood vessels and helps the flow of blood. But the liver usually becomes less efficient with age, and the doctor must, indeed, be very careful in what he advises; what was moderate in youth or middle age may be toxic in old age.

• Severe cases of insomnia among the old may be entirely relieved, not by drugs or sedatives, but by eliminating salt from the diet. After three weeks without salt, old people who had been getting only one or two hours of sleep began to sleep eight hours a night and awaken fully refreshed. There is no obvious explanation for this. In other cases, it has been discovered that the same barbiturates used to tranquilize or help a person sleep may—when that person is older—cause excitement and wakefulness. And some nursing homes in Scandinavia give steaming hot cups of coffee to their residents—at bedtime, to help them sleep.

There are no ready answers to why such changes take place. In the last example, is it because of the inner warmth given by the hot coffee? Some basic shift in response to caffeine with advancing years? Or have the years of taking caffeine dulled its effect? We all know how food affects us from day to day, according to types, quantities, and mixtures taken. It can make us sluggish, give us "heart burn" and other digestive upset. Some people cannot eat shellfish without getting a violent reaction, some cannot take the seasoning of monosodium glutamate without suffering the "Chinese restaurant syndrome"—often a queasy stomach and tightening around the temples. We feel bad, and undoubtedly our mental processes are affected, too.

What food does to us organically throughout the life cycle is even harder to comprehend. To what extent does diet—malnutrition, eating the wrong foods, eating the *right* foods—affect personality and mind? Why is there a stereotype that fat people are jolly and well-motivated while thin people are dour or thoughtful or scheming? ("Let me have men about me that are fat . . . Yond Cassius has a lean and hungry look.") Why is there a superstition among many peoples of the world that fish is a "brain food" and contributes to long life—although neither quality is peculiar to fish or any other type of food?

Increasingly, psychiatrists have come to rely upon chemical therapy—pills—to treat certain kinds of mental disorders, even long-standing ones. Might not the chemical reactions produced by foods, eaten day after day through the years, also have significant impact upon mental health and emotions? And might not some of the disparate attitudes and responses of people throughout the world—the cause of misunderstandings and wars—be caused by dietary differences and deficiencies?

Coming back from the cosmic: In the field of aging and nutrition, there is still an overall dilemma or uncertainty. Dr. Shock sums it up: Science has not yet demonstrated that dietary requirements, or the ability to absorb foods, are "significantly different" as we age. Yet we know that nutrition affects aging. The gradual loss of cells is a primary problem as we grow old, and this, he says, "may stem from environmental conditions, such as inadequacies in cellular nutrition."

Professor W. Ferguson Anderson of the University of Glasgow raises it to a different level—the issue of the relative importance of heredity vs. environment. He asks: Have the people who reach advanced old age been helped to get there by their life-long nutrition pattern? Or did they achieve their years because of their heredity, which also, somehow, shaped that pattern?

In the circumstances, Dr. Shock gives the wisest possible answer. The field of nutrition and aging, he says, "remains an area that must be explored in greater detail."

6 MIND, MEMORY, AND TIME

A man may start getting the message, "Make way for youth with fresh ideas," while in his early middle age. By his fifties, he may be a victim of the burnt-out-case theory—that everyone over 50 has already done his best work—and be reduced to the role of lame-duck preretiree. If he makes mistakes, they will be attributed to his age and mental fatigue, although they may be fewer than those of his youth, when, attributed to an excess of exuberance, they were forgiven.

As we get older, we are hounded by the notion that memory, intelligence, and the ability to learn and be productive must deteriorate, that our mental energies must fail, somewhat slower than our physical energies but in the same way. The idea that mind and memory decline with time is so strongly held that it sometimes becomes self-fulfilling; mind and memory may fail in old age simply because they are expected to.

There is no inexorable reason why this should be so. To the contrary, most of the scientific evidence is that:

- Our mental abilities and competence may remain unchanged long after 80.
- Mental performance may—and should—improve as we age.
- We can continue to learn as long as we live.
- Memory need not have any age limits at all.

The end of the line, the extreme notion, is that senility is the inevitable lot of the old. To many people, its prospect looms certain and darker than death (despite the evidence of all the very old, very bright people in the world about us). Even the dictionary definition caters to the equation of "old" and "senile." "Of, relating to, exhibiting, or characteristic of old age: *esp:* exhibiting a loss of mental faculties associated with old age" is a current, standard way of explaining what senile means.

We apply it to an old person whenever he shows any of the many "senile signs"—lack of personal cleanliness and indifference to dress and grooming; confusion about or forgetting of people, places, and dates; reclusiveness, among them. About twenty-five years ago, a group of scientists developed a more precise "Senility Index," a compendium of commonly accepted "senile signs" which explores many behavior and personality traits: how people relate to family and friends; how they view themselves and keep busy; how satisfied they are with past and present life; their health complaints and neuroticism; their ego-strength and intellectual competence. The Senility Index looks into the host of "regressive signs" of old age; the higher his score on the Index, the more "senile" a person is supposed to be.

Psychologist Frances M. Carp recently decided to put some aspects of the Senility Index to the test: Are those "senile signs" really signs of senility? And what do they have to do with old age? She applied the Index to two samples. One was a group of 295 people ranging in age from 52 to 92, an average age of 72. The other was a group of undergraduates with an age range of 17 to 25, an average age of 20. There were two rounds of tests and interviews for all, eighteen months apart.

Dr. Carp's findings explode some of the misconceptions about "senility" and the old:

• Within the older group, there was no relationship between senility and chronological age. And, after the eighteen-month period, there was no significant change in their scores; senility was not catching up with them.

• The college group did not have a lower score than the older one. In fact, among the college students there was a *higher* proportion of "senile signs" than among the 52-to-92-year-olds.

This does not mean that college students are more "senile" than people fifty or more years their senior. It does show that the "senile signs"—which most of us accept—have little to do with age itself. The way the Senility Index is constructed, its high scorers are bound to be people of lower mental level, socially inept, with greater signs of anxiety, and maladjustment, and all the rest. In this case, the younger people had more of these problems than the old. Dr. Carp reported her findings in an article aptly titled "Senility—or Garden Variety Maladjustment?"

There are many ways in which the equation of "old" and "senile" damns the aged: It reduces their image and function in daily life, puts them beyond the pale. It deprives them of the care they need by masking the real problem: An old man may be called senile because of an acute brain syndrome—a result of malnutrition. Or his problem may be depression or anxiety (which often accounts for the "rigidity" of the old) but with the diagnosis "senility," he is put away and forgotten.

The label of senile has broad social consequences. "For the physician, lawyer, psychiatrist, or family, [it] structures their perception of the person," declare Michael Baizerman and David L. Ellison. The label provides "a social status passage," they say, which makes a patient out of a person, and thus makes it easier to relegate him to an institution, whether commitment is warranted or not.

A diagnosis of senility is a handy way of getting rid of the troublesome old, along with a way of assuaging conscience. It has clearly been abused, and, finally, in 1968, the American Psychiatric Association, in its *Diagnostic and Statistical Manual of Mental Disorders,* sought to end the practice by explicitly prohibiting a diagnosis of senile dementia based on a patient's age.

Senile dementia, of course, does exist. It is a serious medical problem and a fair predictor of mortality. It appears when a pathological process is imposed on top of a psychological one; it concerns a person's general condition of health, not just his mind, memory, or years. Pure senile dementia, attributable to brain atrophy, is a comparatively rare disease. (Psychiatric examination alone cannot identify it; neither can an old person's family or neighbors.) But even patients with advanced organic brain disease are now being helped with "sensory exercise training programs."

They cannot be cured, but they can be put back in touch, and express their joy in being alive.

Why, then, do some old people show acute "senile signs" when they have no medical symptoms of senile dementia at all? Dr. William A. Nolen explains one of the reasons. Memory loss—one of the "senile signs"—is not an essential characteristic of the old. There are too many well-known persons—active, productive, and with incredibly long and sound memories at 80 and beyond—to let us believe that it is. Memory loss may often be voluntary on the part of the aged, Dr. Nolen says. When they lose contact with the outside world, friends, and family, "many people let their memories go to protect themselves from the sad knowledge that they're alone." Reality is grim, so they evade it. When they feel that they are again loved and needed, memory often returns.

This fits into the pattern of what we know about memory, in people of all ages. Burying the painful and remembering the pleasant are characteristic of young and old and essential for survival. The "benign forgetfulness" of old age is well known to psychiatrists, but it is not a mark of senility.

Dr. Nolen—a popular medical writer explains what we need to avoid the appearance of "senility." A good genetic background helps, he says, and so do physical exercise and sane diet. Then, in stressing that deterioriation of intellect and memory is not an inevitable part of the aging process, he says, in effect, that we should "keep using our brains—the more we use them the better we will be able to retain memory and intelligence in old age."

The theme is a consistent one. "There is a positive growth curve for many types of intelligence," says psychologist Henry J. Mark. "The more you have, the more you use; the more you use, the more you grow." The sustained use of our faculties may be the single most important factor in making old age successful. The more our senses and emotions work, the more satisfactions we have and, we shall see, the longer time lasts. The more our minds and intellects work, the brighter and better off we are.

A look at reminiscence among the old also bears this out. Reminiscence is a form of life review, in which the old reach out to infuse others with their memories. It is a universal and inner experience as they come to accept the inevitability of death. And the more they reminisce, the better off they are.

"What makes old age hard to bear is not a failing of one's faculties, mental and physical, but the burden of one's memories," an aged Somerset Maugham said. The unburdening of memories, for whatever reason, is crucially important to the old; the tragedy is that there is often no one to listen. Psychiatrist Robert N. Butler says that even therapists working with the old have difficulty listening to them reminisce: "The older person is often [felt to be] garrulous and 'living in the past.' The content and significance of what he says are often lost or devalued." And an old man's family is often even less interested or more bored.

The young tend to think that an older person reminiscing is out of control, talking aimlessly, or that he is escaping from reality and the void of his old age. And what an old man says is considered to be of dubious reliability—even though many people believe that "remote memory" is better preserved than "recent memory" in the old.

Yet the evidence is that those who do reminisce are less depressed than those who do not. They think of the past in happier terms, and have made better social and personal adjustments. In reminiscing, the old are not unburdening themselves of sorrows and guilt, as the Somerset Maugham line suggests. The memories of the old—unrelated and rambling or not, filled with wisdom or not—are often all they have to pass on to the young. "They're giving us their riches, even when we suspect they're coloring the past to suit their self-concept," a psychiatrist said. "It's entirely possible that what they're telling us is less doctored and colored, more substantial and with greater insight into who and what we are, than the published reminiscences of famous people. We'd better listen . . ."

A person who has listened and listened to the old is Dr. Belle Boone Beard who has spent more than twenty years specializing in research studies on centenarians and, in her words, "has corresponded with, interviewed, recorded, and photographed more 100-year-olds than any other person on earth, past or present." Dr. Beard has made particular study of mind and memory of men and women in their second century of life and has come, for a scientist as least, to an unequivocal conclusion: Memory shows no upper age limit.

Dr. Beard refutes two popular beliefs about memory: the idea that memory declines with age, and recent memory declines more than remote memory—the idea that an old person can remember events of his youth better than he can recall what happened last week. The theory of universal memory decline, she says, bumps too hard into the fact that there are any number of old people around who have good, even remarkable memories.

She arrays on her side the findings of many researchers whose work, over more than forty years, has challenged the universal memory decline theory. What follows is a highly abbreviated tracing of some of her reference points about the course of memory and intelligence:

- 1930: Up to the age of 50, there is no decline in learning ability for those actively engaged in study.
- 1930: Mental functions remain unimpaired to a very advanced age in those gifted in earlier life with lively interests.
- 1938: Rote memory does not show a sudden fall until about the age of 82, when it declines rapidly.
- Memory loss is less in brightest than in less bright people. The brightest do not show as much drop from their original levels as do the others in a 60-year-old group.
- 1947: The unlearned lose the power of clear thinking as they grow old, but scholars gain it as the years advance.
- 1955: Measured intelligence continues to improve through the teens and early twenties, and light but regular increase continues to at least the age of 50.
- 1955: Older people learn less rapidly but for reasons other than the fact of age itself. They may show initial resistance to learning, which can be overcome by pointing out the advantages. They bring with them a range of attitudes, self-concepts, content, and methods acquired throughout their lifetimes; the young are blanker slates and may be more responsive to learning new things. If there is slower comprehension and speed among the old, this can be overcome by adjustment in teaching procedures and techniques.
- 1956: Cross-sectional studies suggest that the "curve" of

intellectual decline relates to educational status. The higher the educational level of a person, the more gradual the curve of his memory decline.

• 1958: The ability of an older person to deal with a new situation may be maintained if he is given more time to understand visual or verbal data and if incoming information is intensified.

• 1962: Cognitive ability declines with age at different rates, depending on the intellectual level of the person.

• 1965: The ability to retain visual information deteriorates markedly after the age of 60.

Dr. Beard notes that the most significant difference in learning between young and old has to do with the material itself. The old simply do not bother with or cannot learn what seems to them to be irrelevant, impractical, trivial—meaningless—information. The young are better at it, or at absorbing, without great discrimination, anything that comes along.

Her own research among centenarians found that their "adaptive intelligence" can remain high. There is no limit to the age at which they can adjust to change, combine knowledge to make new generalizations, or recall "stored information." Results of the standard memory tests she gave to the 100-year-olds indicated that they accepted the popular attitude that memory declines with age. Few felt embarrassed when they showed poor memory: Some considered it an unavoidable nuisance; a few fought valiantly to retain their powers of memory and succeeded.

Among the centenarians, too, those who exercised their memories retained them longest. Dr. Beard found no age limit at all on *any* type of memory: People who were in the habit of exercising their memories tended to maintain both remote and recent memory; the notion that older people have good memory for early events but poor memory for recent events was not at all supported by research among the centenarians.

Dr. Beard's findings are some of the most optimistic among gerontologists; by definition, centenarians are a unique breed, and it may be misleading to generalize from all of her conclusions. But study after study indicates that the popular view of what happens to memory and intelligence as we grow older is awry.

Psychologist Jon Kangas did a 38-year follow-up study of 48 men and women whose intelligence was first examined at the preschool level in 1931, then at junior high school level in 1941, at the young adult level in 1956, and again in 1969. Two of the standard tests for measuring intelligence—Stanford-Binet and the Wechsler Adult Intelligence Scale—were used: Kangas found that the Intelligence Quotients of the 48 men and women, all living in the San Francisco Bay area, went up about 20 points between childhood and early middle age. As preschoolers, the group had a mean IQ of 110.7; by the time they were in the 39-to-44 age group, their mean IQ had risen to 130.1.

Kangas's study reinforces two of the major points of gerontologists: that fears of aging are self-fulfilling and that the more we exercise mind and memory, the better off mind and memory are. He believes that IQ continues to rise even after 44, given the right circumstances. "People tend to have a self-image and become what they envision themselves to be," he says. "If you assume you are going downhill, you will." The men in his study who had the highest IQs as children showed the greatest increase as adults. But the women who were brightest as children made the smallest gains as they grew older. The reason, Kangas believes, is because the men had stimulating jobs that forced them to think; most of the women were housewives or held menial jobs that made no demands at all upon their intellectual equipment.

Different ways of testing intelligence and memory, however, do not show the same results. The study reported by Dr. Kangas covered a period of thirty-eight years in the lives of the same people, a form of longitudinal study. However, much of the testing in the past was cross-sectional, relating, for example, the performance of a sampling of 70-year-olds with that of a sampling of 30-year-olds on the same test, done about the same time. The classical cross-section tests show a decrease in mean IQ as people pass their late teens or early twenties. The major longitudinal studies consistently show a continued rise in mean IQ until at least the age of 50. (And early results of the few longitudinal studies started with older persons indicate that intellectual decline hardly shows up at all in the sixties.)

Longitudinal studies are the harder to make; they cover a long span of time, and people die, move away, or lose interest. But they are probably more valid. In cross-sectional studies, the social and cultural histories of a 70-year-old group and a 30-year-old group may be so different that the two groups cannot be expected to respond to the same tests in a way that allows comparison. But longitudinal studies use the measurements of the same person at various points in his life.

Some of the results of a pioneer longitudinal study of aging twins —organized at the New York State Psychiatric Institute in 1948— were recently reported by psychiatrists June E. Blum, James L. Fosshage, and Lissy F. Jarvik. The study also sought to find out whether men and women have different mental aptitudes that decline at different rates. As early as 1934, a Japanese scientist had found that Japanese men, aged 20 to 70, were consistently better in solving maze, form, and figure search tests. In the United States, men have been found to be better in tests of spatial and arithmetical ability; women have done better on tests involving words, or with a high "verbal loading," including analogies, disarranged sentences, vocabulary, and digit symbol substitution tests.

These differences apparently persist into old age. The Blum-Fosshage-Jarvik report, covering 54 men and women whose mean age was 84 at the close of the twenty-year period, supports some of the earlier findings: Women are somewhat better—or decline less—at high verbal loading tests. But, in the main, there is almost no difference between the intellectual aging of men and women.

There were general declines on all verbal and performance tests. This is understandable; the years 64 to 84 are a time of many great biological and psychological changes. People did not decline in any consistent way and there were many exceptions. The decline in verbal functions begins in the eighth decade of life, becomes significant statistically only in the ninth, and is very small even then. And some of the older people actually did better in verbal tests in their seventies and eighties.

When men seem to decline more sharply—as some did in the verbal tests—the decline is probably a harbinger of death, they found. This bears out a finding of James E. Birren in other studies: "Some of the higher cognitive processes measured by standard intelligence tests were more related to the health status of the individual than his chronological age." Poor health and proximity to death are more the causes of the decline than old age.

Generally, the old do worst in tests that require new associations. But they seem to lose fewer points because of test errors than do young people. Psychologist Alan T. Welford of the University of Cambridge says that the old compensate for their loss of speed by paying more attention to accuracy. This, plus the use of judgment in avoiding wasted effort, is a characteristic of the old in intellectual tests—and probably in their lives.

That seems to be the overwhelming majority view. Even though some of the old may have lost their peak efficiency, they can continue to function in most areas as well as the average young person, says Jeanne G. Gilbert of Mt. Carmel Guild, New Jersey, in describing a thirty-five-year follow-up study of a group of 60-to-74-year-olds. That, too, is the view of Dr. Birren, perhaps the dean of gerontologists studying age and mental performance. For more than twenty-five years, his work has provided guidelines for many others, and his findings may best sum up what we know about aging and mind.

His earliest experiments had to do with the slowing of response speed due to age. Starting with rats, he found that there are indeed age differences in their startle-reaction time to electric shock and noise. Then he began to study human responses and learning abilities with the aid of an electronic device, the Psychomet, which captures differences in response speeds of up to one-hundredth of a second. He compared reactions of 30 young adults and 23 elderly persons in a series of tests. The older persons were consistently slower—but those tests concerned only speed, not other aspects of capacity and intelligence. In a vocabulary test, the scores were higher among the older persons, suggesting little loss of stored information.

In 1963, Dr. Birren began a longitudinal study of 47 healthy men with an average age of 72 years. (It was quickly found that they had higher verbal scores than did younger control subjects.) In the follow-up study made five years later, some of the men—now averaging 77 years—showed no change at all in mental agility and perceptual acuity. A few did show dramatic decline, but they were probably suffering from organic brain damage. Overall, Dr. Birren concluded that "the average person need not expect a typical deterioration of mental functioning in his later years." And, given good health and freedom from cerebral vascular disease and senile dementia, people can expect "mental competence to remain at a high level beyond the age of 80."

The wisdom of the old and their decision strategies were another subject of Dr. Birren's study, this time made with Drs. Bernice Neugarten and Ruth Kraines at the University of Chicago. Older persons, they found, may have better "strategies of thinking" because they look at larger chunks of information at one time, while the younger look at its bits. As a man ages, his experience trains him to deal with important relationships, not small and solitary items, and to discard the irrelevant. That is why Dr. Birren says that most of us—if we stay healthy—can look forward to "a more effective mental pattern" as we age.

This, together with findings of psychologist Dennis B. Bromley of the University of Liverpool, is reassuring news for aging men in professional and managerial positions. In practice, Dr. Bromley says, the "age factor" is of marginal importance in their jobs; there are many more importance influences in a man's background and judgment that bear upon the decision-making process. Furthermore, he adds, the most carefully devised tests do not show any outstanding real age loss in the functions "thought to be relevant to high-level problem-solving and decision-making."

There are, of course, a number of major *ifs* to this: if we stay healthy, if we are not disoriented by time and change and deaths about us, if we are not cast into strange new roles of isolation or dependency, if we are lucky.

                              *   *   *

"At my age, time passes quickly, very quickly," old Uncle Antonin says in a Marcel Aymé novel. "It's a queer sort of feeling —it makes you want to shake yourself—this feeling of being caught up in a machine that never falters and never has an accident. . . . The days when I think about God, I always try to goad him into making the machine go backward . . ."

Backward, no—despite the fascinating time machines of science fiction.* But Uncle Antonin's first observation was solidly based and grounded in scientific fact. For a number of reasons, time actually does pass faster for old people; year by year, the years flow faster. At different times of life—and for different people at the same time of life—the experience of time is of different duration. And time, if we have the energy and will, actually can be made to last longer.

The experience of time is universal and we are all its captives, whether we live with the view that "time is money" or the older, wiser one that "time is life." Everyone's life, from beginning to end, is regulated by feeding and sleeping schedules, which in turn affect our feelings of physical well-being. A child has little conception of what it means to waste time because there seems to be so much of it. But later on in life, "the emotional reaction to time usually changes," say philosophers Maria Reichenbach and Ruth Anna Mather. "The adult often wishes to start all over again; he has regrets over wasted time. Youth is looked upon with nostalgia, childhood is pictured as a paradisean stage, the brevity of life is deplored, and the end is dreaded."

Aging and old are relative terms; at 15, a human being is young, a dog is old, and their experiences of time are substantially different. But time passes more swiftly for the old within the same species, a fact which has a solid mathematical basis. One year in the life of a 70-year-old is less than 1.5 per cent of his life; one year in the life of a 10-year-old is 10% of his life. Each will have a different subjective response to the length of that year. A 10-year-old will return to a summer camp feeling that an interminable

---

* Unless one considers experiments in psychiatry, hypnosis, and with the brain generally. W. Pennfield and L. Roberts, in *Speech and Brain Mechanisms,* report that in working with patients undergoing brain surgery, they sent electrical current through temporal lobes of the brain which recalled the past. "The patient . . . seems to relive some previous period of time and is aware of those things of which he was conscious in that period. It is as though the stream of consciousness were flowing again as it did once in the past," they write. "It is a hearing again and seeing again, a living through moments of past time." This is similar to the phenomenon of ecmnesia, a pathological condition in which adults believe they are, say, 8 or 10 years old again, and experience episodes in their childhood as though they were there.

time has passed since he was there the year before, at 9, because so many things have happened to him since. (And, indeed, many things have happened to him; in childhood, astounding changes take place from year to year in personality, tastes, skills, and interests, to say nothing of physical development.) The 70-year-old, coming back to a place after a year's absence, will hardly feel that he's been away. Alvin Toffler explains the relative meanings of time, based upon the mathematics of the situation, in another way: "Two hours in the life of a 4-year-old may be the felt equivalent of twelve hours in the life of her 24-year-old mother. Asking the child to wait two hours for a piece of candy may be the equivalent of asking the mother to wait fourteen hours for a cup of coffee."

There is a biological basis, too, for the fact that the calendar years seem progressively to shrink with advancing age. For the metabolic processes and biological rhythms of the old are slowing down; hence the world about them appears to be moving faster. The cycles and deep-seated rhythms of life, biological periodicities— "biological clocks"—affect virtually all living organisms. They are related to all the major natural geophysical periods and the interplay of sun, earth, and moon. They appear to persist indefinitely, even when organisms are shielded from the fluctuations in environment— temperature, humidity, light.

The rhythms may be circadian—roughly a 24-hour cycle of peaks and lows for humans in wakefulness and sleep, in body temperature, in activities of the nervous and endocrine systems, heart rate, blood pressure, liver and kidneys. They may be monthly—about the period from one new moon to the next—as in reproductive cycles of certain plants and marine life, or in the human menstrual cycle; traditionally, this has suggested that phases of the moon must have influenced reproduction during millions of years of primate evolution. They may be yearly, as seen in the growth, flowering, and production of seeds of many plants.

Perhaps man feels the effects of his circadian rhythms most strongly when he takes a plane trip covering several time zones. He arrives at his destination with rhythms still set by the place he had left. After a few days in the new time zone, his biological clock will gradually reset itself at about the rate of a day for each hour of change. Local light and temperature play a large role in the resetting

of the biological clock; the daily rhythms may be reset, under laboratory conditions, over a period of several twenty-four-hour cycles of
artificial change of light and temperature—without moving at all.

Another biological clock—a clock that winds down with age—
may mark the limit of the life span. The fact that human life spans
rarely exceed 90 to 100 years suggests that the aging process has
been programmed into the genes during millions of years of evolution,
programmed so that man would not become too multitudinous to
survive as a species.

There is a clock that winds down with age built into inorganic
systems, too: A watch with a steel spring will slow down, eventually
stop, if the spring is given enough time to lose its temper; parts of
an automobile will wear out, rust, or get tired. These are not
endowed with self-maintaining, self-regulating ways to fight wear and
tear. Living organisms are; and, in the processes of taking in nourishment and eliminating waste, there is a continuous exchange of new
material for old in the body. However, this is not quite enough for
the living machine to go on forever. Senescence means, as much as
anything, that the self-regulating mechanisms are beginning to fail;
homeostasis—the stable state of equilibrium of the elements making
up bodily health—diminishes with advancing age. "Some of the
disruptive processes in the tissues of the mature organism always
exceed the corresponding repair processes so that a steady state can
no longer be maintained," writes biologist Herbert D. Landhal, and
eventually, the organism dies. Unless, somehow, science can some-
day find a way to reset *that* biological clock.

Psychologist Robert E. Ornstein of the Langley-Porter Neuropsychiatric Institute in San Francisco has been fascinated by time
much of his life. "What is time? Where does it exist?" are the
questions he sets out to answer in his short, outstanding work, *On
the Experience of Time*. His answer finally is that there is no
answer—time is too diverse a concept. There is "the time of the
poet, the philosopher, the physicist, the psychologist, the biologist,
the times of the sundial, the calendar, the time to boil rice, the
time of the hourglass." And, he might have added, the time of the
pregnant woman, of the man in prison, of the soldier awaiting
battle. And the time of the young, middle aged, and old.

Although not addressed primarily to the subject of age, Professor Ornstein's research offers keys to the question, "How can Uncle Antonin's machine be made to falter?" How, as one gets older, can time be made to pass less quickly? Is it possible, psychologically at least, to prolong life and its pleasures?

Scientists use two major concepts in defining time as it is experienced in daily life. One is the idea of time as a sensory experience, of time made up of periodic intervals. This is the time measured by biological clocks—and by the clock on the wall. Many scientists accept this "time base" approach but Ornstein does not: "The clock is an arbitrary way of defining time," he says—a convenience "no more real than the time for boiling rice is real . . . One may measure out one's life in coffee spoons as well as a calendar, or hourglass." And if time were a sensory experience like vision, "there would exist a 'real time' independent of us, and we would have an organ of time experience such as the eye."

He favors the second concept: The length of time is determined by what we experience, learn, and perceive—all the stimuli we are subjected to—and what we store in our minds. This is a cognitive, information-processing approach, without any kind of time base; thus time's duration can be studied without reference to an external clock, mechanical, biological or not.

To illustrate the concept, Ornstein uses the metaphor of the "storage size" of the memory. Thinking of the mind as a computer, what is fed into it, how it is fed and stored, determines our experience of time. Anything that alters the size of the storage space available for information in a given interval also determines how long that interval lasts.

In both concepts of time—that of clocks with their time base and the cognitive approach favored by Ornstein—one general finding holds up: When the number of stimuli perceived (and presumably stored) are increased, *duration is lengthened*. To mix the metaphor somewhat, the greater the input into the "mental content" can, the longer time lasts.

This is not a recent discovery: Almost ninety years ago, two scientists showed the relation of stimuli to duration of time; they demonstrated that the more sounds a person heard in a given interval, the longer that interval seemed to last. Such tests have been made often; one, conducted in 1959, found that when a metronome beat 92 times a minute instead of 42 times, the duration of time was much longer.

It works the other way, too: When stimuli are reduced, the experience of time is shorter. In one test 33 persons were kept out of contact with the world—in a state of sensory deprivation—for 8- to 96-hour periods. At the end, each was asked to estimate how much time he thought had passed. By the clock, they had been confined an average of 54 hours and 25 minutes; their mean estimate was 50 hours.

Ornstein applies these findings to everyday situations:

• "A watched pot never boils" because expectancy makes us more sensitive to stimuli. "An increase in vigilance results in a great amount of awareness of input . . . and a lengthening of duration," he says. The watched pot does eventually boil, but it has taken longer because we were awaiting it.

• A boring situation seems interminably long. No matter how dull he finds it, a student must listen to every word as his professor drones on; somewhere along the line, he may be called upon or learn something to help him pass his course. His forty-minute class period seems two hours long. When we are forced to attend to more of the "stimulus array" than usual, Ornstein says, the increased attention we have to give makes time longer.

It follows from this that a significant event—one out of the normal, when perceptions are sharper—takes up more "storage space" and seems of longer duration than a commonplace one, when senses are blunt. A communion or wedding day, the day of a friend's funeral, lasts longer than a routine school or workday. Time spent at the theater, seeing a good play or movie, is longer than time spent in bed sleeping. Seeing a memorable event, with senses sharpened, lasts a long time. A televised event—such as the coronation of a queen— will have the same effect. For Americans and, perhaps, much of the world, the sequence of events flowing from the first news of the shooting of President John F. Kennedy in Dallas took up incalculable time: the shooting of Lee Harvey Oswald, the lying in state at the Capitol, the bereaved family, the funeral procession, the dignitaries of the world assembled, the riderless horse, the burial at Arlington. With all emotions at work, those who lived through and watched those days on television cannot only not forget them; they seem to have occupied not four days but a month or a millennium.

So it is in aging. A child's first day at school, filled with new, striking experiences and encounters, is of long duration. At the other extreme, an old man or woman in an institution, living without change of routine or event, is living without "input." Day flows into day, without reference to time. It is true that minutes on the clock may drag if the clock is watched, as the watched pot takes so long to boil. But over the weeks and months, time has escaped. Unless the old man or woman has a visitor or some interest that engrosses the senses, each day is mainly made up of time that never was. This is compounded by the fact that the biological rhythms of the old may be slowing down; in that other kind of time—"time-based" time—all the rest of the world seems to be moving faster and time is shorter still. But this is a lesser fact, a biological problem that may be compensated for in other ways.

With this information, the answer to "How can we make time last longer as we age?" is evident. It is: Increase sensory input. Live to the fullest with all the emotions and perceptions possible.

It is not by accident that modern institutions for the aged stress activities of all sort—arts and crafts, lectures and dramatics, sensory-training programs, and the rest. The more visitors and activity, the more "special days" in a home for the aged, the less disengaged its residents will be—and the more time they will have. Without activity, time is a void and meaningless.

The overwhelming majority of the aging live outside of institutions. For most of us, there are three major ways of increasing cognitive and sensory input and making time last longer:

• *Change the routine and pattern of the days.* Set patterns of life and work may be essential for the productive life. But, in time, they also deaden the senses. We tend no longer to see the beauty or ugliness of things about us. The change of seasons, each with its new stirrings, reminds us how important such change is.

• *Develop a new or deferred interest.* Unless an old person knows how to use his hard-won leisure time, his life becomes aimless and without focus—and all time is lost. Above all, his interest must give him a good deal of ego satisfaction. Education—going back to school—is a choice way. (See Chapter 10, "Retirement and Leisure.")

• *Move to another setting.* At the age of 78, the renowned political commentator Walter Lippmann explained why he was moving from Washington, D.C., to another part of the country: "I have realized that a change and a new start is good for the aging," he said. "Moving is the only known remedy against settling down in a groove. It is the only remedy against doing the same old thing again and again, and gradually doing it less well."

This last will do the job by itself, but the three together contribute to the greatest amount of input. A trip abroad for the first time, for example, combines all three and serves many functions in increasing input and lengthening time's duration. Consider all the elements at work: anticipation and planning of the trip, the stimulation of making choices, getting tickets and passport, telling friends; the journey itself and arrival in a new land, long-pictured but never seen; the strangeness of foods, roads, buildings, sites of all kinds. It is best if the traveler has at least a sketchy knowledge of the language; his emotional responses will be heightened in encounters with local people. The traveler will also have a new sense of self-importance, knowing that he is somewhat exotic to those who are at home. Sending back letters and postcards; playing at photography (but taking it seriously); having small problems which can usually be solved easily (or forgotten about, or made the nucleus for future anecdotes). The absolute charm and novelty of the situation—and then going home to show those photographs and talk about what he felt, saw, and tasted. (No matter that his friends bore him a bit with their counter-observations. That, we have seen, makes time last longer, too.) Three weeks in a strange land is infinitely longer in the time-memory bank than three weeks at home for anyone. It is longer still to an older person simply because he rarely enjoys the freshness of new experience, often felt by the young; the contrast is all the greater. A journey—or a move—will reawaken sensation, give him new life as well as time.

The more you do, the more time you have. Time is a relative thing, without definition or meaning until it is used. A person who says he has no time to read or to go to the theater—if he believes that these are things which gratify him most—is evading a reality. He is letting time escape in a meaningless way. Some of the busiest people in the world, and the most successful, find all the time they need to read widely or go to the theater a dozen times a season. Their input is enormous and, compared to those "without any time," they live several lifetimes.

Even being eccentric is a way of making time last longer. By breaking out of set patterns of behavior, the eccentric subjects himself to new or more experiences and greater input. Uncle Antonin was a strange old man who built eccentric gaudy cars to drive around the streets of Paris. Onlookers were delighted, his family was embarrassed, and there were laughter and tears in his disputes with them. Laughter and tears helped him live a long time. The scientific evidence, as well as the novelist's insight, is that we are undergoing the experience of time only when we think and feel. Ultimately, the time machine is in man's mind.

7 WHAT IT'S LIKE TO BE OLD

Every so often Marlene Dietrich fosters the illusion that she is ageless. In what appear to be diaphanous gowns, she plays the role of femme fatale in night clubs and on television, murmuring her songs and giving the impression that she is no older—well, not much older—than she was as Lola Lola in *Blue Angel* in 1930.* Close-up, without artifice, of course Miss Dietrich looks her age. Undoubtedly she feels her years, too, as we all must until science does much more unraveling of the secrets of biological aging. Miss Dietrich will not discuss her age; when an interviewer brings up the subject, she either shows her annoyance or, at best, smiles enigmatically.

That enigmatic smile is warranted, even if she wanted to discuss how it feels to be approaching the mid-seventies. It is difficult to express what it's like to be old. What aging does to the body is fairly easy to see, and even if we're young we can understand its effects. But what it does to mind, attitude, and behavior—and how it really feels to be old—is something else: a subject filled with wonder and many misconceptions. An enigmatic smile is about as good an answer as most people can give.

There are good reasons why it is not easy to get a universal or

* When she was 29. To be thoroughly ungracious to a good woman: Marlene Dietrich was born in Berlin in 1901.

consistent answer from the old to the question "What is it like to be old?" The interrelated processes of aging are so complex that no two people age the same way or feel exactly the same about aging. Further, the same old people don't feel the same way at all times: They have more aches, depressions, changes of mood than younger persons. They are more susceptible to changes in weather and environment, how and where they live.

How sensitive they may be is revealed in a study made by gerontologist Frances M. Carp. Dr. Carp set out to find how 115 men and women, average age 72, felt about themselves before and after they were admitted to a brand-new housing facility, built especially for the old. When she first interviewed them, all were living in substandard housing, in some social isolation and stress, feeling poor and feeling their age. Miss Carp interviewed them again, after they had been living in their new apartments for a year. They were no longer the same miserable group of old people. More of them now described themselves as middle aged, not elderly or old—a good sign that they were feeling better about themselves. They had a much higher evaluation of their own accomplishments in life. They were less concerned over problems of health and personal adjustment. Indeed, fewer mentioned problems of any kind. Many of them said that the present was the happiest time of their lives. Same people, fifteen months older, living in a new, more desirable environment—with a new self-concept.

For a multitude of reasons, there is a great range of response when people do express, in one way or another, their feelings about being old. This sampling of six types of response gives an idea of that range.

The most successful: A few days before his 73d birthday, a college teacher sat down and did some "autogerontology." The physical losses that come with age, he wrote, did not start in his case in the fifties or sixties but earlier:

"I seemed to have reached a series of successive plateaus . . . I recall that the first indication that I was entering a period of reduced energy (or turning a corner, as I have always called it) came when I was 37. After that, it became a little harder to work both day and night and come up bobbing the next morning. The next turning point came at about age 45, followed by others at ages

52 and 63. I am probably experiencing another this year as I seem to notice a distinct reduction of energy compared with that of previous years . . . I still average a six-hour day and frequently longer. But I am running out of daily energy and am not sure that if I had to gear myself up again to plan and run a conference I could do it." The professor, Andrew Tendrickson, sought to explain his feelings as physical changes occur:

"After the shock of the first turning point at age 37, the others didn't bother me until the one at about age 63 . . . I was impervious to changes because, I think, I was healthy and able to do at least an average amount of work . . . I regretted the reduction in quantity of production, but I found myself compensating in greater quality of product and in improved techniques of working. [But] at age 63 I began to be affected emotionally. I changed from counting the years I had lived to counting those I might have left . . . As my work load continued to increase year by year, and I began to find myself being exhausted beyond the ability to be replenished, I made the decision to retire at age 67—three years before the mandatory age . . ."

The professor wanted to move to a warmer climate—and he also wanted a postretirement career. He easily found an appointment as visiting professor at a university in Florida along with his wife, a professor of child development, who obtained a position in the university's school of home economics:

"It is hard to sort out the thoughts and feelings I have had since beginning my second career. Physical and emotional states seem to react forcefully upon each other. Some days I don't think I can get up in the morning. On others I feel that I can whip the world. I have had a number of rewarding [professional] experiences . . . which have buoyed me up, have provided me with a sense of having contributed to society, and have kept me mentally alert. My mental activity has also been continually stimulated by association with other members of the adult education staff, who are young, lively, and whose teaching and research activities are characterized by freshness and creativity. These lively contacts have undoubtedly kept the adrenalin flowing and helped to maintain body tone. Conversely, physical exercise (swimming, gardening, caring for a large lawn, etc.) has probably contributed to my mental health and emotional satisfaction."

Professor Hendrickson, surely, is among the luckiest of gerontological subjects alive. All the qualities for a successful old age seem to be his: reasonably good physical health, financial security, retirement with his wife to a good climate (but not really retiring or disengaging from his primary interests), association with people of many ages and new ideas, and doing the things that keep ego, mind, and body strong. His is the ideal.

The saddest: Perhaps not in science but in art—in this case the art of journalism—does the stark, often tragic reality of old age come through. "The Old Man in the Bronx" is a moving article by Herb Goro that appeared in *New York* magazine. It tells the story, over a four-year period, of an old Jewish man, born in Russia, religious, with some education, living out his old age as a junk collector in a slum neighborhood. Primarily in the old man's own words, it evokes the circumstances of his and his family's life, his emotions, loves and fears throughout his long life. It is the other extreme from the old age of Professor Henrickson. The beginning of the story is also its ending as the man lies in his institutional bed:

"Ninety years a man and all I do is eat and sleep. I've been in the hospital eight, twelve weeks. I know it's a long time. I can't do anything anymore. People don't want to hear me and I can't hear when somebody else is talking. I don't think. Why think? What I think now never can help nothing no more. When a man comes to my age he's done. He's got no strength. He can't talk right. He can't see right. So he does what he can do. He can eat and he can sleep and that's all. He prays maybe God will take him away, maybe he'll be better off in the next world. I pray to God every day he should take me. Nobody can know me no more. The doctors, the nurses, they don't know what kind of man I was. Who could look at me in bed and know what I was? Who listens to an old man?"

The questions are rhetorical. They are an appeal for understanding, and for recognition of the value of a man's life.

The most acid: It is hard to find two more disparate persons than the old man in the Bronx and Philip Wylie, social critic and author of *Generation of Vipers,* who wrote about old age—his own and others—just before his death at 69. Wylie, a professional iconoclast, said that part of the "lonely exile" of the old is their own fault.

"By and large, I dislike the company of people of my own age. Nine out of ten [people over 60] are bores, and the splendor of the exceptions does nothing to diminish the head-splitting tediousness of the rest. The mass of aged bores tire everybody, often one another most of all . . . They aren't interesting. They aren't even *interested*. They are casualties of what has been called 'future shock,' left behind by a world that has made breathtaking changes since the aged were young."

The burden of Wylie's complaint about the elderly was that they don't keep up with the times, have little practical wisdom to impart, and when they give advice often spout nonsense. Wylie, however, was not angry at the old so much as he was at the rest of the population. The plight of the old, he went on to say, was everyone's fault. "When millions can expect their final years to be spent in pain, solitude, and squalor, a country cannot boast about the quality of life it has achieved. So, while I feel strongly that multitudes of old persons are to blame for some of their massive segregation from the family, and while I feel that the vanities of youth worshippers are another cause, I know, too, that old age itself is so terrible a disaster for many . . . that . . . we cannot take pride in ourselves at any age.

"A life is a whole span and a continuum. I was an infant, boy, and man, and now I am an old man. But I was the same person all the while, and the remembered 'I' is the same one I know today. Age isn't a category but merely where you happen to live at the time. And any younger man who tries to call me 'senior citizen' better beware . . ." *

The most bitter-sweet: Minna Frank leads an active social life, operating in and out of her apartment on Lake Shore Drive facing

* Wylie was hardly alone in reacting to the euphemism. In 1960, John Kenneth Galbraith paid a call on Bernard M. Baruch to ask him to contribute to and endorse the campaign of John F. Kennedy for president of the United States. "My visit to Baruch went well," Galbraith later reported, "thanks not to my irresistible persuasion but to Richard Milhous Nixon. He had asked Baruch (who was then around 90) to head a committee of senior citizens for Nixon. That had left Baruch livid. Did the man think his distinction depended on his age? 'Senior citizen, for God's sake!' "

Lincoln Park in Chicago. She is politically active; the term "radical chic"—pejorative or not—best describes her interests. As well as the next man, she can start a conversation with "What did you think of *Last Tango in Paris?*" She travels to Europe once a year to go shopping and visit old friends. She doesn't tour any more because, she says, there is little left to see. Besides, she has trouble with her eyesight and is partially deaf. Minna Frank is 87 and, a novelty among the old, she is rich—this last item making all else possible.

She is, because she must be, obsessed with her physical well-being and problems of mobility and makes elaborate plans when she leaves her house or travels abroad. Doormen know her and, when ordering a cab, make sure that it is an old-fashioned big one, easier for her to enter. She uses a small wheelchair when tired and knows exactly how and where to get around in it. She travels with a favorite bright reading lamp, along with a small transformer for use in Europe. (Also, extra batteries for her hearing aid.) She is an authority on elevators, distances, hotel beds and bathrooms, and restaurants that best suit her diet. She is lively and intelligent, annoyed only when she cannot hear or is left out of a conversation.

All of her friends are somewhat or much younger than she. They call her "Aunt Minna" to her face; "good old Minna" or "wonderful old Minna" when she's not around. But even those who patronize her seem to love her.

One friend asked her, in the course of a cocktail-party conversation on old age, "What is it like to be old?" She ignored the question and seemed flustered that it had been addressed to *her.* But ten minutes later she called the friend over and whispered, under the party hubbub, "Above all, it's the loneliness."

The most ordinary answers: Minna Frank gave a direct, insightful answer. Few old people can do as well, and the enigmatic smile is often as good an answer as any.

Gerontologists are fascinated by subjective response—the self-portraiture of the old. A few years ago, Robert Havighurst publicly mused, "How does it feel to grow old?" He made a point of disentangling feeling old from being ill—not the same thing at all, he reminded his audience—and asked three general questions:

• Are the old aware of aging? Do they feel that their world is growing older although they retain the same loves, hates, ambitions?

• Do they have a comfortable feeling of achievement now that they are old?

• Do they now feel like observers to the passing scene or do they still feel part of the world about them?

He received much interesting mail. A Florida newspaper columnist picked up the idea and asked his old readers to write to him on the subject. But neither Dr. Havighurst nor the columnist could do much with their material. It is difficult enough for anyone to express a state of mind or feeling with depth and clarity. And many of the old are too inhibited or bound to their roles to respond with more than clichés.

Some proof of this appears in a study made by two psychiatrists who recently followed up on Dr. Havighurst's idea. They interviewed old people in good health at a senior citizens activity day center and asked members of its creative writing class to write unstructured essays on the subject "How does it feel to grow old?" They came back with essays written by five men and six women with an average age of almost 71. Unstructured or not, most of the essays are as trite and self-conscious as one would expect from a class of ten-year-olds, asked to answer: "How does it feel to be young?"

"I have had a good full life in the greatest era in history and in the greatest country on earth. I don't worry about dying. The Grim Reaper can't cheat me now," wrote one. Another said, "Growing old is a wonderful thing." A few were more thoughtful: "There is no questioning the proposition that growing old lessens the enjoyment of life but strange to say increases the desire for continuing to live." Another old person came up with a more challenging view, in support of negative euthanasia: "I feel very strongly that it is wrong, even cruel, to keep life in a worn out body by such means as feeding directly into the stomach by tubes, or intravenous feedings, etc. . . . the spirit should not be imprisoned this way."

Health, finances, and loneliness were cited as the three basic problems facing the old, although, surprisingly, finances were not mentioned as often as the other two.* "Loneliness can destroy an

* Surprisingly, because this took place in the United States where finances are a leading problem among the old, with poor health and loneliness often the by-products. If the reader thinks that this book treats

Elderly Person, both mentally and physically, more quickly and more surely, than one might be inclined to realize," said one. And another: "Life is very dear as long as I have my health." Many other answers were as conventional and as earnest.

The psychiatrists found that the essay writers supported Havighurst's theme: They were aware of aging but felt that they were the same people, and they had a sense of accomplishment and achievement. None of the essayists felt he had changed from participant to observer of life, which is not surprising since all eleven were involved in day center work, taking up creative writing, and feeling on-stage at the moment. The psychiatrists added that throughout the essays "a central theme of loss emerged. And yet it was not depressing to read them. . . ."

It is also, alas, not very illuminating to read them; the idea of old age is difficult to express. But sometimes it blazes through.

---

the economic plight of the old superficially, he is probably right; it is just that the subject is an overwhelming one, worthy of the special treatment it has already received in many works. (Notable among them is *The Golden Years . . . A Tarnished Myth,* a report prepared for the Office of Economic Opportunity by the National Council on the Aging and reprinted March 1972.) If this were another type of book, a primary answer to the question, "What is it like to be old?", would be one word— "Poor." Almost a quarter of all American old live in households with incomes below the poverty level. Some 60% of all older women living alone or with nonrelatives live in poverty, another 10% are on the borderline. Among similar nonwhite older women, 85% live in poverty, another 5% on the borderline. About 31% of the old and poor need dentures, 25% need eyeglasses, 21% need hearing aids—and do not have them. Most are probably poorly nourished, a condition exacerbated by inflation. "Food prices are murdering the aged," said Robert Forest, editor of the *Senior Citizens Sentinel,* recently. "The only two places they can cut costs are food and medicine—and the less food they have the more medicine they need."

A special program called "Forget Me Not," televised in Philadelphia, asked old people to phone in their problems. The largest single bloc of questions—23%—was about income maintenance; 19% called with questions about health, but two-thirds of these were about the economic aspects of medical care, not health itself. In fairness to the American system of providing for the old, however, it should be noted that many old Americans simply do not know about or how to take advantage of benefits available to them.

The most eloquent response: Some 300 alumni of Johns Hopkins University—aged 65 to 97—were asked what it's like to grow old. One answered:
"It is like living on an island that is steadily shrinking in size."

All these men and women, disparate as they are, have something in common—they and all the old. Behind their words is the same theme, almost a plea: I am myself, young or old. I am different from everyone else. Do not judge me or discard me because of my age and appearance.

Loneliness is one of the blights of old age, far worse than it is for youth or middle age. Almost a quarter of the elderly in the United States and Great Britain live alone. But the two facts are *not* coincident. Living alone does not, by itself, mean that an old person is lonely; the losses he has suffered in family, friends, and social world through the years contribute to his loneliness more than the simple fact of physical isolation.

This is one of the most important findings of a major survey of living conditions and behavior of elderly people in Denmark, Britain, and the United States. The report, *Old People in Three Industrial Societies,* may be the single most revealing document of the past decade explaining, scientifically, what it is like to be old.

Old People makes the distinction between living alone and age-related isolation, or "social desolation," which usually is the cause of loneliness. "A person who has lost a social intimate (usually someone he or she loves, such as husband, or wife, a relative, or a close friend) is isolated relative to a previous situation," the report says. This is "desolation." Time "heals" the loss more easily for young people than it does for the old; the young have more opportunity to remarry or replace the lost close relative or friend. And, for the old, the substitutes—when they find them—"tend to fall short of former intimates in the roles they play in [their] lives and affections."

Thus, a man or woman who has been recently widowed is more apt to be lonely than one who has been widowed for many years. But people who do not live alone, and who lead active social lives, may still be lonely if they are not getting the satisfactions or types of relationships which gratify them.

The study found that similarities between the populations of the three countries were more striking than the differences. Almost the same proportion of the old lived alone— just under a quarter in the United States and Britain, just over a quarter in Denmark. Fewer than 5% lived in extreme isolation, but a much larger minority lived in a state of semi-isolation or felt themselves to be alone often. Between 2% and 3% of the old not only lived alone but had no visitors in the previous week *and* had no human contact on the day before the interview. The proportion having no relatives or not having recent contact was not much larger, suggesting that in old age the family plays a primary role in maintaining some degree of integration with society.

The cross-national survey had another surprising finding, challenging the notion that loneliness is pervasive and constant among the old. "Extreme loneliness is not a rare phenomenon [among the old] and occasional loneliness is quite a common one," the report said. But *relatively few old people feel lonely often.*

The sampling that produced this finding was extensive—almost 2,500 men and women were interviewed in each of the three countries. (Still, the authors caution, the interviews were made "at a particular time and should not be regarded as representing uniformly permanent attitudes.")

The authors of *Old People* sum up: Desolation—particularly the loss of someone who is loved—is more responsible for the loneliness of old people than is simple isolation. It may also seriously affect health and state of mind. However, a substitute or some new type of social involvement may help a great deal to get over loneliness.

When the elderly man said that being old is "like living on an island that is steadily shrinking in size," he was undoubtedly thinking of his social world, too—the erosion of his circle of family and friends. Living alone is not the essential problem. It is having no one close to be visited, who will visit and, really, to love. Psychiatrist Andrus Angyal says that "existing in the thought and affection of another really is a very concrete level of existence." Angyal's guiding theme is that keeping close "with another is the center of existence up to the very end of life."

Dr. Marjorie Lowenthal looked into the relationship of loneliness and mental health in her study of more than 1,100 old people, half of them living in psychiatric wards, the rest in neighborhoods with a heavy concentration of the elderly. The happiest and healthiest, she notes, are those involved in one or more personal relationships. People having a "close confidant" are much less likely to be depressed as a result of widowhood or retirement than those who do not: 45% of women widowed for seven years were depressed, even when they had a confidant. But of the widows who had no one close, many more—73%—were depressed. Half the people who had retired within the past seven years, although they had an intimate, were depressed. But 64% of those without an intimate were depressed.

Dr. Lowenthal also found that the rate of psychiatric impairment was only 5% among people who worked actively in one or more voluntary associations. Those who merely visited friends or attended social gatherings had a rate of 11%. But old people whose social life was made up of visits only to relatives had an impairment of 22%. Those who did none of these things had the highest rate of all —31%. There was a fearsome consistency to this: the smaller the amount of emotional involvement, or even human contact, the more serious the degree of psychiatric impairment; it was 6% among those who went to one church meeting a week, 22% among those who never attended church. It was 12% among old people who lived with others, 19% among those who lived alone. People who had a telephone had a rate of 13%. Those without a phone in their homes or even in their buildings had a rate of 46%.

Gerontologist James Peterson summed up these findings in a discussion of loneliness in old age: "People need people" if they are to cope with the shocks of growing old, he said. "The intermediary of someone to love is a buffer between life satisfaction and the blows of widowhood and retirement . . . To love is to be a complete human being."

To be incomplete often means to be lonely. But the quality and type of substitutes for lost intimates or past associations are of crucial importance. As long as they are meaningful, the substitutes need not duplicate what has been lost. This is often difficult for younger people to understand; they have, after all, their own preconceptions of what the old should be like, based upon their own standards and emotions.* Social worker Naomi Brill tells the story of Mr. and Mrs. Johns who came to discuss the problems of Mr. Johns's 72-year-old mother, a widow. She had sold her duplex, moved into a smaller apartment, seemed lonely, avoided socializing—"doesn't even go to church"—and had nothing to do since giving up management of the duplex. Also, they said, the old lady drank.

"As we talked, I got a picture of an anxious couple, devoted to each other and their own way of life, greatly concerned about the mother and perhaps a little guilt-ridden because their late marriage had left her alone," Miss Brill writes. "When I asked how the mother felt about being alone, how much she had socialized before this move, did she enjoy the demands of managing property, what did she do with her time, was she satisfied in her new living arrangement, was the drinking enough to create a problem for her or was it something she wanted to do—they did not know the answers. They perceived her through their own eyes, using their own system of values instead of striving to see her as she was."

It is entirely possible that she was having a roaringly good old age, freed from responsibilities she had never sought. She may have been less lonely and more fulfilled without her duplex—and, possibly, without her husband. Some unhappy marriages continue interminably when divorce or separation seems out of the question because "it isn't done" or "it would hurt the children." A French film of a decade ago, *Little Old Lady,* traced the awakening of a small-town Frenchwoman of 70 after her martinet husband died, showing how she reveled in her new freedom, made new and young friends, shared their intrigues and triumphs, and discovered a joyous new life.

Finding that much happiness in widowhood seems offensive to some, but it shouldn't. The wearing of widow's weeds becomes waste-

* Preconceptions everywhere. Theodore Lidz tells how doctors have them, too. A 76-year-old man was brought into a hospital in heart failure, completely disoriented. After a while, the heart failure subsided, his brain received enough oxygen, and he appeared to be rational. But he kept insisting that now that he was ready to go home, his mother would drive over to pick him up. The doctors decided to keep him in the hospital a few weeks longer, to see if his mental state would improve. One day his mother of 95 did drive over from a town a hundred miles away, accompanied by her 97-year-old sister, to take their little boy home.

ful of life after a while, but few people have the energy, nerve, or opportunity to do much about it; it is easier to mourn the past and cherish it to the exclusion of present and future.

Loneliness, inadequate income, and the state of their health—this is the triad of problems bedeviling the old. The problems of loneliness and money may or may not be solved, and they are not necessarily fatal, but an old person can die or does die because of poor health. "As long as you've got your health" is not a trivial expression to the old. They mean it literally; almost every other problem may be surmounted, they feel, but not physical decay.

Some of the old worry about it more than others. Psychologist Robert Peck says that as they age, old people make the choice between "body transcendence" and "body preoccupation." The old person must decide whether he is to dominate his body or his body is to dominate him. Peck writes:

"For people to whom pleasure and comfort mean predominantly physical wellbeing, [declining health] may be the gravest, most mortal of insults. There are many such people whose elder years seem to move in a decreasing spiral, centered around their growing preoccupation with the state of their bodies. There are other people, however, who suffer just as painful physical unease, yet who enjoy life greatly. In their value system, social and mental sources of pleasure and self-respect may transcend physical comfort alone."

The study of old people in Denmark, Britain, and the United States found that—to an extent—loneliness and concern about health are parts of the same problem. People who think they are sick—according to their own evaluation of their health—are more likely to feel lonely and alienated than those who think they are well. "Overall, it may be the feeling of poor health that brings with it feelings of loneliness," the authors say. In any event, psychic depression is widespread among the old and "overconcern with one's body and associated depressive feelings" are common signs of such depression.

In all three countries, men were more optimistic about the state of their health than women. There was also a marked difference in attitude between people in their seventies and those 80 or more. The recently retired, men seeking a new role in life, are often depressed about their health. But those 80 or more (and still living in the community) are less complaining and more cheerful and optimistic.*

The American and British old did not respond to questions about their health in the same way. The study's authors say that there seems to be enough truth in the national stereotypes—the British are patient, polite, and uncomplaining; the Americans are active and gregarious—to explain the difference. The elderly in Britain seem to accept their impairments and incapacities more easily—with a stiff upper lip—and say their health is good. The American old are more likely to say their health is poor when they have the slightest impairment. "Any restriction on [an American's] activity seems to evoke a maximum response," they say. However, the majority of both Americans and British think their health is better than the health of their respective compatriots. "We may say that the Americans think their health is better than the health of others because they are optimistic, the British because it is unbecoming to complain," they conclude.

The old who are physically failing have good reason to be preoccupied, if not obsessed, with their condition. It is not a matter of worrying about dying; it is a question of getting about each day, of living in a world that is not made for the old or handicapped.

Minna Frank, at 87, can overcome some of the obstacles. She has the good fortune to be rich; she always travels first class, with a companion and much equipment, including a portable wheel chair. But even she steps into the world outside her apartment in a state of high nervous tension. Many old people don't bother to step out.

Some of the problems the old and handicapped face are as intimate as can be. What is an old person with cane or wheelchair to do about getting into a public toilet booth and making use of its facilities? How can a slow-moving old person survive the ordeal of an automatic elevator that closes its doors in less than seven seconds? Or cross a street before the light changes, or climb steep bus steps?

* Elaine Cumming and Mary Lou Parlegreco, in their study of very old people, found "some evidence that living to be over 80 . . . is associated with being a member of a biological and possibly psychological elite. Further, very old people often have a surprisingly high level of social competence and seem able to maintain high spirits . . . [There is] sometimes a mood of using up the last days of life in tranquility and sometimes a genuine carefree quality."

These are not just the problems of the old. It is estimated that in the United States about 25 million and in the United Kingdom about 7 million partially or totally disabled persons find their activities restricted through architectural barriers of one sort or another: steps that cannot be mounted instead of ramps, escalators that start off too quickly, revolving doors that cannot be passed through, public telephone or lunchroom counter chairs too high. According to Dr. Henry Betts of the Rehabilitation Institute of Chicago, architectural barriers not only interfere with the access of the old and disabled but "they interfere—more seriously—with the *quality* of life he can make for himself."

Transportation is one of the most vexing problems of the old; the inability to get around to visit, shop, seek vital services or recreation—can isolate an old person as well as if he or she were bedridden. A study in one American city found that almost half the pensioners over 65 did not have a car in the garage but "depended on the generosity of relatives, neighbors, and friends, in that order." A report on the United States generally found that automobiles were owned in only 56% of the households headed by people over 65, compared to 84% of those headed by younger persons. By the time they are 70, most people no longer drive or cannot afford to maintain cars. (Some car-hire services will not rent a car to a person over 65.) Taxis are too expensive. "Modern transportation systems too often fail to take into account the physical limitations of many older persons," says Cyril F. Brickfield, legislative counsel of the National Retired Teachers Association. "When we consider transportation for the elderly, we are actually considering barriers to mobility— barriers that make it difficult for an older person to leave his apartment building or home to go a corner store, let alone go downtown or travel across the country." *

These, too, are answers to "What is it like to be old?"

* Barriers to mobility are bad enough, but the old have their problems even when staying at home. A U.S. Senate Special Committee on Aging recently held hearings to see whether new protective measures were needed to reduce fire hazards to the old. The urgency of the matter quickly became clear; the committee records were soon filled with many instances of tragedy—and proof that the vulnerable old suffer a disproportionate share of deaths at home by fire and burns. And fires in nursing and other homes for the aged account for a significant number of deaths in the "major disasters" records of our time.

The question the answers raise—Can something be done about the isolation of the old?—is not insoluble. Loss, more than isolation, may be the basic reason why the old are lonely, but finding ways to ease isolation will, unquestionably, help in many ways. It will help them to be again part of the mainstream, to be less alone and afraid. And, by exposing the old to new situations, it will help them find substitutes for what they have lost in family and society or the past.

The guidelines exist. They are drawn explicitly, for example, in an Administration on Aging report called *Let's End Isolation*. This goes through the catalog of problems and tells what professionals and volunteers are doing in many communities, often with government cooperation. The description of what's being done gives the impression of a great stirring in behalf of the old:

• There are the senior centers that eventually "may come to hold a place in the older person's life equivalent to the central role now played by the school in the lives of children." Aside from offering the old a place to meet, work, play, and learn, the centers can serve as a community's clearing house, to coordinate all services available to the old. In 1973, some 1,500 centers in the United States provided programs at least three days a week.

• There are visiting centers, a form of "organized neighborliness" in which volunteers visit the homebound on a regular schedule, to talk, play cards or chess, write letters, go shopping together. The idea is to provide continuing companionship for the lonely. There are also home services in which volunteers, usually mature women with much experience at homemaking, give personal assistance, meet out-of-hospital needs, prepare meals, clean up, and recruit the help of others to do heavier work around the house, such as mowing lawns or moving furniture.

• A variety of programs provide useful work, often with pay, to the old. One is called SERVE (Serve and Enrich Retirement by Volunteer Agencies), which organizes older volunteers to work in state hospitals and schools for the mentally retarded. Some of the old work with patients, some in the office, some with other hospital duties—even the bus ride to hospitals seems to provide a setting for new friendships among older people. Both the National

Council of Senior Citizens and the National Council on the Aging operate programs, with some government funding, employing men and women twenty hours or more a week on a variety of community services. A government-inspired effort is the Foster Grandparent Program in which older people meet regularly with children in temporary care centers, hospitals, and other institutes, give them love and find that they are loved themselves.*

• People living alone are often in dread of accident or illness—with no one knowing and coming to help. This happened to a 72-year-old Michigan woman who spent eight days lying on her kitchen floor, victim of a stroke. She was found, barely alive, by a friend who finally came to check. The friend—Grace Sample McClure—subsequently came up with the idea: Why not initiate a telephone calling service for the old? Others, including the head of a telephone answering service, came to her support. On August 15, 1957, the first "telephone reassurance" call was made—to the 76-year-old Mrs. McClure.

The idea has since spread. Mrs. McClure explained how it usually works. "Older people living alone subscribe to the service for $2.50 a month. They report to the answering service the name of their physician and leave a key to their house. The service calls twice a day (but if the subscriber is going to be away, he must let the service know). Should repeated calls bring no answer, a policeman picks up the key and checks the house."

People who cannot afford to pay can usually get a local church or club to meet the expense. Not only the old but heart patients and others with serious ailments use the service. There are many variations to the idea. In some cases, residents of a home for the aged make the calls to old people living alone. Sometimes, as in Davenport, Iowa, an old person is given a number to call if he just wants to talk; on the receiving end are ten elderly professionals—all good listeners.

• Poor nutrition throughout their lives is a primary cause of poor health among the old. Compounding this, they often eat badly

* These and other voluntary organizations are described in Chapter 10, "Retirement and Leisure."

because they cannot afford to eat better, or cannot get around to shop, or do not know how to balance their meals, or—if they are alone—feel that it is hardly worthwhile to prepare food or to bother to eat regularly. For eating has a social function; it is the time for warmth, companionship, and conversation. Parties, picnics, holidays all the least solitary and most joyful times of life—are associated with food. When the social element is removed, many old people turn to sporadic snacks or hardly eat at all.

There are many plans to get people together and eating. Massachusetts has passed legislation enabling cafeterias in schools and other nonprofit institutions to serve inexpensive luncheons to people over 59. A Los Angeles cafeteria chain offers special low-cost meals to the old in its various locations, seven days a week, in the off-meal hours of 1:30 to 4:30. Some cities have Meals-on-Wheels programs that link the homebound with the outside world on a daily basis. Sometimes the programs are run almost entirely by volunteers; the old who can afford it pay $10 a week while others pay what they can or nothing at all. A Denver Serve-a-Meal-to-Seniors program feeds 700 people each week in eating places scattered throughout the city. The benefits of group eating are so great that many professionals urge that even the blind and other severely handicapped old be included; helping them gives the more active old a chance to be of service and makes the meal more of a social occasion.

• Helping the old to be mobile is one of the major efforts. Hayward McDonald of the National Commission of Architectural Barriers says that "it is not by design or intent that buildings are constructed so as to be inaccessible but primarily a matter of oversight." The problem will be close to solution, he believes, when architects and builders start building "according to minimum standards for the handicapped" and discover that they can do so without undue cost or loss of design and function.

If public transportation is to better serve the old, according to *Let's End Isolation,* the designers of original or replacement equipment must do better: "Buses can be built so that their doors open at curb level . . . ; automatic devices similar to those which collect road tolls could replace inconvenient subway turnstiles; one-way doors to control traffic; and gradual acceleration and deceleration to prevent jolting . . ." *

Meanwhile, many other avenues are being opened to the old. At least fifty American cities with public transportation systems have experimented with reduced fares for older people during nonrush hours. Community and voluntary groups, some with government help, provide special transportation. In Chicago, the Young Men's Christian Association, with the Administration on Aging, set up a Senior Citizens Mobile Service that made some 30,000 trips in a three-year period using special buses or vans. In Austin, Texas, the Texas Roadrunner Volunteers, which calls upon nursing-home residents, leased a station wagon and a small bus to take patients on essential trips. Many senior centers provide bus service between members' homes and the centers, usually without charge. In rural and small town areas, volunteers driving private cars give the old a choice of services in the absence of public transportation—taking them to doctors' offices, to polling booths, to stores. The cars are not necessarily driven by their owners; some people drive to work and park, then turn the keys over to volunteers who use the cars during the business day to drive old people around.

There is a great range in substance and value in these ideas. However, all they really do is suggest what a compassionate government and people might achieve if they wished to. *Let's End Isolation* is more a note of encouragement than a serious report on American progress in one special field. Commissioner John B. Martin of the Administration on Aging clearly faces that fact—his introduction to the publication is headed "We Have the Tools—Now Let's Use Them." Some of the programs described here have already been modified or curtailed for lack of public funds.

It takes a great deal of energy to reach and help many people, and enthusiasm, even among the most devoted of volunteers, is hard

---

* None of these problems is exclusively American. The French subway system has special provisions for seating the blind, war wounded, and pregnant women—but nothing for the old. Further, doors to *Métro* cars are manually opened by passengers themselves, both for mounting and dismounting. They are heavy and they stick and it takes a special knack to raise the handle, all nerve-wracking and sometimes impossible to a person feeling his years.

to sustain.* The promise is real, but it is still only promise. For example, the above facts on transportation—although listed here in highly condensed form from the government report—give the impression that older Americans receive organized help in getting about. They do not: A study of retired persons living in a major American city found that "an almost trivial proportion (3%) were ever driven anywhere by a volunteer or staff member of a community agency or other service organization." That enigmatic smile of the old may also hide some skepticism.

* From an editorial in *Modern Maturity,* February-March 1971: "A woman in her eighties wrote the *Los Angeles Times* recently saying she was so lonely she 'could die.' She had moved to an apartment downtown from out of state about a year before. She was able to go shopping from time to time, taking the bus to get around. But, she said, she had nobody to talk to. No one even phoned her.

"Naturally, the *Times* ran a story about the letter. And naturally within a few days she was inundated with letters, got so many phone calls she had to have her line disconnected, and couldn't take a bath because her bathtub was filled with flowers.

"A few days after that, a reader in another letter to the *Times* suggested that the newspaper check the lady of the story in a few months' time. How many letters, phone calls, and flowers would she have then?

"This episode demonstrates America's tremendous generosity when its heart is wrenched—and its impersonal apathy at other times . . ."

8 THE OLD AND THEIR FAMILIES

These are some of the conventional wisdoms about the "plight" of the old in their families today:

• Families used to be tightly knit, self-sustaining units. Grand-parents, children—the extended family—lived together in an atmosphere of warmth, love, and mutual respect. The old were patriarchs (or at least treated like patriarchs—the center of attention), their counsel heeded. When necessary, they were supported by the young, but often it was the old who controlled the family's finances.

• Today, all has changed. There is little respect or compassion for the old. The family unit has disintegrated into, at best, the nuclear unit—the smallest unit possible that may still be considered a family, the single kinship of parents and their children. Parents, aunts, uncles, children, all go their own way, often to widely scattered places. The old are left behind, neglected, put away in institutions whenever possible, unlike the old days when their children looked after them tenderly. When they do live at home with their families, their children are usually locked in squabbles—filled with heat and emotion—about who is responsible for their care and who should pay.

If all this were true, it would be tragic, indeed. The family situation—with all its supports—is one key to the good long life. As we age, home and family life become even more the center and whole of existence. In mid-life, we may have spent only sleeping, eating, and a few recreational hours at home. After 65, our orbit shrinks and we spend 80% to 90% of the time there; in advanced old age, virtually all the time. Away from the family, an old man or woman is usually just that—an old man or woman. Within the family, the old are something else; they have status and role, as progenitors, matriarchs, or patriarchs, as links with the past, as major figures in shared memories. Old people who are married or live with their families live longer and better than those who do not.

All this is as true today as it was in the past. The individual old person's place in the family structure is far more important than is generally assumed. There is a new awareness that the family, changes and all, has never been stronger or more solidly based and is as extended as ever. There is also a new phenomenon: As people marry younger and live longer, more and more families are being extended into the fourth generation.

And, as society has taken over a greater role in caring for the old, it is likely that there are fewer, not more, intrafamily squabbles than in the past over who pays and cares for the old. In short, the old in their families may be better off today than ever before.

We hold to the myths of the past—the images of life in Tennysonian country homes or Thackerayan drawing rooms or idyllic scenes of Mark Twain. One image is that of grandfather putting down his cane and hitching up his pants to throw a horseshoe or two with the kids, while grandmother tats away in her corner of the sitting room—both, somehow, always in the bosom of their families.

The reality is that most people, until the recent past, didn't live that well or share in the bounties of life. Daily existence was a much greater struggle, toil harder, and leisure and recreation often unknown. The rights of workers were barely considered, and few people were covered by pensions or had financial security at any time. Society showed little concern for the welfare of the individual—and the "useless" old were far worse off than they are now.*

Simone de Beauvoir has looked at the past and stripped it of its

---

* Not that there were so many old people around in "the good old days." Life expectancy at birth in Elizabethan days was 32, in Abraham Lincoln's day 40, in 1920 under 60. Today in Western Europe and the United States, it is over 70 for all. More than a quarter of all the people in the history of the world who have ever reached the age of 65 are alive today.

nimbus. The Industrial Revolution changed family structure in the 19th century. As people moved away from the countryside and the proletariat first appeared, the old were among those most victimized. Many people died from their toil amid wretched working conditions. Those who survived were usually reduced to extreme poverty when they were too old or sick to go on.

Among well-to-do peasants in France, an old man often continued in a harsh patriarchal role—as long as he could keep on working or hire laborers. But most peasants, in their old age, were at their children's mercy; the children themselves lived near destitution and had nothing to spare. Their parents were often abandoned to alms houses or asylums.

Often a father, no longer able to work, would turn over all he had to his children who could then mistreat or starve him. French law tried to help. A father who gave his property to his child became legally entitled to receive a life annuity in return. Now the child was bound to pay a specific amount at regular intervals to his father—making the situation more deadly.

The murder of old parents, by violence or privation, was common, "Most of these killings remained buried in the silence of the countryside," says Beauvoir, "but the fact that in the 19th century public opinion was uneasily aware of them proves that they must have been frequent. Many people spoke out about the dangers that lay in wait for the aged."

The great majority of the old, proletarians or peasants, received little help even when the government was in the hands of the old; the ruling old came from the upper middle classes and seemed to accept the exploitation of the workers. Within the bourgeoisie, old and young were bound together in common cause in the face of the "dangerous" classes.*

* One change in family attitudes inherited from those days: New jobs and some broadening of social life made the family less patriarchal. Young couples often began to set up housekeeping for themselves. The idea of the extended family—all generations living together—was still venerated; the grandfather remained its symbol and he was treated with all respect possible. But he was no longer the head of the family. This led to a new alliance between children and grandparents, somewhat over the head of parents. Children came to think of their grandparents not as the authoritarian heads of households but as indulgent companions— as we tend to think of them today.

The upper classes lived longer than the rest. In the mid-18th century, French peasants began "to decay before the age of 40 for want of nourishment in proportion to their labor." One hundred years later, a visitor to a British or American factory or mine might have come to the same conclusion. A visitor to the living quarters of the urban masses throughout the 19th century might have been even more aghast. Lewis Mumford describes how families lived in the cities:

"In Liverpool, one-sixth of the population lived in 'underground cellars,' and most of the other port cities were not far behind: London and New York were close rivals. . . . The crude results of all these conditions may be followed in the mortality rates for adults, in the disease rates for urban workers compared with agricultural workers, in the expectation of life enjoyed by the various occupational diseases." Industrial workers and their families were exposed to "cancer-producing chemicals which pervaded the atmosphere and sapped vitality." It was a world filled with despair, fatigue, sickness, and death; people had little time, will, or the resources to care for their old. Social mobility, standards of living, housing, working conditions, general security, have improved incalculably in our century. In the good old days, the prospects for the good long life—for most families—barely existed.

It is easy to see the improvement in living conditions; it has not been as easy to understand the change in family structure. Today, most of the old—70% of all people over 65—live at home in families made up of two or more persons. (Another 25% live alone, the rest in institutions.) In all, about 8% of all families are three-generational, the same percentage as at the turn of the century. There has been no long-term decline in the number of multigenerational families—they are as rare now as they were a century ago.

The view among sociologists and others that the family is more solidly based than ever is a recent one. Until a few years ago, it was assumed that the extended family was breaking up into the single kinship unit, that the family was being shattered because the married children first moved out of the household, then even away from the neighborhood of other relatives. This theory lagged behind the evidence. For one thing, it was based upon an idealization of what the extended family was like in the past: The large household was often neither as stable nor as integrated as we recall it. The theory was also based on the fact that today's family may not live under the same roof. But the modern family continues to adapt itself to changes in society, and what we have now, according to sociologists Marvin Sussman and Lee Burchinal, is "an extended family system functioning within a network of relationships and mutual assistance patterns . . . encompassing several generations."

These are some of the reasons why sociologists now conclude that the family is as sound and as extended as ever:

• *Separate households do not mean the end of family ties.* They may have in the past, but today, with all the means of communication possible, physical distance has far less of a disintegrating effect on the family. Children may move far away from their parents but establish a new network of contact with them, including telephoning, correspondence, and visits. There is a change of function within the family structure—some responsibilities lost, some gained—but the family may feel as close as ever, with more anticipation and appreciation of the time spent together, of the messages and progress reports exchanged.*

• *Living together is not a sign of family stability.* There was probably more tension than harmony in the old-time autocratic family, no matter how stable it seemed from the outside. Living together is not at all the most important factor in relations between old people and their grown-up children and does not mean that they are closely knit. To the contrary: The problems of an adult couple who live with the still-active parents of either mate are often insurmountable. Attitudes, social worlds, and self-concepts of the two couples are bound to clash. Each couple has a distinctive life-style. Who is in charge of what? Who does the cooking and according to whose taste? Who sits at the head of the table? Who pays for

* Jane Howard gives another view of the old-time autocratic extended family. She tells of Nelba Chavez, a Chicana psychiatric social worker, at a conference where the "Anglo" psychiatrists persisted in talking of the need to "rediscover" the extended family. "Hell, we've been living in extended families for years," Ms. Chavez said. "Some of what you say about closeness and security is true, of course, but those ties can be *too* close. What you're trying to bring back is what we're trying to get away from."

the new furniture—and who decides what new furniture to buy? Should the older couple retire to their bedroom when the younger couple have guests (and vice versa)? A superhuman amount of courtesy, sensitivity, and patience—and loss of privacy—is required to make such an arrangement work. That and, most likely, separate kitchens, living rooms, bathrooms, cars, and television sets. In short, the overwhelming odds are that separate households best permit a stable, strong, and congenial relationship between adult couples of different generations.

• *People now marry younger and live longer.* In 1890, on the average, a man married at the age of 26, a woman at 22. In 1970, the ages were 23 for the man, 20.8 for the woman. The 1970 mother was almost seven years younger at the time of the birth of her last child than was her grandmother in 1890, the 1970 father at least eight years younger than his great-grandfather at that time.

There are trends toward more marriages, earlier childbirth, and fewer large families. It is these facts that have brought about the new, relatively common phenomena of our time: great-grandparents and the emergence of the four-generation family—something that rarely existed in the past.

With fewer years between the generations, parents and children are now closer in interests, problems, even physical condition.* This does not mean that they can live together in harmony under one roof. Their ego clashes are bound to be more frequent than ever as there are fewer years to separate them. But the greater proximity in age also strengthens the relationship—helps the generations to understand each other—and, say the authors of *Old People in Three Industrial Societies,* makes for "greater stability at the center" of the family today.

These trends may bring dramatic changes in the family of the future. Old people will be divided into two broad categories—the "young-old" who are grandparents (the third generation) and the "old-old" who are great-grandparents (the fourth generation). Increasingly, both husband and wife will survive to become grandparents; they will have more energy and time to spare for their

---

* Today's new grandparents have good reason for feeling that they're not as old as their grandparents were. They're not—they're actually younger in years as well as in social and biological ages.

grandchildren because they will have retired earlier and will be younger than grandparents of the past. A new conflict may arise: grandmothers competing with great-grandmothers for the attention of the two younger generations. The second and third generations —parents and grandparents—may have more in common in the future, including the fact that both will have a set of parents of their own—an emotionally dependent older generation—to cope with.

Today, adult children often ponder (and quarrel) and meet in family council to decide who will look after a widowed parent, usually the mother. The future problem may be: How can a middle-aged man and wife reconcile dependent relationships with *both* sets of their parents, fill their emotional needs and care for them? The extended family of the future—although living apart—will be more extended and complex than ever, and as mutually dependent.

• *People are more understanding.* Or at least they try to sound more understanding. In a post-Freudian age, people have somewhat greater insight into why they think, behave, and react as they do. The popularization of psychology and the mass awareness—even in jargon—of such things as Oedipal and superego problems have had many effects. One is that we tend to be more reflective in our dealings with others. Temper, vanity, and pride are more controlled, speech is more euphemistic to avoid injured feelings. And we tend to examine our own motives more than we did in the past and, perhaps, act more humanely.

This is true in many of our relationships in which a knowledge of psychology has taken hold. If only because he thinks it will be more productive in the long run, the modern employer reasons with, persuades, and even flatters an employee when, in the past, he would simply have ordered him. An army officer tries to "define the mission" to a private soldier instead of merely pointing him in the direction of an enemy. Teachers don't scold or slap a child who can't read or add but try to "develop his personality."

We are more sensitive—or try to be—in our family relationships too. The old family was, to an extent, made up of "personnel." Each person had a role and duties to perform to keep the family afloat and functioning. Today, the blurring of lines of authority, the diminishing of family duties, and a new atmosphere of equality

among family members have brought with them something else
—a greater sense of understanding and affection among family
members.

The decline in the pattern of duties and authority may have
weakened the family in some ways but it has strengthened them
in others. The ties of affection are probably stronger now than in
the past. Sociologists Gordon F. Streib and Wayne E. Thompson
of Cornell University quote as typical a response from an old man
describing his life as a child:

"When I was a kid, there was stricter discipline, I can tell you!
My mother kept a willow switch handy and she knew how to
switch us where it would hurt the most . . . We had plenty of
opportunity to play—used to have all the kids in the neighborhood
in our backyard. But we knew how to work too, and when my
folks said do something, we did it . . . we didn't question why we
had to, we just did it. My folks were fair . . . but there was stricter
discipline, I can tell you!"

Streib and Thompson then asked old people whether they feel
there is less affection in families today. Here, too, they received a
typical response, this one from a 70-year old:

"Less affection? No, not at all, There is *more* affection today.
I'm not saying I didn't hold my parents in high regard, because
I did. But it was that I respected and kind of feared them, too, I
guess. I thought they had all the answers. Now take my kids: they
know more than I do, but they love the 'old man' and even let me
spoil my grandkids. What more could I ask?"

Young people assume that they are more important to the
old than the old are to them, according to Streib and Thompson. A
younger person still feels guilty if, say, he has neglected to visit
or write his parents. But guilt aside, he really regrets his negligence
only because he fears it might jeopardize his friendly relationship
with them. Such regrets usually take the form "I hate to hurt their
feelings but . . ."

This points up some of the hazards of the new understanding
within the family. Friendship and familiarity may also breed
condescension. "Good old Dad" suggests affection. It also suggests
that Dad may be a bit of a slob, innocuous and helpless. "Mom's a
real Auntie Mame type" may sound complimentary; it may also

mean that a widowed mother is acting up too much or somehow not playing the docile role her children expect of her.

Countless books on child psychology and care have helped shape the new and generally positive way parents treat their young. Unfortunately, many parents believe they can apply the techniques and idiom of child psychology in handling *their* parents. The treatment amounts to: Let's pretend we're equals but never forget who's really got the authority (and the money). This can be destructive of the personality of the old; if an old man is dependent on his children for love, care, and money and treated this way, he may be reduced to acting like a child—be alternately petulant and arrogant, servile and tearful, knowing he needs his children more than they need him and hating the role he must play.

We may be thankful that there are not an equal number of books on how to treat old parents. The trick in dealing with the old is not to use any tricks, just intelligence and understanding. The old are adults and not children, at least as sensitive and often more proud than other adults.

But there are hazards, too, when their children see the old with a measure of psychological insight. They may think they see them more clearly—and conclude that they dislike them. Somewhat freed from guilt feelings, a grown child may abandon even the pretense of loving his parents. He may follow the commandment "Honor thy father and thy mother" in the most limited of ways—by paying their expenses if necessary but giving them nothing else. Gerontologist Bertha G. Simos quotes this view:

"My mother was always a taker, never a giver. I know she is old and sick now and needs care, I want to see she has the best care I can get for her, because she is my mother, but I don't want to see her if I can avoid it. She is still demanding, and all I can think of when I am with her is: 'Where were you when I needed you?'"

Dr. Simos says that some of the people she interviewed—all with parents ranging in age from 60 to 94—were surprised to discover how little intrinsic pleasure they found in their relationship with their parents. She concludes that parents, like others, may be judged solely on the basis of past performance and that they are apt to get the treatment they have earned from their children.

There may be a considerable amount of rationalization in this. A man of 50, say, may have unbudgeable financial problems made worse by the dependence of his parents. With little or no money in the bank, having just finished paying for his children's education, he now looks forward to his retirement (and reduced income) with apprehension. The money he must dole out to his parents stands between himself and a somewhat better way of life—and he doesn't know when he'll be able to stop paying it. He deeply resents the burden and feels that he would be much better off if his parents were dead. That is an unutterable thought, so he transforms it to "What did my mother (or father) ever do for me anyway?" *

Most likely the reference is to a mother, not a father: Women marry younger and live longer, and there are four times as many widows as there are widowers. No matter how close children feel to their aging parents, it is virtually impossible for them to understand the depth of a parent's loss when her mate dies. After a serious affective loss, "the structure of one's inner world . . . will never be the same," Freud once wrote. "Not only is the identity of self changed but also that of the outer world is different."

A new widow may seem calm at first, almost unchanged, appearing to cope with her problems as her husband would. Then she becomes numb and seems to fall apart, as she truly perceives the finality of loss. There is a characteristic process in mourning: impact, recoil, and then recovery or adjustment—but still the world is never quite the same.

As she ages, the widow may feel that she is traveling along

* A small amount of "psychological insight" may indeed be a dangerous thing. In a family dispute, for example, an older person may wind up saying: "How can you treat me this way after all I've done for you?" A son or daughter may rationalize away filial responsibility by thinking (or saying out loud, if the fight is heated enough), "I didn't ask to be born. I didn't ask for a thing. Everything you did for me was to gratify your own ego. Why should I drown myself in guilt over you?" Psychological parricide may be preferable to the real parricide of centuries past, but it is still deadly. A wiser child would relent in his struggle for independence, assume a more mature role toward his parent's dependencies— and accept the responsibility.

the road to institutionalization and sees, with greater clarity than her children, that each year is a step along the way. There is a process here, too: being taken into the children's home, giving up her own furniture and way of life, seeing the children's life and problems first hand and realizing that they have a life-style and needs entirely apart from her own. She may become dissatisfied with the dependent role, feeling that she is a burden and in the way, even though the children try hard not to express such feelings. She finds herself living a strangely disoriented and useless life in the circle of those she knows best.

It is at that point that she may start to show the "rigidity" of the old. She may seem inflexible, demanding, or completely un-cooperative with the family. The children may assume that this is just an exaggeration of past tendencies—"Mother was always set in her ways and now she's getting much worse"—when in fact she is really expressing her anxiety. It is hard to be old and dependent when you've been an independent homemaker all your adult life. Further, the old person is as aware as the young of the bleakness of her future—more so because she thinks about it a good deal of the time. Anxious and apprehensive, an old person may herself raise the subject of institutionalization no matter how she dreads the prospect. She wants to put an end to an uncertain and provisional situation.

Despite these attitudes—and the myths—there is no great tendency to pack the old off to institutions to live out their days. In the United States, only 3.7% of all persons over 65 live in residential or nursing homes or, for long terms, in chronic disease or mental hospitals (2.3% in nursing homes alone). In Britain, 3.6% live in institutions, 1.6% in nursing homes. Thus more than 95% of the old in the two countries have their own households or share them with their families or companions.

These figures come from *Old People in Three Industrial Societies,* which also—through the use of four major tests of involvement—gives a profile of the old and their family relationships. The tests are: Do they share a household? How far away do they live from each other? How often do they get together? And does the family exchange services?

Of all the old with children, 42% in Britain and 28% in the United States live with them. Of those who do not live with their children, in the United States almost 50% live within a thirty-minute trip of one or more of them—in Britain, 40%. This despite the notion that, in a mobile age, families are scattered far and wide. Altogether, more than 75% of old people with children either live with them or live no more than thirty minutes away.

About two-thirds of all the old said they had seen their children that day or the day before. Even the old living alone had, for the most part, seen their children within the past day. And more than a third of the old with brothers or sisters said they had seen at least one of them within the past week.

They do exchange services: A half or more of the old people in the United States and Britain said they give help—in the form of money or household services—to their children or grandchildren. About two-thirds of the old said they receive help from their families, including money or gifts. From 35% to 40% depend upon children or other relatives for help with housework, meals, or shopping in the event of illness. If they are handicapped or have other difficulties, the great majority of the old rely upon husbands, wives, children, or other relatives for help in such tasks as housework, meals, shopping, dressing. If they are confined to bed at home, almost nine out of ten depend primarily on family members for these services. Less than a quarter of all the old said they rely upon persons or agencies outside the family or that they have no source of help at all.

These figures give only a sketchy profile; there is too much diversity in the family structure of the old for them to provide much more. About 90% of all the old with children also have grandchildren; 40% in the United States and 23% in Britain also have great-grandchildren. About 20% of those with children have six or more. Yet up to 25% of the old are single or otherwise childless; 3% to 5% of the single or widowed old have neither children nor brothers or sisters. A minority of the old have no kin at all; many of the rest are "knitted in a complex network of surviving kin spanning several generations," say the authors of *Old People*.

They found that elderly men and women seem to be about equally integrated, enjoy approximately the same proportion of contacts with their children, and have similar living arrangements, but more of them live with married daughters than with married sons.

One pattern is sustained throughout: As they get older, more old people live with or closer to their children and have more contacts with them. They also get more help from their children and give less themselves. With advancing age and disability, the role of the old person changes from independence to dependence. And it is the old who now become the visited instead of the visitor.

This brings up a commonplace: One reason for having children is to have someone to look after you in your old age. If any further proof were needed, it comes in the form of a sociologist's findings—findings that are generally applicable although they are based on a study of old people in working-class London.

Peter Townsend found that the normal environment for old people is the three-generation extended family—grandparents, parents, children. Family ties are far more important to the old than are ties of friendship and neighborliness, of club and church membership; many of the old Townsend interviewed did not have one close friend outside the family. With increasing age, "friends died or passed out of knowledge, money was shorter, and it was more difficult to get about," he writes.

This was the case whether or not the old shared a household. Many of the old live with relatives but prefer a "supported" independence. Even the old who do not live with their children rarely live alone in a literal sense: Townsend found that three generations of relatives were generally distributed over two or more households near one another and that the old had very close ties with their families. But at any time, he says, there is an isolated minority —from 10% to 20% of old people—who have no close relatives, no family.

The poorest people, not only financially, are those without an active family life, he writes. They have the fewest resources in times of need. They are "more desolated than isolated, and the loneliest." They also make the heaviest demands on outside and government health and social services.

Old people who have daughters at hand make the least claim

of all—partly because there is a particular tie between the women in a family, between a grandmother and her daughter (and the daughter's child). But the reason why an old person will call upon a daughter instead of a son may be the most obvious one: Giving such personal services—shopping, preparing food, cleaning, providing care during sickness—is considered a domestic matter, to be attended to by a daughter along with her other domestic tasks. If the old also have a son, it is understood that his role is to be out of the house earning a living (and providing money, not household services). In his absence from the house, they are less inclined to call upon his wife—their daughter-in-law—than upon their own daughter for such services.*

Assuming the parents have been reasonably good ones, there is good reason for children to get fonder of them as they grow older. Youthful rebellion is far behind them. The children have made their marks in life (or at least their adjustments to it). If the parents were once authoritarian, they are now far much less so, particularly as they foresee greater dependence on their children in the future. They appreciate their children's accomplishments and possessions, and speak of them openly, often boastfully. (It is not uncommon for a parent to refer to "my son, the doctor," when that son is, at best, a registered pharmacist, or to claim that a daughter is of *cordon bleu* quality in the kitchen, when she has not gone beyond Betty Crocker.) Together, adult children and their parents selectively remember the good times of the past and savor them.

A son may have had a period of hostility toward his father—until he himself gets a job, marries, and has a family. Then he may find himself in just about the same position as his father before him, with the same kinds of problems. He becomes more tolerant, and accepts what he used to consider his father's idiosyncrasies. At this

---

* In-law problems are not the province of this book. It is interesting, however, that older people are usually closer to a child-in-law when they do not have a child of their own of the same sex. A mother-in-law, for example, will get along better with her son-in-law if she does not have a son of her own to compare him to and to command her affections. They get along better still if the parents of the son-in-law are dead or live at a distance; the mother-son surrogate relationship is closer and there are greater mutual need and more services exchanged. (This is true for in-law relationships generally, not just mothers and sons-in-law.)

stage of their lives, many sons go through a kind of reconciliation with their fathers, Townsend says. Now the sons can share the burden of being a father with their own fathers "just as many fathers can continue to fulfill, through their sons, the need to procreate and teach the younger generation."

The birth of grandchildren is, obviously, of great importance to a family, to both generations. Parents recognize the value of having grandparents on call and thus feel reliant and closer to their fathers and mothers. The older person feels that there has been a renewal of his life; the older he is the more he feels the need to communicate with a younger generation, to pass on his experience and knowledge—and his reminiscences—to assure himself of at least a measure of immortality. If an older person has no grandchildren he may seek substitutes in the young children of nieces or nephews or other relatives. Some older people without families of their own attach themselves to other families with young children, for the same purposes.

The old who eagerly join groups like Foster Grandparents, in which they develop relationships with and help institutionalized children, are expressing the same need. Anthropologist Margaret Mead stresses how important it is for old people to think in terms of what they can do for someone else and says that the old must "take the lead by finding ways to relate to either their own grandchildren or someone else's."

Dr. Mead believes that society today lacks the close relationship of grandparents and grandchildren—a loss to both society and the child: "Children need three generations to grow up with," she says. "Grandparents give you a sense of how things were, how things are . . . The older generation has lived through change, and the young need to know about it."

She attributes some of the responsibility for the situation to grandparents themselves. "Older people who are close to their grandchildren are themselves very different from people who are not." She is most critical of parents who place on grandparents the obligation "to keep themselves out of the picture, not to interfere, not to spoil, not to insist, not to intrude. . . . Perhaps that was the way the parents felt when they were young toward their own parents and grandparents. They resented interference. But I had none of this. I loved my grandmother and I valued the way my mother nursed and loved her children."

Peter Townsend docs not share her view. He sees no lessening of the role of grandparents at all. He cites studies which show that more than half of all elderly grandparents have a role in the regular care of their grandchildren (with grandmothers involved more than grandfathers). That is true for all classes of people. He cites two examples:

• A woman living in an East London attic said that her grandson had stayed with her the previous night. "I'm taking him to Trafalgar Square and Buckingham Palace today," she said. "I'm doing it for his history. He stays with me every week like this. I like learning him about things."

• Another woman, the wife of a baronet, said she read to her grandchildren every night when they were small. Now "my husband and I have put aside a large sum in trust for our grandchildren's education," she declared. "It will cover all their school needs."

The two women have different resources but the same hopes for and interest in their grandchildren.

Townsend concludes that "the major function" of the grandparent may be the most important fact to emerge from his study. He says that it is remarkable how often grandparents reciprocate help in the form of midday meals, care of grandchildren, and other services. Much, but not all of this help, is needed and cherished by parents.

Margaret Mead deplores the fact that younger adults often try to keep grandparents out of their children's lives; she urges that grandparents have a more active role. But others question what that role should be. Grandparents today have relative affluence and, often, a lot of free time, and, warns psychologist Joseph Weinreb of Vanderbilt University, through their gifts and attention they may unwittingly create conflict and confusion in the lives of both their children and grandchildren. According to writer Lillian G. Genn, many grandparents find that they are resented or rebuked by their children. She quotes as typical these complaints of parents about grandparents: "They're spoiling our children." Or "They're trying to own us." Or "Why don't they let us do things our own way?"

With too much zeal, grandparents may undercut parental authority and self-esteem or may somehow seem to be conspiring with their grandchildren. Their behavior is well motivated; they are, after all, just competing for love, and they cannot understand why it affronts. But it can drive parents to fights among themselves, to vexations with the grandparents, and to the muttering—sometimes rising to a shriek—"Why don't they leave us alone?"

Miss Genn has come up with guidelines for avoiding the problem —a primer, in effect, addressed to grandparents, on how to be good ones. Among her points:
• Don't interfere with the way parents are managing their children. If you must speak up, do it when the children are not around.
• Don't assume the major responsibility of being the parent under any circumstances. It can only cause great harm. This is especially true when the children's parents have been divorced. Children belong to their parents, for better or worse.
• Don't take over the house under any circumstances, unless asked. And don't do such annoying things as telling parents how to handle a child's illness or spoiling children with foods you know the parents don't want them to have.
On gifts: Don't bring fine presents every time you visit; reserve them for special occasions such as Christmas or birthdays. (Children can get blasé too, and parents start resenting the flow.) Don't give gifts of money because you think their parents don't give your grandchildren enough. And don't vie with other grandparents—or great-grandparents—to see who can give more.
On personal behavior: Unless there is a warm, intimate relationship, don't ask intimate questions. If you're not living with your children, you may invite yourself over to their house—but not too often. Don't be a constant baby-sitter at the expense of your own social life. No grandparent should be exploited in the hope of winning the love of his or her children. Try, instead, to join them in meaningful events—but live your own life, too.

This is simple, sensible, and somewhat obvious advice. It appears in a popular magazine, addressed to a mass audience. That it should appear there is, in a way, a tribute to the vitality of the extended family and the fullness of our times. However, it should not, for one minute, be taken to mean that too much bounty is *the* problem —or even a serious problem—in the relationships of the old with their families.

The real problem has always been the matter of resources: the time, money, living accommodations, knowledge, and all the facilities needed to meet the needs of the old. Change and improvement have been agonizingly slow, but they have taken place, in the most basic of ways. Overall, there has been this realization: The problems of older families are no longer merely a private matter. It is now "a vestigial idea" that the family alone is responsible for its old, says sociologist Gordon F. Streib. Our times have seen the growth of organizations—public and private, governmental and nongovernmental, voluntary and professional—that offer to the old a variety of services, most of them undreamt of a generation ago. The services are still inadequate. Often the old and their families don't know about them or are loath to take advantage of them. But they are there and growing. The fact that society has taken on some of the responsibility for the old may be the single best assurance of the good long life for more people in the future.

9 SEX AND MARRIAGE

For the old, the sexual revolution came fifty years too late. They can hear and read about it but they cannot touch. For they are burdened with the idea—society's and often their own—that sex isn't for them.

The jokes about the old, usually bad and sometimes terrible, suggest their predicament. A study of "Attitudes Toward Aging as Shown by Humor," by Duke University's Erdman Palmore, found that most of the jokes—"especially those dealing with physical ability or appearance, age concealment, old maids, and mental abilities"—reflect a negative view of aging. Some were downright hostile.

His analysis begins with the comment of a 75-year-old acquaintance: "After you reach a certain age, you discover that most jokes about aging aren't funny anymore"—a line which echoes Will Roger's "Everything is funny as long as it happens to somebody else." Dr. Palmore's collection of jokes about the old, as they appear in *The Gerontologist,* surrounded by interpretation and summary, must be the saddest ever. Among them:

- On death: The funeral of a comedian in London was attended by many old-time comedians who had gathered to say a last farewell. During the ceremony, one looked up at his neighbor and asked, " 'Ow old are you, Charlie?" "Ninety," replied the old-timer. " 'Ardly worth going 'ome, eh?"
- On declining mental ability: "Four stages of memory loss:

(*1*) forget names; (*2*) forget faces; (*3*) forget to zip up fly; (*4*) forget to zip down fly."

Many of the 264 jokes analyzed by Dr. Palmore are specifically about sexual ability or interest. This is a sampling:

- Definition of old age: "The time of life when a man flirts with girls but can't remember why."
- Oscar Wilde: "Young men want to be faithful and are not; old men want to be faithless and cannot."
- Description of the sexual life cycle of a man: "Triweekly. Try weekly. Try weakly."
- "A 90-year-old man married a beautiful 18-year-old girl. He lasted only five days but it took the undertaker three days to get the smile off his face."

Old women are viewed as lonely, frustrated, and shriveled:
- Definition of an old maid: "A lemon that has never been squeezed."
- "An old woman was held up by a robber who proceeded to frisk her for money. After a thorough search all over her body, he gave up. She exclaimed, 'Heavens, young man, don't stop now—I'll write you a check.' "

Dr. Palmore also weighs the significance of the facts that there are no "old bachelor" jokes and that more of the jokes about women are negative (77%) than are the jokes about men (51%).

Dr. Palmore's material came from such Middle American standbys as *The Speaker's Treasury of Stories for All Occasions.* There are countless other sources and types of jokes about the old, often more felicitously phrased if more ribald. Frank Harris, in *My Life and Loves,* wrote about a witticism of Degas, who lived to 83. Degas heard someone condemning cunnilingus, to which he replied with an old French saying: *"Quelle triste vieillesse vous vous préparez!"* ("What a dreary old age you are making for yourself!"). In his *Rationale of the Dirty Joke,* G. Legman, an authority on erotica, devotes a forty-page chapter to jokes about old age, with section headings such as "Old Wives for New" and "Impotence of Husbands." Among his example are:

- "A young man sees his father coming out of a notorious

brothel. 'Father!' he says, shocked. 'Son,' says the father, 'Say nothing. I prefer the simulated enthusiasm of a paid prostitute to the dignified acquiescence of your mother.' "

• "An elderly roué at a brothel insists he wants his usual girl, Mamie, who happens to be occupied. The madam vainly offers him various other girls and finally asks: 'Well, what has Mamie got that the other girls don't have?' 'Patience,' he replies."

Mr. Legman also includes the French proverb, *"Si jeunesse savait; si vieillesse pouvait,"* which has its English equivalent, "If youth only knew; if age only could." Actually, age can. And particularly in marriage or in remarriage. All these jokes about the old are gross caricature, cruel and misleading.

There are "two great invalid and destructive myths" about the old, according to sociologist James A. Peterson. One is the idea, held by almost all young and middle-aged persons, that a new marriage for the elderly is foolish and inappropriate. The second myth, "even more devitalizing, is that sexual joy is reserved for those in the first decades of life and that physical intimacy is somehow proscribed" in later years. "These myths are so pervasive and powerful," he says, "that they have caused millions of older persons to live lives of loneliness and frustration." Dr. Peterson cites a number of scientific findings, including those of Dr. William H. Masters and Virginia E. Johnson of the Reproductive Biology Research Foundation and authors of *Human Sexual Response* and *Human Sexual Inadequacy*. There are changes, of course, as there are in any phase of aging, but Masters and Johnson found that there is no age limit to sexual responsiveness and "sexual interaction between older marital partners can be established easily, warmly and with dignity."

Dr. Peterson, an admirer of the Masters and Johnson studies, says that they assure a man, for example, that he need not ejaculate to have a "rewarding physical closeness" with his wife. "As the male ages, he becomes alarmed when intercourse does not result in ejaculation and he fears that he is becoming impotent," Dr. Peterson says. But if the man understood that intercourse can be rewarding with or without ejaculation, he would soon find out that he can ejaculate periodically and without stress. If he is anxious, he may become impotent and fail in his sexual attempts.

The facts of life for aging women are given in a direct quotation from Masters and Johnson: "There are only two basic needs for regularity of sexual expression in the 70-80-year-old woman. These necessities are a reasonably good state of health and an interested and interesting partner."

The ability to be an interested and interesting partner is often difficult to sustain after four or five years of marriage. To sustain it after forty or fifty years of the same marriage requires more than simple passion. It also requires more than the repetition of sexual stimuli. Routinized love making is no more exciting than dressing. "As a couple ages, both the man and the woman require new experiences. Habit is the master of the unimaginative . . ."

In explaining about the increasing joy of sexual play, Dr. Peterson does everything but draw pictures for exciting new approaches to love among the old. As interesting as his statements is the fact that they appear in an article he wrote for *Modern Maturity,* not a scientific journal but a magazine edited with the popular appeal and professionalism of the *Reader's Digest,* and published by the American Association of Retired Persons, an organization with about 6 million members. The magazine is a fine blend of history, current events, criticism, nostalgia, and practical advice for its readers of post-retirement age; the fact that its editors approached the subject of sex in old age so directly is an indication of how seriously the problem is felt.*

Perhaps no mass-circulation, middlebrow magazine in the world published articles with such candid talk about orgasm, ejaculation, and masturbation until 1948, when Dr. Alfred C. Kinsey and his associates at Indiana University issued *Sexual Behavior in the Human Male.* Its publishers felt the need to include a foreword explaining that the book was intended primarily for scientists and other professionals. But mass interest in the subject matter was ready and waiting; Dr. Kinsey and his colleagues handled their studies and the publicizing of their findings with such care, skill,

* In a study of a community made up of 10,000 old people, Dr. Peterson notes that psychologists and therapists report that twice as many problems revolve around sex as around anything else.

and taste that their breakthrough into the mass media—and mass idiom—was revolutionary, irreversible, and almost painless. The two Kinsey books (the one on women was published in 1953) are now almost unavoidable first citations for new studies of sexual behavior. Kinsey didn't mean it that way but his studies did little to make the aging feel better. For example, he concluded that—despite all the variables going into sexual behavior—"in the sexual history of the male, there is not a single factor which affects frequency of outlet as much as age." Kinsey was a professor of zoology, not a psychologist or sociologist. Love, life adjustment, and the psyche were not his professional fields; "sexual outlet" and its frequency made up his base for measuring sexual behavior. He was looking at the entire *biological* life-span of man when he talked of aging:

"As far as human sexuality is concerned, aging begins with the onset of adolescence . . . It seems more correct to think of aging as a process that sets in soon after the initiation of growth. The sexagenarian—or octogenarian—who suddenly becomes interested in the problems of aging is nearly a lifetime beyond the point at which he became involved in that process."

His wisdom was circumscribed only by the limits of his professional interest when he said that "aging studies need to be reoriented around the origins of biologic decline, and that will mean pre-adolescence or early adolescence in . . . at least some aspects of human physiology."

Kinsey had a missionary spirit in his fight against the sexual hypocrisy of his time—the difference between what people did and what they talked about or pretended they did. He noted that at least 90% of all American males over 17 years old had experience with masturbation and that, "as a question of physical outcome," there was no evidence of harm to it. The harm came, he felt, in telling children or adolescents gruesome tales about the effects of masturbation; it was through his influence that the manual of the Boy Scouts of America finally dropped its unscientific warning about the damage masturbation would do to the mind and body of a scout.

He was not above chiding his subjects. He reported that "highest-rating" males masturbate on an average of 23 times a week in early adolescence, 15 times a week by the age of 20, six times a week by 50, and once in two weeks by 60. He added: "It is about then that the older males are most inclined to warn the adolescent boy that masturbation will certainly harm him if he does it to excess."

Kinsey's butt was dishonest men, not "dirty old men." There is no scientific credence given that term, despite the widespread stereotype. For one thing, "old" is a highly relative term, particularly from the point of view of the young. Vladimir Nabokov's memorable specimen, Humbert Humbert, corrupter of Lolita and any nymphet he could get his hands on, died—even in fiction—at the tender age of 42. An "older man" started molesting real-life Virginia Woolf when she was 6; he was her half-brother, then 20. If the accounts of Marilyn Monroe's tragic youth are to be believed, the "old man" who raped her when she was 9 or 10 was no more than 45 years old.

In the mid-1960s, the Kinsey-founded Institute for Sex Research published a report based upon case histories of more than 1,500 men convicted of sex offenses. Most were committed by men in their twenties and thirties. The report noted that the public thinks of the child molester as an old man: "It is true that the average offender versus children was older at the time of his offense than any other sex offenders, except the incest offenders. Yet scarcely can he be described on the verge of senility since he was, on the average, aged 35."

A 1954 study of "psychiatrically-deviated sexual offenders" found that certain of the men who returned to prison did fall in the aging category. But these men were not true deviates; instead, they had reverted to an infantile sexual level because of physical regression. A 1967 study of geriatric sex offenders attributed the problem to "chronic brain syndrome, loss of inhibitions, persistence of sexual problems from youth, and efforts to salvage remnants of previous powers."

Dr. Joseph T. Freeman of Lankenau Hospital, Philadelphia, says that such behavior is notable mainly because it is unusual. Deviations in the elderly may disclose sexual conflicts that were unresolved through life or they may herald a new pathologic situation, he says. Since both interest and capacity usually wane with age, odd and compulsive behavior usually means that there has been "a mutation in normal habits and an escape from social restraints."

Dr. Freeman cites, from the annals of pre-World War II French medicine, "a classic example of bizarre sexual behavior": "In a member of the French Academy, sudden excitation and compulsion on a visit to the zoo precipitated an attempt at sodomy on an animal. The deed, which he performed while he was in a crowd and without self-consciousness or embarrassment, was a clue to a pathologic condition identified as cerebral disease. Death from a cerebral hemorrhage occurred within six months."

Classic example indeed. Still, the incidence among the elderly of abnormal sex behavior is low. And there are relatively far more dirty young men, to judge from the crime statistics, than there are dirty old men. The term itself, and that of "old maid," are hardly defensible. All such stereotypes punish the old and are cruelly unfair. There are old men and women, in varying degrees of physical and mental health and sexual adjustment, all with about the same needs for love and dignity.

It is true, say, that masturbation persists among men and women into their sixties and beyond; although infrequent, it is sometimes a more important source of outlet than coitus as opportunities shrink, within or without marriage. But to condemn masturbation, or to consider it deviate behavior, is a sanctimony which suits few people. Most authorities go quite the other way. "Masturbation presents no significant problem for the older-age group women," say Masters and Johnson. "When heterosexual contacts are limited or unavailable the widowed or divorced woman also may revert to the masturbatory practices of her teens and twenties when sexual tensions become intolerable." Dr. Isadore Rubin, a specialist on problems of sex in the aging, notes that "every study of older people has shown that large numbers of them engage in masturbation as an alternative method of gaining release from sexual tension," although they may feel something is wrong in doing so. He quotes, with obvious approval, the advice of marriage counselor Lester W. Dearborn: "It is to be hoped that those interested in the field of geriatrics will take into consideration the sexual needs of the aging and encourage them to accept masturbation as a perfectly valid outlet" when other means are unavailable.

Any study of attitudes or behavior among the old must consider the cultural and social forces which shape, restrain, or threaten them. The notion that the old do not really need or cannot partake in sexual activity is a self-fulfilling one; it implies criticism and ridicule and limits the enjoyment of their years.

The old *are* old, born in another time with different ways. Dr. Frederick E. Whiskin, psychiatrist at Cushing Hospital, Framingham, Massachusetts, observed the reading habits of old patients. He found that a number enjoyed rereading bestsellers of a 1900 vintage. Biographies of major figures and tales of adventure were popular, too. So were tender love stories, in which all ends well, and religious works.

"Leanings toward genuine intellectual challenge were found to be lacking in our subjects," Dr. Whiskin said. "Wit, humor, drama held little appeal. This lack of interest may be more on the basis of cultural differences than the age factor. Contemporary frankness in discussing sexual matters was generally offensive to the older readers. This could be related in part to their own strict early training, and also a general feeling that older people should not be interested in sex."

Of course, many are—although they are loath to show it. The DeWitt Nursing Home in New York City is a modern home run with considerable imagination and style by Dr. A. Lee Lichtman, Its residents, whose average age is about 83, elect their own local government. A male resident sneaked into a woman resident's room one night and tried to get into bed with her; she did not complain to the doctors but to the residents' government which took it upon itself to admonish the man. Dr. Lichtman found out about the incident later when another resident confided in him. He was satisfied that it had gone to the local government to handle but was not surprised by the incident. "They keep their sex lives pretty quiet," he said. "But it's definitely there. I get it through the grapevine." *

It *is* there and slowly becoming tolerated. We've suffered a long time from the idea that "what was considered virility at 25 becomes lechery at 65," says Martin Berezin, past president of the Boston Society for Geriatric Psychiatry. But now institutions have become

---

* A much longer grapevine has it that there is a senior citizens' community in Florida with its own brothel just outside its confines. The customers are 65 or older, the "girls" from 30 to middle age. The grapevine does not tell what the customers' wives have to say about it.

somewhat more understanding of sexual contact between unmarried residents who, "in the old days, would have to slip out
into the woods like adolescents," he says.

The feeling that it is repulsive for people over 70 to hold hands,
kiss, or make love may be about the last barrier of prejudice against
the old to fall. Still, that is exactly what the old are doing in
greater number, whenever—as in retirement villages—they find
the chance and atmosphere that allow it. The fact that the old have
strong sexual cravings is hardly a secret to the medical profession.

Perhaps the most illuminating examples of sex as a clinical
problem among them come from patient records described by
Dr. Freeman. Among them:

- A 72-year-old widow had periodic abdominal distress but no
  organic cause could be found. Finally, alone with the doctor,
  she started to cry and unburden herself. Her conscience was
  troubled because she had been dreaming every night that her
  late husband was returning to her; in the dreams he often made
  love to her and she found the sexual relation completely
  satisfying. Now she had a deep sense of guilt, felt that she
  was cursed, and was afraid that her unmarried daughter might
  learn of her disgrace. The woman was told that the situation
  was "one of normal possibilities." She rejected this and broke
  off treatment. However, it was later learned that her abdominal
  symptoms had disappeared.

- A 91-year-old man, highly intelligent and still working daily,
  was distraught because his wife had denied him a sexual relationship for fifty years. His principles forbade extramarital
  intercourse and he had relied on masturbation for release. He
  now masturbated once a month but was depressed each time.
  He feared and disliked his 89-year-old wife, who was extremely
  active, still housekeeping, shopping, and cooking, and whose
  virtues were constantly being repeated to him. "This increased
  not only his distaste but also his self-concern."

- A retired fireman, 71, and his wife, 70, were concerned because
  they enjoyed a vigorous sex life, with coitus at least once
  a day. They had fourteen children. Both had the impression
  that what they were doing was somehow unnatural for older

people. The patient record concludes: "A simple expression of reassurance was sufficient to relieve their suspicions of ill-health or ill-doing."
- A man having a general physical review complained that he was upset by his wife's persistent sexual urges. She was a diabetic suffering from atrophic vaginitis and demanded intercourse as the only way of getting rid of her vaginal discomfort. The husband always obliged but said that he was getting "a little tired of it" at his age—84. His wife was 79, and he felt that frequent intercourse was no longer "natural." He asked that his wife be treated vaginally to relieve the problem.

In their report on women, Kinsey and his associates concluded that the decline in intercourse in marriage is the product of the aging process in the male, not in the female. But others believe that it is the man's "fear of failure" in sexual activity more than aging itself that accounts for the decline. "There is no way to over-emphasize this," say Masters and Johnson.

Once impotent under any circumstances, a man may withdraw from all coital activity rather than have his ego shattered by repeated failure r he may turn to other, young women for reassurance.) But they repeat that sex among married couples—given the right circumstances—can be a joy almost forever: Regular sexual expression, together with physical well-being and a healthy mental attitude toward the aging process, provides a "sexually stimulative climate within a marriage," they say. And this climate will, in turn, "improve sexual tension and provide a capacity for sexual performance that frequently may extend to and beyond the 80-year level."

This is set against an ideal background. "Fear of failure" on the part of the man has at least its share of counterparts among aging women. After menopause, there are the "mechanical" factors caused by endocrine imbalance. Among them are the thinning of the vaginal walls, reduction in size of the vaginal barrel, shrinking of the major labia. During orgasm, uterine contractions frequently become painful, a condition which, Masters and Johnson say, may be relieved by a balanced combination of estrogen and pro-gesterone. But they note that many facets of the relationship between steroid starvation and female sexual response "remain to be defined" and that, in any event, the psyche—and sexual habits in earlier years—plays an equal or greater part than that of an unbalanced endocrine system after menopause.

The menopause itself is not, apparently, the traumatic ordeal many women fear it to be. In a study of attitudes toward the menopause made by Bernice L. Neugarten, Vivian Wood, Ruth J. Kraines, and Barbara Loomis, women of varying ages were asked to respond to the statement, "Women generally feel better after the menopause than they have in years." About 68% of the women between 45 and 65 years old agreed to the statement; only 26% of the women between 21 and 44 had that hope. Another statement put before them was, "Going through the menopause really does not change a woman in any important way." 83% of the women between 56 and 65, postmenopausal age, agreed, but only 58% of the women between 21 and 30 felt the same way. In the same age groups, 21% of the older women felt that "a woman is concerned about how her husband will feel toward her after menopause"; more than half—58%—of the younger women had that concern. And 21% of the women between 56 and 65 agreed that "after the menopause, a woman is more interested in sex than she was before." Only 14% of the 21-to-30-year-old group felt that to be the case.

Older women seem to feel more confident and freer after the menopause; young women look at it differently, as an ordeal related to aging, something dim and unpleasant. Older women also regard it as unpleasant, but as less important. "It's just the pause that depresses," one said.

This study found that loss of fertility is not an important concern of women, consciously or unconsciously, as they get older. Only 4 out of 100 women between 45 and 55 said that "not being able to have children" was the worst thing about menopause. (Twenty-six said "not knowing what to expect" was the worst; 19 said "the discomfort and pain," and 18 singled out "it's a sign you're getting old.") This finding disputes the assumption in much psychological literature that "the closing of the gates" is a considerable blow to women. Men—theoretically—never lose the ability to initiate pregnancy. A few years ago, Soviet gerontologists, interviewing men of advanced years, asked at what age they had become impotent. They found that some of the centenarians had not yet reached that stage; indeed, a few had recently become fathers. This bit of knowledge may be comforting but meaningless to most men in more industrial Western society; after middle age their ability or desire to have children has usually long since left them for a dozen other nonbiological reasons.

There are now more and more studies of sex in old age. One made under the auspices of the Langley-Porter Institute in San Francisco suggests that *most* elderly persons are vitally interested in the subject and eager to learn more about the norms of sexual behavior for their years. Back in 1960, psychiatrists Gustave Newman and Claude R. Nichols felt it necessary to explain—in reporting a study of the subject in the *Journal of the American Medical Association*—that "guilt or anxiety over sexual feelings may interfere with the adjustment of the older person and with his interpersonal relationships, among which is the doctor-patient relationship" and thus "thwart the therapeutic efforts of the physician." This parochial note still crops up in professional literature. Of course, more than guilt, anxiety, and the doctor-patient relationship are involved in sexual feelings in the old. So are drives, expectancies, tensions, romance, eroticism, happiness, and general states of physical and emotional health—even as in younger people. Withal, also involved is the length of life.*

The pioneering study of Newman and Nichols was based upon interviews with 250 men and women who were 60 to 93 years old,

---

* At least among people of "normal intelligence." Castrated males tended to live longer than intact ones—69.3 years to 55.7 years, in a thirty-year study of inmates of an institution for the mentally retarded in Kansas. Males castrated before reaching sexual maturity lived longer than those castrated later. The study has a number of scientific points to make (there is a lower incidence of death from infections among eunuchs, for example) but shuns the notion that becoming a eunuch is a good way to the long life. Its authors, James B. Hamilton and Gordon E. Mestler, point out that, in ordinary populations, the loss of highly valued organs and functions such as the testes and reproductive behavior has great psychological impact and is known to have a "deleterious effect on longevity."

with the average age 70. One hundred of them were single, divorced, or widowed; of these only 7 reported any sexual activity. However, 81, or 54%, of the still-married men and women, were, indeed, still in the game. Newman and Nichols too concluded that, despite the decline in sexual drive and activity, reasonably healthy elderly persons with reasonably healthy partners can continue to be active into their seventh, eight, and ninth decades.

It is easy to understand why so many of the married old people continue to enjoy sex while so few of the unmarried do. In the absence of a legally or socially sanctioned mate, an older person simply doesn't have the kind of sex drive that will send him or her out of the house looking for a sexual partner. But some researchers make another point: Not just aging but inactivity is the cause of some of the decline in sexual vigor. Dr. Freeman says that reduction in sexual activity can be retarded, if aging persons have the "opportunity and mobility." Others have blamed "non-use rather than abuse" as a cause of impotency. It seems that sustained and regular sexual activity carries with it its own reward.*

More recently, Adriaan Verwoerdt, Eric Pfeiffer, and Hsioh-Shan Wang, of the Duke University Medical Center, studied the effects of age, sex, and marital status on 254 men and women, 60 to 94 years old, over a three-year period. They found that men were generally more active than women; activity was no great rarity among men surviving into the eighties and nineties. In women, sexual interest was at relatively low ebb during their late sixties and

---

* There is no discussion in this book of "sexual rejuvenation" or the use of aphrodisiacs and other devices to sustain sexual interest or activity, a complex subject made up of folklore, scientific fact, and desperation. Individual doctors may have their own ideas. Individual *statesmen* also may have their own ideas; Henry A. Kissinger is reported to have said that "power is the ultimate aphrodisiac," a line which falls short of explaining why the birth rate is so high among the under-privileged. There are only two prescriptions to be cited here. One comes from Kinsey *et al:* "Good health, sufficient exercise, and plenty of sleep still remain the most effective of aphrodisiacs known to man." The other comes from Dr. Jean Mayer of the Harvard University School of Public Health. When asked how nutrition affects sex, he said, "It's interesting that practically every food you can think of has been mentioned [as an aphrodisiac]—and at the proper time and in the right company it probably is."

early seventies, probably because of the condition of their husbands, a few years older than they. The Duke University doctors found that there was "a rather sharp drop" in sexual activity among men of the 72-to-74 range. However, there is a greater discrepancy between sexual activity and interest in men than in women at that age and later. They attribute this to psychological stress, as men try to reorient their sexual aims. It may well be that many men in their mid-seventies are faced with the "the task of finding new outlets for the sexual drive and developing new ways of intimacy," they suggest.

Among those who stopped intercourse before the study was completed, there was general agreement—86% of the women and even 58% of the men said so—that it was the husband who was responsible. The reasons for stopping—with percentages of blame suitably attributed—are given in this table:

Reason Given	Men	Women
	(in percentages)	
Spouse to blame	42	86
Because of:		
death	10	48
illness	19	23
loss of interest	10	1
loss of potency	1	14
Self to blame	58	14
Because of:		
illness	15	4
loss of interest	15	10
loss of potency	29	0

In this study the median age for stopping intercourse was 68 for the men and 60 for the women—much earlier for women than the normal difference in age between husband and wife would indicate. Almost all such studies support the idea that women are far more dependent on men than men on women for continuing or stopping and for frequency and type of sexual outlet. Even in reporting their studies, some researchers take time out to comment on the problems of women—and the problems they have with women—in getting direct answers from them. Psychologist Jack Botwinick observes that the problem of determining the effects of age in the female sex drive is more complex than in the male. Dr. Freeman asked a group of older people to give a self-evaluation of their sexual activities throughout their lives and noted, almost parenthetically, how difficult it was for the women to reply. He had sent questionnaires under identical conditions to both men and women, but only one-fourth as many women responded; their answers tended to be unformed and indecisive, with "an increased number of free expressions, ranging from indignation to elaboration." Even simple questions would be answered with "I don't know," or "This all depends on my husband."

Women have different attitudes toward sex—and respond differently to questions about sexual behavior—because of their psychologic and sociologic conditioning, Dr. Freeman says. And then, in words that could preface a manifesto for older women's liberation, he says that society "has been less understanding of and less prepared for a continuation of sexual needs and activities in older women— single, married, or widowed. Only an occasional woman has the combination of qualities by which to break through this average pattern of her aging, her husband's influence, and general customs."

*　　*　　*

Women have these burdens and more, made worse by the realities of growing old. Among the reasons why it is difficult for older women to marry or remarry is the extreme shortage of older available men. Statistics coming out of the 1970 U.S. Census give an idea of the problem. Overall, there are about 95 males to every 100 females in the United States. But men are usually about two-and-a-half years older than their brides when they marry the first time and they do not live as long. By the time Americans reach the 55-to-64 year age group, there are about 80 men to every 100 women; by 65 to 74, about 72 men to every 100 women; after 75, only 63 men to every 100 women. The ratio of widows to widowers is four to one, with three-quarters of the widows 60 or older.* There are so many more

* The situation in Great Britain, with its greater percentage of older people, may be worse. Not only does Britain have many more widows than widowers; it also has an excess of spinsters—14% of its women over 65 have never married at all compared to 6% in the United States.

old women around than old men that, if a man survives his wife, he is apt to step into a bustling marriage market, with himself as a prize. More than two-thirds of men over 65 are married (for the first, second, or more times) but only one-third of the women. To borrow again from Dr. Freeman, this time his most poignant line, "Apparently old widowers get married and old widows get lonesome."

It is not the statistics of the situation alone that limit a woman's options. Susan Sontag recently wrote about "the double standard of aging—the social convention that aging enhances a man but progressively destroys a woman." Sontag says that most women of "a certain age" either lie or feel tempted to lie when asked their age. A man doesn't have the same reaction; he knows that he can remain eligible well into old age while even good-looking women become ineligible much younger.* Sontag noted that when such men as Pablo Casals, Charles Chaplin, U.S. Supreme Court Justice William O. Douglas, or Senator Strom Thurmond take brides many years younger than themselves, it strikes people as remarkable but still plausible. "For the man, a late marriage is always good public relations. It adds to the impression that, despite his advanced age, he is still to be reckoned with."

But an elderly woman who marries a young man is greeted quite differently. It is felt that she has broken a fierce taboo, and she gets no credit for her courage. Rather than being admired for her vitality, she is apt to be condemned as predatory, willful, selfish, or exhibitionist. She is also likely to be pitied, since such a marriage is taken as evidence that she is in her dotage. And the younger man who marries her may be thought to be "extremely neurotic, if not mildly contemptible." Sontag says that only three well-known older women who dared such unions—even then only at the end of their lives—come to mind: George Eliot, Colette, and Edith Piaf. And all were creative artists or entertainers who had "special license from society to behave scandalously."

---

* For a totally different view of the desirability of older women, see the charming letter, "Advice on the Choice of a Mistress," written by a barely middle-aged Benjamin Franklin (*A Treasury of Ribaldry*, edited by Louis Untermeyer, Doubleday & Company, New York, 1956). It gives a young man eight persuasive reasons why he will find an old woman infinitely more enjoyable as a lover than a young one.

There are other obstacles to remarriage which older women have in common with men. One, certainly, is the memory of the first marriage, whether that marriage was good or bad. There is, according to sociologist Peter C. Pineo, a prevalence of "disenchantment" in the later years of marriage, a general drop in marital satisfaction and adjustment. The grounds upon which one decides to marry deteriorate through the years; the "fit" between two individuals, which led them to marry in the first place, reduces with time.

The last years of a marriage may be marked by invalidism or chronic illness; the stresses are great and often haunt the survivor because of compassion for the sufferer, or a feeling of guilt over not having done enough to help, or because of all these together. Whether widow or widower were happy or not in the first marriage, many of them idealize the memory of the dead mate, although the truth may be that, toward the end, the marriage was sustained mainly by memories shared but seen from a different perspective, simple convenience and habit, an easy-to-upset financial structure, and a sense that divorce was impossible, out-of-convention, or pointless.

When it comes to marriage, the children of the old don't help much either. Dr. Peterson, in challenging the "almost universal attitude" of younger persons that a new marriage for those in their later years is "stupid and inappropriate," puts considerable blame on sons and daughters.

"Some . . . feel that their mother or father ought to spend the remaining years in celibacy in honor of the deceased mate," he writes. "Others fear that a second marriage will not be successful. Still others are afraid that a new mate for the surviving parent will sever their own relationship. A few plot against such remarriages because they think they will lose part of their parent's estate. Others feel that nature intended all sexual life to cease when reproduction is no longer possible."

Dr. Peterson adds that these attitudes—"many selfish, all inaccurate"—prevail at a time of loneliness and isolation for many old people who no longer get companionship or comfort from children and grandchildren.

The situation forces an increasing number of elderly couples to marry in secret. A 69-year-old widow wrote for advice to syndicated advice-to-the-lovelorn columnist Abigail Van Buren in some desperation: "Is there a state near Iowa where a couple can go to be married in a hurry? We would like to get married as soon as possible as his children want to put him in a rest home."

Ann Landers, Miss Van Buren's sister and a competitive columnist, received a letter from a 59-year-old widow who said she was having a difficult time getting a proposal from an elderly widower because "his children are against it. They do not dislike me but they don't want me to inherit any part of their father's estate . . . I'd be happy to sign a premarital agreement leaving everything to his children. (I will leave what I have to my daughter.) All I want is his love and companionship."

These two samples of the perils of the old come from the study, *Retirement Marriage,* by Walter C. McKain. McKain and his staff located 100 old couples, all of them previously married and widowed, with a median age of 71 for the women, 76 for the men. The oldest man was 95; he had been 90 when he took a bride of 74. The oldest bride was 78, her husband 76. All the couples had been remarried for five or more years at the time of their interviews.

McKain is a professor of *rural* sociology, which seems to make a difference; his little book describing the study is written in charming, anecdotal, somewhat pastoral style. He says that only a few of the older couples interviewed made even oblique references to their sex life and the interviewers had been instructed not to raise the subject or to appear unduly interested in it. Still, it came up among a few; others got around to it indirectly when they discussed the importance of companionship or falling in love. McKain says that older men may use remarriage as proof of their masculinity although having a sexual partner available to them is probably more important than the sex act itself. His conclusion: "The role of sex in the lives of these older people extended far beyond love making and coitus; a woman's gentle touch, the perfume of her hair, a word of endearment—all these and many more reminders that he is married help to satisfy a man's urge for the opposite sex. The same is true for the older wife. One woman had this comment on her remarriage. 'I like the little things; the smell of his pipe, the sound of steps on the back porch, his shaving mug—even his muddy shoes.' The sex life of older married couples is not confined to the bedroom."

This quaintly romantic attitude seems to blend with an acutely realistic one. Nearly three-fourths of the men and two-thirds of the women mentioned the need for companionship as a major reason for remarriage. "I was lonesome. I hated to be alone. I wanted to share my life with someone who needed me and cared whether I was alive or not," was a characteristic response, age-old and fundamental. Yet they showed much care before deciding on a mate. Some couples mentioned finances as a reason for getting married: a second income, usually from Social Security, would be helpful. "It was either get married or lose my home," one man said bluntly and then, in mitigation, gave other reasons as well. Most couples would have short courtships, small and quiet or secret weddings, and forgo honeymoons as being inappropriate to their years. But later they often were eager to spread the news. "We wanted everyone to know so we sent a casserole to the annual church meeting and signed the note 'Mr. and Mrs.'," one couple said. A few spoke of "love at first sight," but were embarrassed to have other old people overhear them.

McKain notes an idea proposed by Dr. Victor Kassel in *Geriatrics* which would permit any man past 60 to marry from two to five women in the same age group. Such a form of polygamy, Kassel says, would lead to a genuine interrelated family unit with many advantages over the present pattern which "condemns a growing number of older women to celibacy."

"It would enable one man and several women to pool their financial resources," Kassel wrote. It would insure a better diet and provide more hands to care for any member of the marriage group who became ill . . . It would lead to better grooming and more cheerful dispositions" and "elminate the loneliness and neglect that has accompanied the disappearance of the consanguine family . . . With the American concept of equal rights and opportunity, not only all older men but also older women should have the chance to remarry following the death of a spouse."

McKain seems to approve this plan since there are not enough men to go around, but fully understands that it is not going to be sanctioned by American society today, if ever. Besides, he says, "in our sample of older marriages, the brides and grooms are very conservative and a radical change in the institution of marriage would be highly repugnant to them. Many of them did some intensive soul searching before they even considered a second marriage."

McKain concludes that the marriages in his sample had the greatest chance of success if both bride and groom knew each other well and shared activities before marriage, if the marriage had approval of friends and relatives, if the couple had enough money, and if each partner was well adjusted and satisfied with life generally. There was less chance for success if, implying a lack of trust, they kept separate financial accounts and did not pool their resources, or if they continued to live in a house belonging to either mate in a previous marriage. A woman tends to be uncomfortable living in a house, with all its associations, furnished by an earlier wife; a man to feel that home ownership also makes him the head of the household.

Being head of a household, or at least being a full partner in a household, is important. Children take in a widowed parent and think they're being long suffering and wonderfully tolerant of the weaknesses of the old. But intergenerational stress takes its toll both ways. Older people do not like being reminded of their infirmities and often shudder to hear, "Let me thread that needle, Mother," or "Dad, you shouldn't try to lift that chair." One old man summed up his feelings: "Who wants to spend his life with a big brute of a son-in-law and three children who stay up all night?" And he remarried, to become his own man again.

Whether their widowed parents live with them or apart, many, or most, children hardly ever consider seriously the possibility that a parent will remarry. When that prospect does occur, they suffer surprise, shock, and often embarrassment over mother's making a fool of herself or father's turning out to be a dirty old man. About 25% of the remarried old couples said that at one point or another they had almost given in to their children's objections or hostility and called off the marriage. (McKain assumes that many more possible remarriages simply don't happen for this reason.) But after five years of remarriage, more than 80% of the children were pleased with the outcome; more than half who had opposed it had changed their minds.

One of McKain's chief aims—to determine whether remarriage in old age can, indeed, be successful—was clearly served by the study. He used careful techniques to judge "success." One was an independent evaluation of the marriage by each husband and wife; a negative note from either placed the marriage in the doubtful or unsuccessful category. Another was "internal evidence" based upon a couple's response to a series of questions about their decision-making processes. Finally, each couple was closely observed during the interview, often lasting several hours, for just this purpose: "Outward signs of respect, consideration, affection, pride, together with obvious enjoyment of each other's company were evidence of success while any serious complaints led to an appraisal of unsatisfactory."

Only six of the 100 marriages appeared to be failures. (In the general United States population, there were 33 divorces for every 100 marriages in 1970.) Twenty others were mainly successful, but "still had problems to overcome." This leaves all the rest, just under three-quarters of the 100 old couples. "Despite the secrecy and shame involved," McKain says, they emerged as "highly successful." And, presumably, bride and groom lived happily ever after.

10 RETIREMENT AND LEISURE

In the year 1973 it was finally recorded that, on the occasion of his retirement dinner after 32 years of devoted service, a man got up and said: "I'll be brief. The working conditions here are terrible. I haven't liked a day of it. I'm glad I'm out of it." And sat down. The news story does not go into reactions of boss, colleagues, friends, or family. Nor does it tell of the new retiree's feelings the morning after. But clearly before making his brief speech, he had faced a moment of truth—and decided, for once, not to play the game.

Work ethic and guilt feelings aside, the truth is that most people do not like their daily toil. Abraham Lincoln once said, "My father taught me to work, but not to love it. I never did like to work and I don't deny it. I'd rather read, tell stories, crack jokes, talk, laugh—anything but work." It is different for some professionals and creative workers or for those who are specially driven. But for the great majority, work is hardly the soul-satisfying experience that the "joy-in-work" philosophers have assumed. Juanita M. Kreps of Duke University, a pioneer in the study of the economics of aging, says that "work is often tiring, boring, and quite unpleasant. It is no accident that the pressure for shorter working hours (albeit, with no reduction in pay) has come from industrial and commercial workers, who are much less satisfied with their working conditions than the professional."

To those who remember the Great Depression—and the desperation of men seeking any kind of job—the result of a study of attitudes today must seem astonishing. Nearly 400 white male blue-collar workers were asked: "If you could retire with as much money as you need for a good pension, and not have to work anymore, would you do it right away, or would you wait a while?" The level of the job bears upon the answer. Two-thirds of all men over 55 in low-level tasks (with little variety, responsibility, or autonomy) said, "Yes. I want to retire right away." So, too, did fully half of all the men *under 40* in low-level tasks. Of men in higher-level tasks, half of those over 55 and a third of those under 40 also said they preferred immediate retirement.

In practice, a growing number of presons do indeed pick early retirement—age 60 or even 55—and tighten their belts, accept lower pensions and Social Security benefits (even in face of rising prices and taxes) in order to get out from under their work a few years earlier. It is not just physical surroundings or tedium or rigors of the job they wish to escape. "Health" is often given as the reason for retiring; emotional, as well as physical, health is at stake. For there are also the matters of not being one's own man or woman, of subservience in countless ways, of being pigeonholed and frustrated and angry and insecure.

Why then is there so often the fear of being retired—and of having all that long-cherished leisure time to fill up? The business-man or executive considers the prospects gloomily and says, in some desperation: "Golf is not enough. I'll take up painting or pottery—or something." A working man worries about having enough to live on, about spending all his days around the house, and says, "Maybe I can find a part-time job, here or somewhere else." Even those who calculate they can get by on their pensions often try at the last moment to cling to their jobs—although they may have spent the previous twenty years cursing boss, rat-race, or the stupidity of the job itself. Trade unions talk of lowering retire-ment ages—and also of bargaining for "flexible retirement" so that a worker can stay on a few more years, according to his ability. Wives of retirees have their doubts about it, too. They've been heard to define retirement as "twice as much husband on half as much income." That they don't really mean this as a joke is borne out by a Duke University finding that 55% of the wives of retired men (and

67% of the wives of early retirees) are sorry about the whole thing. Still, the loss of occupation is felt much more acutely by men than by women. The women continue to have care of home and family to busy themselves with. "To many working class men, retirement is a social disaster," notes Peter Townsend.

There are at least three good reasons why those who retire often seem to be victims as well as beneficiaries of the pension system. One is the matter of reduced income; a second is the tradition of the work ethic and the loss of role in society; and a third is lack of preparation for retirement and simply not knowing how to use leisure time. Sociologist A. J. Jaffe, taking the extreme view, is not at all sure the problem can be solved for many of the old. "Retirement in our society is a contradiction of the work ethic," he says, and training a man to enjoy retirement after a lifetime spent in the throes of work (and in the belief that work is moral and right) "seems to be difficult, if not impossible."

Even if the contradiction can be overcome, Dr. Jaffe is not sure the results may be desirable. "For men to enjoy their retirement, they will need years of practice to overcome the work ethic," he says. "And with the diminution of our work ethic we may ask: What will happen to our economy? There is reason to believe that societies that value leisure greatly have trouble in achieving large economic growth."

Society must be served; industry must be served; fortunately there are spokesmen for the individual man and woman, too. As we seek to reconcile many interests, the subjects of retirement and the use of postretirement time have become the most hotly and lengthily discussed of all aspects of aging. The conflict of interests is seen most clearly in the debate on "compulsory" versus "flexible" retirement, a debate which has escalated as more and more workers are affected by retirement policies (and as national costs of maintaining incomes and health care go up, too). The charge has been raised in the United States and Great Britain that compulsory retirement is a clear case of discrimination against an age group and should be banned, along with other forms of age, sex, and race discrimination in employment. Leonard Davis, honorary president of the American Association of Retired Persons, says unequivocally that the United States must abolish mandatory retirement if it is to meet its responsibilities to its older population. Still, it takes an enlightened big-scale industrial employer to see it that way; if any employer thinks of his workers as cogs in a machine, he may also think that it is easier and more profitable to treat them as cogs, disposing of them and replacing them in uniform fashion as they wear out.*

The issue is being resolved to some degree: More and more companies are adopting forms of flexible retirement, with valued or key employees staying on beyond normal retirement age, negotiating and renegotiating the length of their service from time to time, depending on their health and function.

All the while, the counter-trend toward earlier retirement continues. In 1970, the United Auto Workers union first adopted the slogan, "30 and out," calling for full retirement benefits at any age after thirty years of service. The UAW settled for improved benefits at age 58 in 1971, and at age 56 in 1972. "30 and out" has caught on with blue-collar and professional workers alike, but agreeing on what is adequate income—and getting it—will be a critical issue in labor-management negotiations for a long time to come. This is, indeed, the paradox of the moment: There are greater social and economic pressures to have the elderly retire earlier from the labor market. But, in the United States most of all, millions of the old must continue to work if they are to avoid ending their lives in poverty. More than a quarter of all Americans over 65 still work full or part time because they must. Leonard Davis says that "as things now stand, the overwhelming majority of older Americans must retire on less—often much less—than half their preretirement income." Among others, he and William E. Oriol, staff director of the U.S. Senate Committee on Aging, call inadequate retirement income "the number one problem of older Americans."

The problem, alas, does not end there. A statement of the United Steelworkers gives an idea of the scope of other union concern. Apart from income, there are still "vital needs" to be met: "Ap-

* There is considerably more to the issue and a better case may be made for mandatory retirement than suggested here. A fair listing of both sides is presented in "Compulsory versus Flexible Retirement: Issues and Facts," by Erdman Palmore in *The Gerontologist,* Winter 1972.

propriate housing and enjoyable use of leisure time are not available to large numbers of retirees and pensioners. Too often, drabness and loss of pride and dignity are the lot of many who were unprepared for retirement or who live in a community that has failed to provide services and living conditions suitable for retirees . . ."

Leisure, as retirement's blessing, seems to be a mixed one—even when the financial problem is held at bay. An international gerontological conference was held in 1972 devoted solely to leisure as a contemporary problem; one of its reports stressed that many old people spend several hours a day doing "absolutely nothing." (The term was not further defined.) Sociologist Jaffe warns that societies that value leisure greatly may have trouble with their economic growth. Joseph J. Spengler of Duke University has an apocalyptic view: "Ultimately, no issue is of greater long-run concern than the question of *how* man uses his increasing income and discretionary time. Poets have told us that every empire expires in the soft lap of luxury. Gibbon describes how, in a few years, indolence and luxurious living reduced the Vandals, once fierce conquerors of the Romans, to cowardice, ignominy, and self-pity. Manifestations of dissipative processes are already evident in the West . . ."

It may take a long, long time for the "dissipative processes" to take effect. Retirement and the new leisure have already produced their own burgeoning industries—sometimes frantic ones—which allow no one involved any rest or chance to become decadent. Dozens of books and hundreds of articles are published each year explaining "how to make the most of your retirement" and exploring "the creative use of the new freedom." There are a host of organizations concerned with the rights and opportunities of retirees and preretirees. Probably the largest is the American Association of Retired Persons—"pioneering the new world of retirement"—which has about 6 million members, two magazines, *Dynamic Maturity* (for preretirees from 50 to 65 years old) and *Modern Maturity* (for all persons 55 and over), and—with its sister organization, the National Retired Teachers Association—a score of "better retirement" booklets and other publications, along with the rest of its genuinely creative and valuable program. Other voluntary and professional groups of many types are also devoted to the practical aspects—helping retirees to find new jobs or careers, make money, get all available government benefits, meet their budgetary, housing, health, nutritional, social, and recreational needs. The business of keeping old people active and well in retirement extends into dozens of fields; a well-directed letter or phone call from an anxious retiree may start him on the road to receiving more guidance and advice than he can keep up with.*

On the road—but it still may take him years to adjust success-fully to his new station in life. The act of retirement, its immediate prospects, continue to be a fearsome thing. Gerontologists consider that retirement—along with the death of a mate—are the two most shattering, traumatic events of later life. The day his retirement starts, a man is apt suddenly to feel very old. (It is an actuarial cliché that the first year of retirement has among the highest of all mortality rates.) It is, of course, not just the end of his usual job and the prospect of living on a reduced income that so affect him. The state of being retired is a new and difficult category in society, just beginning to be defined; past societies had aged people, but not retired ones. With retirement comes loss of status, association, and role—that and the fear of uncertainty of change. At a retiree's fare-well dinner, those around him may feel a sense of relief; some deadwood is being removed, their chances for advancement enhanced. He, in turn, may feel that he cannot be replaced and things will never be the same after he leaves—or, at least, he hopes so. Unlike the case that opens this chapter, both parties usually lie a lot about their real feelings, all in a spirit of bonhomie and farewell. But the feelings are there, the damage done. After the shows of goodwill and appreciation—and the presentations of watch, luggage, or loving cup—the retiree is unalterably alone, no longer a member of any team, on his own as he slips into the uncharted and final phase of his life.

*   *   *

* There is good reason for this emphasis on postretirement activities and problems in the United States. In most countries, retirement is ac-cepted as a time of rest after a lifetime of work. In the United States, it is seen as something else, according to *Old People in Three Industrial Societies*. Comparing postretirement practices in the United States, Britain, and Denmark, the study says that "the data suggest that activity is so highly valued by older Americans that the pastimes of retirement take on the aspects of work."

The prospect of living ten, fifteen, or more years without working —on any kind of pension—would have been a source of pure joy in earlier times. In the past, when most men were farmers, a man did not suddenly pass from full activity to inactivity; he worked as long as he could, and neither he nor his society nor government paid much attention to his age.* Emile Thomas, writing about the French condition in 1850, said that "old age arrives before it has been thought of. And it is because it has not been thought of that the worker and his family are ruined by illness and that old age is nearly always an age of poverty and despair." Always the manual worker suffered most because physical strength ebbs first. He made the least money and, unless he could somehow find easier work, was doomed to a dismal old age unless his children could—and were willing to— help him.

The situation is far removed from that today. Perhaps most of all it is the abruptness of change—and the lack of preparation for it—that most stuns the new retiree. There is critical need for all those burgeoning pre- and postretirement programs, those and many more in the future that can penetrate into the mainstream of life. In its abruptness, "the present system of retirement acts like a guillotine," writes Professor Alfred Sauvy of the Collège de France, in urging a more flexible and humane way of doing things. Professor Sauvy offers two principles as a basis for solving the problem:

• A man should have the right, as far as possible, to choose the moment when he will give up his regular occupation or profession. He should also have freedom to work after he has been granted a pension.

* Not that so much work was done in pre-industrial days, and society was hardly the anthill we imagine it to have been, says Professor Alfred Sauvy. Underemployment is a modern word; it was so much the rule in past centuries that there was no concept for it. "Men out of work were not even referred to as 'unemployed.' They were called vagabonds, beggars, thieves, or outlaws, and sometimes were officially listed under those terms," Sauvy writes. Winter was a time of prolonged inactivity; holidays were numerous throughout the year. "Full employment and overemployment only occurred at peak periods such as at harvest or vintage time. It is these periods which have given rise to the belief that an intense activity was characteristic of those times, in contrast with the comparative leisure of modern times."

• There should be gradual change—a series of transitions—from full activity to inactivity.

The two principles are the generally accepted ones—dogma to most specialists. ("First and foremost, people should be allowed to work without penalty," says Herman Kahn.) All men age differently; a man's physical, social, or psychological age may barely relate to the fact that he is 62 or 65 by the calendar. And the nature of the job—the skills it requires and the demands it makes— are basic in considering retirement. It would be inane to compel a philosopher to leave his university post at 62. At the same age, a bus driver, whose reflexes and eyesight have been dimming for a decade, *has* a problem. (Certainly his passengers do.) He may have good years ahead of him—up the scale as a supervisor or down the scale as a watchman—but some change must take place. Many progressive employers and organizations are, indeed, taking steps to retrain or somehow make use of older employees—often with good and mutually satisfying results.*

Professor Sauvy, among others, recommends that the transition and new job and career guidance start long before the age of retirement. "Perhaps it should begin at the age of 50 or 45 with a view to adapting the job to the man, instead of demanding the opposite," he says. Others would start earlier. John W. Gardner, educator and former secretary of the U.S. Department of Health, Education, and Welfare, observes that most men "find it virtually impossible to think realistically—or even to think at all—about their own retirement." Mr. Gardner believes that preparation for retirement should begin in mid-career. Perhaps, he says, there should be clinics to

---

* In a charming aside with which I do not agree, Professor Sauvy suggests that men past 50, whose strength is declining, be given jobs as ticket punchers in the Paris Métro because "the work is not strenuous, except perhaps in the more crowded stations, and requires practically no qualifications or skill."

"On the other hand," he adds, "this kind of monotonous job is not recommended for persons of 20 or 30 years of age [and] can even cause them to develop a psychosis like the one reflected in the popular French song, *'Des p'tits trous, des p'tits trous,'* about a Métro ticket puncher obsessed to the point of insanity by 'those little holes.'" I dispute his point because I am past 50 and would probably have the same reaction as a 30-year-old to the *"p'tits trous."*

help people think things through, to determine whether they are doing what they want to be doing; the time to change or seek greater satisfaction might be at 35 or 40, not 65. J. Cloyd Miller, director of the retirement education program of the National Retired Teachers Association, goes beyond that; he believes that planning for retirement properly should begin when a teacher starts out on a career. (An idea which, it is granted, may be difficult to apply in many jobs or professions.)

The generally approved idea is that it is never too early to start planning for retirement. Many psychologists put it another way. The word "retirement"—all that it connotes—may be the enemy. It suggests withdrawal and disengagement from life, not just from occupation.* But 62 or 65 or whatever, they say, we are the same as we always were, the product of all our experience, not a strange new breed merely because we have become known by a new term.

The key to successful retirement and use of leisure, they say, lies in our youths and middle years. We know now that the capacity to learn and grow continues long after 60 and 70. Our interests throughout our lifetime, our year-in, year-out levels of intelligence and creativity, determine how we shall live out our later years. So, they urge, do not think of retirement or the end of a job as a different phase of life, just as a continuation of it. If it can be seen that way, it will bring no more trauma and require hardly any more adjustment than a move to another house: some strangeness at first but many opportunities for new discovery and redecorating.

The fact is that there are many people who have no problem with retirement at all and never give a thought to leisure as a burden. An appendix to this book gives the statements of a number of extraordinary people past 70 and 80, reflecting on old age and their own roles. The men and women are extraordinary mainly because

---

* I moved to the south of France several years ago simply because I had tired of life in New York City. I was then 49 and in no sense a retiree; I planned to and have here resumed my work as editor and writer. But because I live in a community (and in a style) of many retirees, people often say on first meeting: "Oh, you're in retirement." I see them consigning me to the geriatric scrap heap; I instantly feel twenty years older and fall apart.

their talents have brought them renown; their attitudes, however, are shared by many persons not nearly as famous or not famous at all. It is an attitude expressed by Victor Hugo, who said at 80, "I have only begun to live." Architect Edward Durell Stone was asked, at the age of 71, whether he thought retirement communities were a good thing. He instantly went to the heart of the question: "I don't think *retirement* is a very good idea, and I don't ever intend to retire . . . I think man seeks his own justification through work and feeling useful, so giving up the enormous personal satisfaction of being useful to your fellow man is, I think, a mistake. Retirement communities are not a good idea—they're places where you assemble a lot of people who've given up striving for a realization of their life's work." Anthropologist Margaret Mead published her first well-known work, *Coming of Age in Samoa,* when she was 27. More than 40 years and many achievements later, she is still at it. At 70, she summed up her feelings brusquely because she had little time for so academic a subject: "Leisure is seen as something that you want to do that is of no use to anybody. I'm not impressed. I dislike the idea of leisure very much. I think a person should live."

Miss Mead is singularly blessed. She holds eminent positions at Columbia University and the American Museum of Natural History. She continues to write books and articles and to lead a wonderfully active and creative professional life. She enjoys her work and would not want to be doing anything else. The idea of leisure is repugnant to her because it seems without meaning; her work is her hobby, her joy, her life, and to be away from it is life wasted.

Ideally, work may be completely fulfilling. Most people are goaded to work because they need the money. But in its course, work brings other values to a person's life which, in the long run, are equally indispensable: social participation, the experiences that give substance and flavor to life; creative self-expression, self-respect, and gaining the respect of others. Satisfactory work—and good working conditions —also add a desirable routine and rhythm to life. Most people are not as favored as Dr. Mead; some or all of these values are lacking and work becomes drudgery. *"This* is the life," people say when they go boating, fishing, or to the beach. "Real life"—the image people have of the way they would like to live—is only to be enjoyed outside of office, shop, or factory.

The fear of retirement, too, stems from the fear that these values will be missing in the future, that once outside the ordered universe of work, there will be less money, less companionship, fewer experiences, no chance to be creative, less self-respect, less respect from others. And time, it is feared, will become an amorphous glob; the minutes may seem long but the days will pass blankly and unnoted, the calendar pages turning too quickly toward oblivion.

There are many needs and drives that must be accounted for if older people are to achieve the good long life in retirement. They are hardly different from the needs and drives of younger people but this list, drawn up by the Institute of Gerontology of the University of Iowa, is intended specifically for use in developing leisure programs for the old:

- The need to render some socially useful service.
- The need to be considered a part of the community.
- The need to enjoy normal companionships.
- The need for recognition as an individual.
- The need for opportunity for self-expression and a sense of achievement.
- The need for health protection and care.
- The need for suitable mental stimulation.
- The need for suitable living arrangements and family relationships.
- The need for spiritual satisfaction.

These are real needs for almost all people, basic guidelines in determining how to use free time. Unless they are met, a person is bound to suffer self-preoccupation, an inner restlessness, a sense of futility and even shame. Finding suitable leisure activities is complicated by the fact that our work-minded culture "has not yet developed an attitude toward leisure as *end time*," notes Max Kaplan, director of the Arts Center of Boston University. Today's old have been forced to be the pioneers in forging a path that is "substantively unrelated to work, relatively free of family obligations, and increasingly available over a span of years rather than hours— and ideologically open to new and creative directions," he says.

It is not an easy path, and the old take many byways. Some do achieve the realization of hidden or long postponed ambitions—

to travel, write, go to school—or even learn how to fly.* To others, free time signifies nothing but a void—and they face the prospect of quick demoralization and debilitation. In all ways, the better educated and more active a person, the better off he is in old age. A person accustomed to using his memory and brain will have a better memory and brain in old age than one who is not. One lesson we have learned from the studies of time is that "the busier you are, the more time you have." Time is better organized; a person has more experiences; time becomes more meaningful, each moment more important. A study made of people over 65 who are still employed shows that they enjoy their leisure more, with greater intensity— even with a wider scope of activities—than people who are retired and have all the leisure time in the world. And laborers and unskilled workers, with less money, less education, and—presumably— fewer intellectual interests, spend more time just loafing or doing nothing in their leisure time than those with better education.

There is tragedy to this. Death is hastened by demoralization and debilitation—the penalties for using leisure time badly. For most people, the "new and creative directions" in leisure mentioned by Dr. Kaplan are nowhere in sight. In their *Aging and Society,*

* Travel is a splendid way to enrich life, and many people look forward to retirement as the time to do it. Frances M. Carp, who has made special study of travel and transportation among the elderly, once asked older adults what they were planning or would like to do most in the years ahead. The most common answer was "travel." In 1972, she got down to practice in a study made in the homes of 709 retired persons, average age 67.5 years. Only half had taken a yearly vacation; about 40% had not been out of town for three years; many said they never traveled. Primary obstacles were lack of money, poor health, lack of an automobile, and the inconvenience and stress of public transportation. Dr. Carp notes that passenger trains in the United States are almost obsolete, air travel is becoming less and less attractive for the old with its crowding, jostling, and pressure of speedy movement. About half the travelers in her sample traveled by bus but said that its main advantage was that "it beats walking." Still, the bus and airplane may be their only options left. She concludes: "Unless there is special attention to their needs, both as older persons and as leisure-oriented travelers, many may decide that the disadvantages of the trip outweigh the pleasures and decide to stay home. . . . The future of retirement travel does not look promising."

Matilda White Riley and Anne Foner give a sharp picture of how older people spend their time. The study was made of people over 65 who do not work and are receiving Social Security benefits:

Total hours available	24.0
Sleep	9.0
Obligated time	6.7
Meals (preparing, eating, cleaning up)	3.0
Housekeeping	1.6
Personal care	1.2
Shopping	0.7
Care of others	0.2
High-participation leisure time	6.5
Television, radio	2.8
Visiting	1.6
Napping	1.4
Reading	0.7
Low-participation leisure time	1.9
Gardening	0.5
Handicrafts	0.4
Entertaining	0.3
Club and church activities	0.2
Writing	0.2
Meditation, worship	0.1
Walking, sports	0.1
Rides, outings	0.1

This is a composite view. Perhaps a few of the persons included in the study are really striking out in "new and creative directions." But not very many. Television is the greatest single consumer of leisure time. Perhaps a third of all free time—once all sleeping and "obligated" times are subtracted—is spent watching it. Authors Riley and Foner report that a majority of older persons have a favorable opinion about television. "Favorable" may not be the right word: Many feel that they can't do without it, and some keep the numbers of their television repairmen alongside their telephones, on the same list as those of police, fire department, doctor, and other emergency numbers. Television sets are often gifts from their children—"Television is a Godsend to the old" is their view. Institutions, too, rely upon television to entertain and distract the old. A good position in the television room, or television corner, is the privilege of older or more favored residents. If an old person can't have his own set, his Golden Age Club or senior citizens center will have one for him. Television—having favorite programs and performers and knowing them intimately—has become a way of life for many old, particularly in the United States where massive home viewing started first. What they see on television is often more real to them than their own lives.

The trouble with television is, no matter how pat this observation, that it is the opiate of the old. Being drugged by it is one sure way of abandoning all those great hopes for constructive, fulfilling use of the time after retirement. It fills none of the needs listed by the Iowa Institute of Gerontology or any other need described here. It is not creative, it does not help the ego or give recognition to the individual. It does not allow for self-expression or provide normal companionship. It does not help one's self-respect or win the esteem of others—all basic to the good long life. The Iowa list mentions the need for "suitable mental stimulation," but the television programs generally favored by the old—unfortunately the least sophisticated or educational of programs—are hardly "suitable."

This is not an attack on television but a condemnation of its use —as television is now programmed—as *the* major leisure activity of the old. It has almost no value except for the filling up of time—and even though time may seem endless to some of the old, time is precisely what the old don't have to spare. Watching television is like doing nothing, and the consequences of doing nothing are deterioration and dilapidation; in this sense, television is a killer of the old. Today's younger generations are giving more time to the arts of leisure; perhaps, when they are old, they will know better how to use their time after they have stopped working. There is no real assurance of this; the young, nurtured and raised on television, may be even more addicted when they grow old.

Retirement and leisure need not be the bugaboos they are. There are, at this moment, countless ways to supplement retirement income and to spend leisure in satisfying ways. The obstacles are largely psychological ones. Most of today's old come from generations which have lived through wars and depressions that shocked and frightened them; their memories and fears inhibit them still. And they have had little experience with leisure or the kind and amounts of leisure time available to them now.

The professional and voluntary organizations are responding to their needs; what is needed on the part of the aging is some enterprise, some searching out, and a measure of good health.* Again, it is the professional—particularly the self-employed one— who has the advantage as he gets older. He has various degrees of retirement open to him; he can, if he wishes, simply slow down or drop to a lower job level. It is the professional—the doctor, lawyer, teacher, and others—who is most likely to love his work, to be so engrossed in it that it amounts to a calling. Witness the responses of Architect Stone and Anthropologist Mead. In study after study, professional workers are quoted as saying, "I can't imagine doing anything else." The professional has other concomitant advantages, too: He is generally from the middle class and is healthier than men in low-status occupations. Thus he is singularly blessed; he reaches 65 with good health, work he likes, and his own options in continuing it.

Assuming that the artist may also be called a professional, he is the most fortunate of all. Many people assume that artists live longer than others; they do not, but it seems that way because those who do live long—like Chagall, Picasso, Matisse—may continue working until their last days. The artist has fused both work and leisure in his career. When he stops seeking economic benefit from his work, he can go on doing what he has always done for the joy of it. The artist who wins great fame and wealth is the unusual one, but for most artists, work is a source of positive self-

* Far more people retire for reasons of health than because of company rules. A study by Duke University's Erdman Palmore showed that about two-thirds of the men in a U.S. national sample made their own decisions about retirement; about half of these said that they retired because of their health—or fears for their health. Overall, it is believed that less than one in five persons stops working because of company policy; the problem of "compulsory retirement" is not as universal as it appears to be.

identification and a means of self-expression. A study by sociologist Hershel L. Hearn found that artists—both those who had started early and those who started painting later, as a second career— agreed that art would be their work until they died. The current emphasis on art as an activity for the old does not stem at all from the phenomenal success of Grandma Moses in her nineties; there are many valid reasons why painting gratifies—most of them on the Iowa list—and Dr. Hearn concludes that it can alleviate a great many problems of aging persons.

In stereotype, the company executive is a harried, driven man, prey to ulcers and heart attacks, and a burnt-out case by retirement. The picture is out of focus. Many executives are dedicated to their work and find it satisfying; the studies show they put in more hours than they have to because they want to. The laborer or manual worker comes off worst here, too; he has the greater record of absenteeism, he likes his job least and is involved with it least. He also has fewer resources and is least likely to make good use of his retirement time—a condition mitigated, in the unhappiest of ways, by the fact that he dies earlier, too.

The self-employed business man is in much better shape, although he probably lacks the sense of calling of the professional or artist. He may, indeed, have spent so many hours at his work that he can't wait to get out from under it—only to discover that he is just as bewildered by his change of status and with even less notion of how to spend his leisure time. If he re-enters business, as some do, he may come across some new competition: the retired white-collar worker who has decided to go into genteel commerce as a second career, running a book or antique shop, or a tea room, or—somewhat less genteel—a motel. In fact, few retired people start new business careers (although this may change somewhat with the help of "franchise" opportunities). Only the more energetic dare; many more would like to but are discouraged by the risk to their usually small capital. There are, however, enough cases of true second careers starting and succeeding to encourage others. Some persons start out with hobbies and find, after a while, they have enough skill to make money with them. Painting, pottery making, tinting old bottles, making models, and a variety of other crafts are favorites. But the reality is that—unless the hobbyist is unusually gifted—the old person living in an institution has the better chance to sell his wares, through the institution's gift shop. Most old people at home cannot reach out and sell their products —even when they are superbly done—unless someone helps them do so.

Mail order businesses, run from the home, have special appeal to the old; they can be run at one's own pace without physical exertion. However, here the old are competing with others, often larger organizations with more skill and organization and the ability to buy in large quantities at lower prices. Like most anyone in business, the old can succeed only if they have a special product, formula, or service. One example of this is 85-year-old Gladwin Ross, former owner of a Chicago bookshop. His hours were long, his neighborhood had changed, his rent was high. He decided to give up the store and operate out of his apartment. Through the years he had kept about two hundred customers who know him well and, above all, whom he knows well; he knows their interests and reading habits perfectly. He reads about new and current books carefully and makes up a monthly list for each customer with his book recommendations. His is a highly personal book service, and his customers do not mind that he charges them $10 a year for making his recommendations, plus the full book price and postage. They enjoy the special attention and his expertise. They also save considerable time since they know they can rely on him and do not have to shop around or read publishers' catalogs. His volume of business is lower than it was in the book store but his profit is greater, enough to supplement his other income and allow him to live comfortably and productively.

A different type of business is that of Sal Cangelosi, a New Yorker who had an indifferent career doing odd jobs and running elevators until he was almost 60. He then decided that his Lower East Side neighbors would appreciate fresh eggs, delivered to them directly from the farm, something he remembered from his boyhood. A more sophisticated businessman might have considered the idea unsound or pointless; unfresh eggs are not one of New York's problems. But Mr. Cangelosi bought a small farm in New Jersey and started bringing eggs into New York to deliver to whatever customers he could find. He soon discovered his customers would come to him; he then opened a small store and has flourished mightily. His is the only shop in New York City selling eggs alone, and it is becoming a landmark of sorts, not merely to his Lower East Side neighbors but to people from the chic Upper East Side, too. He is open but one day a week—Thursday—when he sells about 500 dozen eggs. Mr. and Mrs. Cangelosi spend half their time on the farm (their son now maintains it), the rest of the week in the East 7th Street area of New York which he loves and where, over 70 years old now, he has achieved comfortable new status.

These are two special cases. One man had experience and a plausible idea; one had no experience and an unlikely idea. Both seem to be working out. Their stories are presented here not as case studies but merely to show that it can be done. Few retirees will need this precautionary note: As creative people in many fields have discovered, the idea is usually much easier to come by than the execution.

* * *

The Nixon years will hardly go down in American history as years of pioneering social welfare legislation and progress. There have been cost-of-living increments to long-established benefits —little more. There was a Second White House Conference on Aging held in 1971, made up of some 3,500 delegates representing a broad range of organizations and interests. Policy and specifics were discussed in every conceivable area; the delegates' recommendations fill up much of the 250 pages of Volume Two of the Conference report. A letter of transmittal from the Secretary of Health, Education, and Welfare to the President notes that the recommendations are "remarkably practical, and concerned with many of the issues and objectives to which your Administration is addressing itself." The extent to which the Administration will, in fact, actively try to implement the recommendations is, to understate it, a matter of high conjecture. In the past few years, there have been many legislative initiatives in behalf of the elderly—and much Administration resistance.

The National Council of Senior Citizens was one of the organizations particularly active in the Conference.* The Council was founded in 1961 with the enactment of Medicare its first priority. Now among its principal goals are Medicare and Medicaid improvements, better housing, adequate retirement income and "employment programs in local community service, designed for the elderly who arc physically capable and want to work." Some of its frustrations are sharply expressed in a recent report, "The Nation's Stake in the Employment of Middle-Aged and Older Persons," prepared for the Special Committee on Aging of the U.S. Senate.

The Older Americans Act, passed in 1965, called for "pursuit of meaningful activity for the elderly within the widest range of civic, cultural, and recreational opportunities." One of its objectives was to provide employment opportunities "without age discrimination." By the end of 1970, only fifteen court proceedings to enforce compliance had been started. "It's true that there are a lot of steps to pass through—conciliation, conference, and persuasion—before the legal proceedings start," said a cynical Administration on Aging official. "I thought that only about 100 or so cases would get to the courts each year. But fifteen cases in four years is a remarkable under-achievement." Apparently the old are hesitant to make and follow up on their complaints and they are not encouraged to do so.

In late 1970, both Senate and House passed an Employment and Training Opportunities Act which was meant to set up a major national effort to provide special job development, training, and supporting programs for older and middle-aged workers. One provision was the basic one, propounded and endorsed by virtually all industrial gerontologists: the establishment of "a midcareer development services program in the Department of Labor to assist persons of 45 and older to find employment." The middle aged thus would have been given the necessary training, counseling, and other services—but President Nixon vetoed the bill, mainly on the grounds that it would create "deadend WPA-type jobs." The Senate failed by eight votes to override his veto.

* A brave use of a term which is not uniformly appreciated. In 1973 it was reported that lapel buttons were being sold in St. Petersburg, Florida, with the inscription: "CALL ME SENIOR CITIZEN AND I'LL ZAP YOU."

More recently, while signing a bill to increase Social Security benefits for eight million elderly, President Nixon vetoed two others that would have increased some medical services under the Older Americans Act and set up a government-financed institute to study the problems of the old. The two bills, which would have authorized the expenditure of $2.2 billion over three years, were vetoed on the grounds that they would "feed inflation." *

In 1972, the creation of a separate institute for aging in the National Institute of Child Health and Human Development was blocked by a presidential pocket veto. The same year, in reporting to members, Bernard Nash, executive director of the American Association of Retired Persons, gave an encouraging report on the overall results of the 1971 White House Conference on Aging and said, in carefully chosen words, that President Nixon's conference address "brought new hope that the Administration will indeed commit itself"—the word "indeed," perhaps, accenting the forlorn quality of that hope.

A year later, such nuance was abandoned. Appearing before a unit of the House Banking and Currency Committee in October 1973, Cyrus F. Brickfield, legislative counsel for the AARP and the National Retired Teachers Association, noted that the Nixon Administration—on the advice of its own experts—had supported the idea of 70,000 new housing starts for the elderly following the White House Conference. But now, he said, the President's latest message on the subject called only for a continued moratorium on building to gain time "for the study and evaluation of existing programs." The elderly do not have time to wait, Brickfield said, and "it is our associations' view that this proposal [of the President] breaks faith with older Americans."

President Nixon has repeatedly made appeals to the old with such statements as "I call today for a new alliance in this country

---

* Inflation was fed anyway, and the old probably suffered most. In reporting on soaring prices in the summer of 1973, *Time* magazine told of the case of an aged shopper in a Milwaukee supermarket whose grocery bill exceeded the amount in her purse by 18¢. She asked the check-out clerk to remove a can of cat food from her order. The clerk offered to pay for it because "I wouldn't want your cat to go hungry." The woman replied with a weak smile, "I'm the cat."

between Americans who are under 65 and those who are over 65." But fundamental Administration support for new (and many old) programs for the aging continues to be lacking. One issue of *Aging,* published by the Administration on Aging of the Department of Health, Education, and Welfare, includes a photograph of Julie Nixon Eisenhower visiting participants in a Philadelphia Retired Senior Volunteer Program (RSVP). Mrs. Eisenhower is quoted in the caption: "RSVP was established by my father in the belief that many older people, if only given a chance, would like to volunteer their time and talents in the service of others . . . You have more than fulfilled his expectations." Readers who knew of President Nixon's interest in establishing and funding new programs for the old could only wince.

A most creative social venture is the Foster Grandparents Program, initiated by the Administration on Aging. The program is based upon the perfectly sound ideas that (*1*) the old—particularly the retired old—have a vague and diffuse role in the United States, and (*2*) it is important for young children to have sustained and affectionate contacts with an adult or adults. The plan—as formulated by sociologists Marvin Taves, Donald Kent, and Clark Tibbitts—led to an Office of Economic Opportunity program to employ people over 60 with low income. They were paid $1.25 an hour (the figure was later raised slightly) to work four hours a day, five days a week, with children under 5 years old. The children, living in orphanages and other institutions, are often neglected, disturbed, or disabled. In its testing period, the program was considered an inspiring success. The lives of both young and old were touched and changed. The young received the love, warmth, and attention necessary for growth; the old had new pride, interest, and self-esteem, a social role in the community—as well as additional income.

The program received great publicity and was treated in the press as though it had swept the country. The trouble—according to the National Council of Senior Citizens' working paper prepared for the Senate Committee—is that the program never really got off the ground. "As an experiment in 1968, it employed 4,000 foster grandparents. As an ongoing nationwide program in 1970, it had 4,300." Then the Administration suggested that Foster Grandparents become a volunteer program, not supported by the Administration on Aging at all; it has since found at least temporary shelter in ACTION. This, indeed, has been the way with scores of federally funded programs, handed down from the Great Society days of President Johnson. The future of all such programs for the welfare of the aged (and the young and middle aged, too) is uncertain, particularly since the dismemberment of the Office of Economic Opportunity. It is moot which will have the more serious and far-reaching effects on the old, the loss of funds for active programs (which also upsets the fine balance of government support and voluntary, public-spirited efforts) or the drastic curtailment of federal allocations for scientific research.

At the moment, it seems that there must be greater reliance on private funds and voluntary effort than in the recent past. A major effort (originally supported in part by the Administration on Aging) is SERVE (Serve and Enrich Retirement by Volunteer Experience). It was started on Staten Island, New York, in 1967 by the Community Service Society of New York, a nonprofit, non-sectarian social agency and, aside from some federal support, is funded by private foundations and individuals. It seeks to give retirees the chance to make good use of their time and experience by serving, as volunteers, with a variety of community agencies and programs. The concept of the old as a source of untapped manpower is a recent one; SERVE's aim is even more original in that it makes use of the "nontraditional volunteer"—not the middle-aged man or woman of comfortable income with an impulse for public service but older persons of lower economic status. Three-quarters of SERVE's men and half its women have never done any volunteer work before; two-thirds did not graduate from high school; their average age is 71.

SERVE's first emphasis was on the needs of the old, not the agencies they voluntarily serve, but the work they do is real enough. The 1967 demonstration project started with 23 volunteers who served weekly at the Willowbrook State School for the Retarded in Staten Island; after three years it had 600 older volunteers serving 24 agencies and programs. (By the end of 1971, another 750 volunteers were serving in pilot programs throughout New

York State.) The volunteers at Willowbrook assist the occupational therapist, tend and give love to the children, teach folk-dancing to adolescents, and sew and repair strollers, among other jobs. In other SERVE projects, they serve as "friendly visitors" to hospital patients and the institutionalized aged or as office volunteers to such organizations as the American Cancer Society or Red Cross.

One of SERVE's methods is the group approach—volunteers are recruited in groups and serve in groups (although each person has an individual assignment). The group approach has several functions: Transportation—a basic problem for the old—is made simpler; each unit has a weekly group discussion as a form of in-service training; the older men and women get the chance to have more social contact and make new friends, and to lessen their feelings of isolation. SERVE has been the model for a national program—called RSVP (Retired Senior Volunteer Programs)— open to people 60 or more, which now has hundreds of locally sponsored volunteer efforts in action.

SERVE's director, Janet S. Sainer, and her associates have developed guidelines for recruiting, training, and finding new roles for volunteers and have gained many insights since starting the original project. Among them: Volunteers should not have to undergo complicated training but be assigned to tasks they can start doing right away—they will readily learn more complicated skills, if necessary, while in service. If volunteers miss a day, their absences must be followed up, so that they will know that they are important and have been missed. And reward and recognition must be given if the volunteer is to stay with the program and flourish—and do his essential job well.

SERVE is one of the most successful of organized efforts to make use of services and skills of the old and help them live a fuller life. Another is SCORE (Service Corps of Retired Executives), which was started in 1964 by Maurice du Pont Lee, a retired Delaware businessman, who found that lack of experience —not lack of financial support—was the major cause of small business failures. Under SCORE, retired businessmen and executives advise and work with small businessmen, giving them the benefit of their years as sales and production managers, retailers, manufacturers, accountants, administrators, whatever set of skills is required. The 4,000 men and women retirees in SCORE work for nothing and are reimbursed only for out-of-pocket expenses. In its first six years, SCORE served more than 165,000 small businesses. SCORE is a nationwide effort, coming under the new citizen service agency called ACTION, which now includes as its components the Peace Corps, the Foster Grandparents Program, RSVP, VISTA (which also makes use of older people working in poverty areas), and two other programs. The SCORE idea has had many local and independent offshoots. In a number of cities, retired businessmen—usually three or four—have banded together to set up consulting firms to hire out their skills or to help younger people without charge just for the satisfaction of being productive. Another type of national organization is Green Thumb, Inc., funded by the U.S. Department of Labor and sponsored by the National Farmers Union. Green Thumbers are mainly retired rural men, with low income, ranging in age from 55 to 94. They work on any publicly owned land or on property owned by nonprofit organizations; they plant, trim, and cultivate trees, help beautify the landscape, work in state parks, along highways, and around public buildings. Green Thumbers work on an average of twenty-four hours a week for the federal minimum wage, supplementing retirement income or Social Security payments. "But the dollar value does not equal the physical and psychological impact that being useful, meaningful, and independent can have," explains a Green Thumb official.

Another program, also funded by the Department of Labor but administered by AARP and other private organizations, is Senior AIDES, which utilizes low-income people over 55 who work in urban areas in jobs in adult education, child care, homemaker and health services. Senior AIDES also receive the federal minimum wage for up to twenty hours of work. There is also a Teacher Corps, designed to improve the opportunities of retarded children by using the services of retired teachers. There is, in fact, no end to ways of using that natural resource—the skills of the retired. The organizations need not be solely for the old: V.I.P. (Volunteers in Probation) is open to adult citizens of any age, but it is the old who have the time, experience, and will to serve it well. The professional probation officer may have as many as a hundred teen-age or adult offenders to handle. A V.I.P. is given just one case and becomes counselor, guide, and friend to the man or woman on probation. There have been instances in V.I.P. experience of a mother asking that her son be kept on probation after his term had ended—his relationship with his V.I.P. had become so important to him. The fact that the volunteer is rarely paid (a few retirees are subsidized up to their Social Security maximums) makes the "probationer feel he is sincere," according to one professional in the field. V.I.P. gives personal care and attention, which a government agency cannot afford, brings the court closer to the community, and helps probationers flow more easily back into general society.

There is an even greater variety of local or community programs to occupy the old: seasonal work at Christmas, their use as traffic guards at school crossings, as homemakers for families with emergency or special needs, as baby or pet sitters. Then there is the growing movement of the multipurpose senior citizens center mentioned in the following chapter. The first was opened in New York barely thirty years ago; there are probably more than 1,500 across the nation today. They started mainly to provide recreation for the old, then added the wide-ranging educational and cultural facilities. One of their most important roles is still emerging: their place as a site to recruit old people to undertake new jobs, new lives in community service.

Not all the old respond to the growing opportunities, even when leisure and recreation alone are the goals. A research team of the St. Louis Jewish Community Center Association recently set out to find who among the old are most apt to join in and enjoy leisure activities organized for older adults—clubs, committees, arts and crafts. They studied more than a hundred men and women over 60, members of a community center with such activities. They found that 42% were regular users of the leisure program, 36% were erratic users, and 21% made no use of the programs at all. Using two standard scientific tests—the Lawton Morale and the Havighurst Life Satisfaction Indexes—they made the correlation: Those with the highest morale and greatest life satisfaction were the most consistent users of leisure programs. Those with low scores were the most erratic or nonusers. Their conclusion, as submitted

to other gerontologists: Pay particular attention to the intermittent
or nonusers of leisure programs—they're the least happy, the
ones who can most easily be overlooked, and the ones who probably
need them most.

The converse of this may be true, too: that the happiest people
don't need organized leisure programs or can make their own
activities. Or—a blessed few like Margaret Mead—have their
calling and don't need or want leisure at all. This is an awful
truth in a way. It emphasizes again that there are no miraculous
new roads to the good life in retirement, that all that has come
before in life clearly points to what will come later. Reasonable
good health and adequate income *are* the *sine qua non,* these along
with a sense of well-being, self-esteem, good intelligence, and
curiosity sustained.

This is not to minimize the value of the movement toward
organized leisure and recreation. It serves many functions; it serves
the cause of health, cuts individual costs, opens opportunities for
human contacts and new roles that would not have existed before.
The very fact that others are doing it, too, serves a basic function
—getting over the feeling that it is wrong to enjoy oneself.
Dr. Alexander Reid Martin stated the problem at a meeting of
the National Council on Aging: "We must disabuse ourselves of
the notion that when effort begins to become enjoyable, we must
stop to make it difficult or shift to something else less enjoyable . . ."
For Americans particularly, there is the search for what sociologist
James A. Peterson calls "leisure without guilt." He has interviewed
many persons to find out what, indeed, gratifies people in their
leisure hours. His four points represent, in essence, a restatement
of the University of Iowa's leisure "needs and drives" of older
people:

• *Sharing experiences,* which, for most people, takes the form
of club or group activity. Peterson found that watching television
or listening to the radio are precisely the pursuits that many old
people would like (and need) to get away from.

• *"Enjoying the beautiful,"* by indulging one's appreciation for
music, or birdwatching, or reading poetry, or going to a museum
—or in any way refreshing the spirit.

- *Service,* which means, among other things, forgetting about one's aches and problems and wondering instead about a child—or another man.
- *Education,* which to most gerontologists is the key and answer to most problems having to do with the use of postretirement time.

The more education in youth and middle age, the more resources we have to enjoy later life. We have seen that the ability to learn does not deteriorate with age, unless that ability is unused and wasted. The need and value of education remain with us always. There have been experiments with the teaching of Russian to Americans between the ages of 45 and 70; Russian was chosen because none of the students had previous experience with it. Some of the 45-to-70-year-olds learned as much in two months as students of usual college age did in a full semester; their interest and craving to learn were stronger.

Education—for the old, about the old—heads the list of recommendations coming out of the 1971 White House Conference on Aging. The opening exhortation reads: "Education is a basic right for all persons of all age groups. It is . . . one of the ways of enabling older people to have a full and meaningful life, and [of helping them] develop their potential as a resource for the betterment of society." Among other things, the recommendations call for more education for the old, either apart or integrated with other age groups, depending on need and choice; flexible hours and convenient locations; greater use of public school libraries as a community learning resource; and some emphasis on the educational needs of people in poor health, of low income, or non-English speaking or of different ethnic backgrounds.

And more federal funds and help. Howard Y. McClusky, professor emeritus of the University of Michigan and cochairman of the conference's education section, spoke up bluntly: "Nowhere does the federal government take specific and primary responsibility for leadership in the field of education for aging—neither in the Administration on Aging nor in the Office of Education. This deficit is a scandal and should be liquidated in the immediate future."

Professor McClusky pointed up a common problem. Many of the aging are not interested in education: "What can it do for me?

Why do I need any more education? It is too late for that," they say. But interest in education can be awakened, he asserts, by showing how it may help the old cope with their problems—how it plays a role in producing and protecting health and income, how it can solve problems in housing, family relationships, adjustment to change. (He also made clear that education for aging should not start after retirement but at least as early as 45 or 55.) But Professor McClusky and the education section went far beyond self-help education; they urged that education for the old be devoted to general understanding of the world and its cultures, progress, and problems. Here one of their recommendations coped head-on with the notion that "not working is demeaning." Education, it said, should be directed to help people understand "the dignity and worth of nonwork pursuits as well as development of leisure skills and appreciations." And one of the objectives of education is the "worthy use of leisure."

In fact, education is now usually available to the old if they want it. Adult education courses are a growing phenomenon, and the increased number of community or junior colleges—often requiring neither tuition fees nor special entrance requirements—make it easier still for an older person to go back to school or somehow have access to educational services. By franchise and budget alloca- tion, the new breed of community colleges is designed to make community services and adult education a principal part of its overall program. "The potential of the community college to serve the elderly is there and could soon be realized," Professor McClusky believes. He also calls the widespread development of the community school a good augury for the old. "The essence of the community school idea is that of service to all people of all ages," he says, adding that the community school—either alone or in combination with the community college—may become the most feasible and universal vehicle for educating the old.

The catalog of the Institute of Lifetime Learning of the National Retired Teachers Association/American Association of Retired Persons gives an idea of the courses most interesting to the old. It lists more than seventy weekly courses, ranging from real estate (a good second career opportunity) to creative writing, to Italian, to advanced portrait oil and watercolor, to music appreciation, to genealogy, to bridge. There are, in fact, so many courses readily available to adults throughout the United States that the sole problem for an older person may be that of transportation—not in getting to another or larger town but in getting a mile or two across his own hometown.

In its way, education meets all the psychological and social needs of the older person, and the spiritual ones. A prime loss in retirement is the loss of occupational identity; the retired person becomes an *ex*-businessman, an *ex*-farmer, an *ex*-postman, an *ex*-teacher, and is relegated accordingly. By going back to school, he becomes a *present* student and assumes a perfectly acceptable and honorable new identity. He will also be on the way to the role which traditionally belongs to the old but which only some achieve—that of wise man.

11 THE OLD IN THEIR INSTITUTIONS

There was some astonishment when Eamon de Valera, at age 90, left his official residence as president of Ireland and went, with his 92-year-old wife, to live in a Dublin old people's home operated by the Sisters of Charity. De Valera is nearly blind and needs constant attention wherever he lives. Still, the idea of a man of such renown voluntarily putting himself into an institution when, presumably, he had other choices, somehow seems shocking. For the best that most people can find to say about old-age residential and nursing homes and hospitals for long-term care is that they are better than they used to be and that they serve a purpose. The worst is that they are abysmal horrors and "I'd rather die than be put away."

Visitors, particularly first-time ones, may come away acutely depressed. Children who have placed their parents in old-age homes may feel that they have committed a mortal sin but are powerless to find an alternative.

There is sound emotional reason for the strong reaction to old-age homes. To many, they seem a step removed from the old-time almshouse (no matter how expensive they may be). The spectacle of people living collectively in various stages of senescence, awaiting death away from family and possessions, seems to be the ultimate tragedy of life. The child fears that he will be judged as having cast out his parent, condemning him or her to die. Nowhere, aside from the entrance to a prison death cell, does the warning

193

seem more appropriate, "All Hope Abandon, Ye Who Enter Here."
The impressions are overwhelming and sad. Yet there is evidence
—offered by the old themselves—that institutional life for many of
them is neither shattering nor demoralizing, that it is indeed more
suitable for some than life at home. And, most hopeful, to those
now growing old, is the promise of new and better alternatives
to today's conventional old-age and nursing homes.

The "plight" of the old in institutions is dramatized often enough
to give the idea that it is *the* problem of people over 65; in fact,
less than 5% of them in the United States and Europe live outside
their homes or away from their families.* An article in the French
magazine *Elle* illustrates a common approach. Entitled "The Embers
of Life" and based upon a book by Annie Lauran, it explains the
facts of prejudice toward and poverty among France's 6,240,000
old. But it starts off with the woeful headline: "It is inhuman to
pen up the old in beautiful buildings where they have nothing
to do but watch themselves die." The old, if they really are
living in beautiful buildings, may have far more to do than await
death; most modern institutions have advanced programs to stimulate
and engross them, including rehabilitation and sensory training,
field trips, self-government, dramatics, editing a house organ, and,
to say the least, a variety of arts and craft activities. Still, the
outsider's reaction—born of fear of age or death, or of guilt, or of

---

* The problem is somehow more egregious in Japan where, traditionally, the aged have been venerated. Since World War II, much of its
family system has broken down in the course of the westernization of
Japan, the rush to the cities for work, and the severe housing shortage
that followed. There are more old and fewer young people, since family
size has shrunk but life expectancy has increased since the war, from
47 to 69 for men, 50 to 75 years for women. One result is the existence
of many bleak housing projects and crowded nursing homes for the
old. *Time* magazine quotes a 70-year-old widow, Take Kikuchi, who
now lives in a nursing home outside Tokyo: "Both my sons have one-
room houses and are married. I shuttled endlessly between them, but
at last the message was so deafening that I had to leave them and come
here." Japan has another particularly difficult problem: It has no social
security system in the Western sense, and 60% of the 7 million Japanese
over 65 have little income ot any kind.

the situation itself—is one of distaste and sometimes irrational. The institution, good or bad, becomes the culprit.

"Don't tell me about nursing homes," a woman said after a visit to her 83-year-old invalid father. "Sure it looks great outside, flowers and sprinklers watering the lawn. Inside, they're giving those programs to reactivate the senses, someone is lecturing about current events, a lot of people are smearing paint—and all the time my father is dying."

It takes time to adjust to any new universe. An old-age home or hospital—perhaps any home or hospital—is a world unto itself, and my own reactions on first visiting one were as confused. An official of a large, modern institution in New York City took it upon herself to show me around. The place was air conditioned and bright. The basement had a boutique selling donated used clothing at bargain prices. It also had beauty and barber shops, and a gift store selling the handiwork of residents. Teen-age volunteers were on hand that day, to help serve an outdoor barbecue held in a garden behind the building. Other volunteers, some as old as the residents, staffed lunchroom counters and "creative activity" rooms. All seemed to be planned well. Residential, nursing, and hospital facilities were on different floors; everywhere, including the large assembly room and theater, there were ramps for wheel-chairs and railings to help steady the feeble. I did not mind the saccharine qualities of the woman showing me around; she was a professional handling a tough job, and nobody is really sweet all of the time. I felt I was trespassing as I looked over the shoulders of old people painting or doing needlepoint. "Not at all," she assured me. "They welcome the attention." She addressed every resident by his or her name. "You'll notice we always do that. If they have a title—doctor or whatever—we use that, too. It's very important to them to know they're individuals with identities, not just residents."

Her good cheer clashed with reality the very first time she introduced me to a resident I was to interview. It was in a large dayroom, complete with Calder mobiles, where residents were watching television.

"And this is Mrs. Rosalie Hummel," she said. "She's 94 and one of our dearest residents. Mrs. Hummel, this gentleman would like to speak with you." *

Mrs. Hummel would have none of it. "It's you I want to speak to," she said directly to the woman.

"Yes, dear?"

"Four walls. I want my own four walls around me," Mrs. Hummel said. "Can't you get them to take me out of here?"

"Yes, dear. Are you enjoying the television?"

The official and I went upstairs to the nursing section and looked at several rooms. "You'll notice that they're all single or double rooms at most, each with its own bath," she said. "And every resident is allowed to have one piece of her own furniture and as many family pictures as she wants." (About 80% of the residents are women.) We walked into a double room where a woman was lying in bed, eyes open. Disaster Two:

Institution Official: "Oh, Mrs. Banks. We have a guest."

Mrs. Banks: "That bathroom light. I reported it ten times."

Institution Official: "What bathroom light?"

Mrs. Banks: "The one in the bathroom, of course. Whenever she [waving toward the adjacent empty bed] gets up to go to the toilet at night, she turns on the bathroom light and it wakes me up. She goes to the toilet a dozen times a night."

Institution Official: "Yes, dear. I'll speak to the building engineer about it. Maybe he can build a partition to screen the light."

Mrs. Banks (voice trailing away as we leave): "Ten times I've already reported it . . ."

Outside the room, the official explained that incontinence is a problem of the old but that a dozen times a night was probably an exaggeration. "Mrs. Banks is cranky today," she added.

I was to discover that most everyone—including the professionals in the field—has a story to tell about old-age homes to make any one of a hundred points. Naomi Brill of the Graduate School of Social Work, University of Nebraska, tells of Mrs. Z, a peasant woman born in Central Europe who had come to the United States as a young mother. She was placed in a nursing home in her old age. She cried and cried, and no one in the home could tell what was wrong. The social worker involved was finally called in—and

* Names of residents are altered.

quickly diagnosed the problem. She remembered that she had always seen Mrs. Z wearing a babushka. She had worn one all her life, indoors and out. In the nursing home it had been taken away from her because it was dirty and had not been returned or replaced. When it was, Mrs. Z stopped crying. This story has, more or less, a happy ending. Many others do not.

The point is: Some of the old are troubled people, institutional life is far from the ideal, and few are there by choice. Further, it is the old who most need a tranquil life, with a familiar rhythm, and adjustment to the new life of an institution is usually harrowing for them, no matter how gentle and sympathetic the institutional personnel may be.

I have since visited many institutions for the old and stayed long enough to enter their worlds. It is impossible to have any one reaction or judgment. Another nursing home, small but superbly equipped, is animated by the medical doctor who runs it. I heard not a single grumble about anything—food, room, loss of privacy, other residents. I had come to know the doctor well and accused him of brainwashing his residents before my visit. He answered seriously: "We're small enough to have developed an *esprit de corps* among the residents. Many have been here a long time. We have a form of self-government. My wife and I live here most of the time. We feel that we're a family, in this life together—and a resident would no more complain to you than would any family member complain to an outsider on first meeting."

In some old-age homes, pilferage by lower-paid employees is a problem. "Do you have any problems with petty theft?" I asked the doctor. "None at all," he said. "Here *everyone* is part of the family." In this nursing home, I had seen a Puerto Rican orderly, wheeling an old lady into the elevator, greet another resident with the words, *"L'Shanah tovah."* (It was the time of the Jewish New Year.)

This is a sanguine, hopeful view of the institutional condition. Usually, no matter how immersed he may be in the activities of institutional life, the old person usually dwells upon his real family, his children and grandchildren. They, their visits, and their gifts give him status. His relations with them continue to be of great importance long after he is institutionalized.

Here, too, there is a great range. Margrit Kessi, of the School of Social Work in Zurich, studied the relations of children and parents living in old people's homes in Switzerland. She found that most of the children kept up a relationship with their parents, usually through mutual visits. Less often were letters exchanged, trips undertaken together, or services provided. Gift-giving was a one-way affair; only the children could afford to give them.

She asked both parents and children how they rated their relationship. Barely half said they were good, the rest said they were average or bad. (The answers of young and old of the same family did not always correspond.) Miss Kessi found that external factors—social class, states of health, living accommodations—were not primary in making for good, bad, or indifferent relations. "The attitudes to one another of parents, children, and grandchildren counted far more," she wrote.

How the old felt about entering an institution most influenced mutual relations. Mainly the old reported good relations with their children only if they had reconciled themselves to living there. Others were embittered by not being able to live with a son or daughter, and relations were bad.

When the children report other than a good relationship, the overwhelming cause is that "in childhood they experienced too little parental love," Miss Kessi says. "Nevertheless they worry about their progenitors because of feelings of duty. Yet very few of these would take the father or mother to live with them." She ends her report sadly: It is almost impossible to cheer up the old who feel rejected by their children, although "a regular hearing of their grief can somewhat mitigate the bitterness of the feeling."

Dr. A. Lee Lichtman, education director of the Metropolitan New York Nursing Home Association, is more hopeful and positive about improving relations between children and their institutionalized parents. Dr. Lichtman is director of New York's DeWitt Nursing Home, which has about 500 residents referred to it by social services departments of various hospitals. Their average age is about 83.

Dr. Lichtman, too, stresses the relationship of child-parent attitudes and institutional living. About half the problems in the nursing home field are psychological, he told a *New York Times* interviewer, and "related to the children, not to the parents."

He has initiated Sunday afternoon meetings—"rap sessions"—among the children of residents and himself. The children, usually middle aged, discuss how they feel about having their parents live in a nursing home instead of at home or with them. The sessions are held at DeWitt; usually the children have just come from visiting their parents. He encourages them to air their doubts and feelings of guilt. He also explains what he is trying to do in behalf of their parents.

"We have to fight dehumanizing here," he says. "The activities group is trying to make the elderly feel that they are important persons. There are little ways to do that. The hairdresser, just having her here, means something . . . When a woman no longer cares to have her hair done, it means she's no longer interested in herself as a person."

The children keep returning to the subject of guilt. "I know my mother is better off here. I couldn't take care of her and she couldn't take care of herself. Still, I feel so badly about it . . ."

Others say they are still keeping their parents' apartment for them, or are trying to, or are lying to their parents and say they've kept their apartment or kept furniture in storage when they've really given them up. Dr. Lichtman makes clear there are no easy solutions, that he and many others share the same problems. "The outside apartment is a problem," he says. "It's like a root to the person who lives there, an anchor. Even the welfare authorities will try to keep a welfare case in one if it is at all possible. But of course sometimes the apartment must be given up. Living among one's things gives a sense of security. Sometimes we try to move the furniture into the room here."

Some of the children visit every day of the week. One, an English professor, explained how he tries to help his 89-year-old mother "in little ways. I feel that my presence helps her. She had a stroke but likes me to touch her. I feel very uneasy when I'm not here. She calls me by my name, she says, 'Oh, my son,' although she is partially paralyzed and very forgetful."

A woman asked Dr. Lichtman, "This coming to see them every day, this touching—is it good for them? Or for us?" "For them," Dr. Lichtman said.

Some report that their parents are happier than before. A

woman said that her 93-year-old father "knows I couldn't take care
of him, but I come every day . . . This is a place to live, not to die;
that's the way I look at it." A woman with both mother and mother-
in-law at DeWitt also expressed little doubt: "What my mother
likes very much is having her own phone in her room. I come twice
a week. She now wonders how she stayed so long in her own
apartment."

Throughout a session, Dr. Lichtman—who is younger than many
of the children of residents—shows both compassion and authority.
"Some of the children who come develop a fear of old age as soon
as they walk in, and they get depressed because of their own fear
of getting old and being sick," he says. "That ends up with a guilt
feeling because their parent is here." In helping the children resolve
their own feelings, he is improving their relationships with their
parents—and thus helping the aged parents, too.

Dr. Lichtman's wife, Marilyn, works closely with him. She is
particularly concerned with activities and art programs. So varied
are the programs, so involved are many of the residents, that
DeWitt's day rooms hum with an air of industry. "We are trying
to help people grow here," Mrs. Lichtman explains. "There's no
reason why they can't."

The resident-edited monthly, *The DeWitt Bugle,* gives news of
sing-a-longs and talk-a-longs, of awards given in their art exhibitions
(open to and well attended by the community outside DeWitt),
profiles of residents and staff, rehearsal dates and news of forth-
coming musical shows. Outsiders, naturally, respond with their
own biases. You can look at them showing off their paintings or
watch 80-year-olds cavorting around in something called "The
Spring Roundup," dressed as cowboys and cowgirls, and find them
grotesque—or see them simply as a group of men and women, a
bit along in years, having a rousing good time. A Broadway
producer, Robert E. Richardson, visited a residents' art exhibit,
felt the sense of community in DeWitt, and was delighted by it
all. He sent to the editor of *The Bugle* a sample of the lyrics from
a musical, "Love! Love! Love!" he was then planning: "Age is a
state of mind / nothing to do with time at all / nothing to do
with wrinkles / unless the wrinkles are in your soul. / If you live
with love / you will live to find / age is a state of mind."

DeWitt and other such homes may be havens for the old who find it increasingly difficult to get around in a big city. Dr. Lichtman is among the gerontologists who are distressed by the predicament of the old in a society built around the young. "Can you imagine what it's like if you're old and trying to get through a revolving door?" he said. "Or trying to get off a bus, or into a government building with all its steps, or into an automatic elevator that closes its doors in a few seconds?"

He does not, however, pretend that life in a nursing home represents any kind of ideal. He asked me what I thought of my tour of DeWitt. I said that I could not sum up any one feeling; I had seen sickness and tragedy and hope and laughter all in the same place. And besides, it *is* an institution. He addressed himself perfectly to my quandary. "You cannot understand what it's like to live in an institution unless you live there. Or, perhaps, unless you read Thomas Mann's *Magic Mountain*."

Everyone who comes to Dr. Lichtman's Sunday afternoon sessions has already gone through *the* ordeal, perhaps the most agonizing of problems concerning the aged: What do you do about a parent living at home who is obviously failing and requires more care, attention—and expense—than you can provide?

You may own up to yourself that your parent should be institutionalized but don't know how to go about it—and, more difficult, cannot bring yourself to do it.

How do you face your parent, explain or cajole or lie so that she will not feel that this is the ultimate rejection by her child? ("She" because the problem usually involves an old mother; there are many more old widows than widowers.)

The problem is a universal one. We have all been through it ourselves or seen the ordeal of friends—good, compassionate people—their lives haunted, family life sometimes shattered, by it. If the aged parent is, say, the mother of the wife, the husband may have strong feelings about putting the old woman in an institution but hesitates to utter them; he can be answered too easily by his wife's "You don't understand" or "It's not your mother" or "You never liked her anyway." (It works the other way too, if the old person is the mother of the husband.) If the mother is very old and sick, both husband and wife may secretly wish her dead, a wish that fills the daughter with even more guilt and anguish. The wife may steel herself to a decision, set the machinery in motion to place her mother in an institution, and, in the middle of the night, change her mind: "My God—how can I do this to my mother? I must keep her with me (or in her own home) no matter what the pain and cost." And wonders, with dread, how she would feel if this were happening to her—if her children were seeking ways to "send her away."

Even when a firm decision is made, it is contingent on what's available in old age homes, the length of waiting lists, and a fair amount of paper work. Shopping around for an institution can be a dismal affair; along with Dr. Lichtman, I recommend a reading of *The Magic Mountain* to fortify yourself. Along the way, you learn the tricks. Do you indeed tell your parent that "it's only temporary, until you get over this siege" or "until winter is over and you can get outside by yourself again"? If your parent is living in her own home, do you assure her that you're keeping apartment or furniture intact "until you move back in"? The devices abound and are often cruel and demeaning: Many children are reduced to having their parents transfer all their property to them, so that parents may be considered indigent—or at least property-less—and thus qualified for government benefits which pay for most of the cost of institutionalization.

All the while, the emotional ordeal is sapping everyone's strength, certainly including that of the old person to whom the waiting period is usually a time of great apprehension. The choice of institution is, of course, of crucial importance. There are good and bad ones, and the good ones usually seem to be the farthest away and with the longest waiting lists. The choice is limited by many factors: type of care provided, costs, even sectarian qualities. No matter how universalist you may feel, you cannot put a devout old Jewish lady into a home staffed by nuns if she will feel uncomfortable with them, and you cannot *not* put a devout old Catholic lady in a home without nuns if their presence will make her feel better.

Social workers know very well: The decision to institutionalize a parent is usually made in a time of crisis—a serious family blow-up over the drain on energies or morale, a turn for the worse

THE OLD IN THEIR INSTITUTIONS

in the old person's condition, the sudden influx of huge bills for her care. Still, the decisions are often recanted—until the next time. The anguish of the problem is here expressed in the cold language of an actual situation from a social worker's casebook:

> Case #4, Applicant Mrs. D.
> Eighty-seven-year-old Mrs. D had lived with son-in-law and daughter, Mr. and Mrs. X, for twenty years. In the screening interview arranged by her son-in-law, she evidenced severe disorientation and confusion, clung to her daughter, and pleaded to be taken home. The daughter denied the mother's obvious memory defect, insisted that incontinence of urine and feces was "normal" for an older person, and saw no need for medical evaluation. She blamed her husband for the tense home situation. No application was made. A year later, again under pressure from her husband, the daughter telephoned (the home for the aged). Mr. X was angrily refusing to "clean up" after his mother-in-law and was threatening divorce. Mrs. X was unable to leave her home even for brief intervals to shop because, left alone even for a few minutes, Mrs. D would start a fire or wander out and get lost. This time, Mrs. X went through the motions of filing an application to placate her husband. The case record noted the social worker's judgment that Mrs. X probably would not be able to carry through an actual placement.

Later in this chapter we will see why old-age homes—including nursing homes—may eventually be reduced in number and function. At the moment, however, they are often the best solutions available; they may immeasurably relieve some situations. The only practical help I can give here is to offer the assurance that the problem comes close to being everyman's. Many or most families face it at one time or another, and the issue should be confined to what is best for the principals involved, not what others will say. Every community has social workers greatly experienced with the problem; they can give practical guidance about local institutions and their respective values, services, and costs. Their professionalism itself may be reassuring; you will realize how many others, not unlike yourself, have faced the problem and survived it.

And I can offer the hope that if the time comes for ourselves, we can face it with the dignity and wisdom of Eamon de Valera.

Among gerontologists themselves there is no certain view of the impact of institutions upon the lives of the old. Margaret Blenkner reported at the Seventh International Congress of Gerontology, held in Vienna, that it is very easy to document "a negative relationship between survival and institutionalization"—that older people die at an excessively high rate during the first year and, particularly, during the first three months after admission to an institution. But, she added, there is no proof that the higher death rate is caused by being placed there or because of removal from familiar surroundings. "People tend to be admitted to instiutions, particularly nursing homes and hospitals, in a state of crisis," Dr. Blenkner said. Or they are "often in a seriously debilitated or incapacitated state which may, in itself, explain the high death rates." *

Do the old lose self-esteem by living in institutions? This assumption, too, is challenged. Sociologist Nancy N. Anderson used a "self-esteem scale" to study both residents and applicants for admission to a retirement home. The applicants were younger than the residents and, presumably, should have had more self-esteem since they were still living at home. All were asked to respond to such statements as "I am able to do things as well as most older people." Dr. Anderson found not enough difference to matter between the two samples and concluded that institutionalization itself does not necessarily reduce self-esteem. Those who "socially interact" and participate in the work of the retirement home and identify with its community, she found, had higher self-esteem than those who did not—suggesting that home directors plan more activties to involve their residents.

* One thing *is* clear: Dr. Blenkner said that any evidence of severe brain dysfunction is unequivocally an indicator of "high risk." If an older person's mind, memory, and orientation to time, place, and person are seriously impaired, his chances for survival after relocation are poor—considerably lower than for those who show little or no such signs no matter how emotionally disturbed or socially maladjusted they may be.

These are examples of the scores of studies and observations made by gerontologists on a most controversial subject. Peter Townsend, in his survey of homes for the aged in England and Wales, summed up the view of those who believe that institutions "dehumanize" and "depersonalize," and that they tend to be dumping grounds for many who need not live there. His view is a bleak one:

"In the institution people live communally with a minimum of privacy and yet their relationships with each other are slender. Many subsist in a kind of defensive shell of isolation. Their mobility is restricted, and they have little access to a general society. The social experiences are limited, and the staff lead a rather separate existence from them. They are subtly oriented toward a system in which they submit to orderly routine, noncreative occupation, and cannot exercise as much self-determination. They are deprived of intimate family relationships and can rarely find substitutes which seem to be more than a pale imitation of those enjoyed by most people in a general community. The result for the individual seems fairly often to be a gradual process of depersonalization. He has had too little opportunity to develop the talents he possesses and they atrophy through disuse. He may become resigned and depressed and he may display no interest in the future or in things not immediately personal. He sometimes becomes apathetic, talks little, and lacks initiative. His personal habits and toilet may deteriorate. Occasionally he seems to withdraw into a private world of fantasy."

Psychiatrist Morton A. Lieberman of the University of Chicago is a foremost specialist on the effects of institutionalization on the aged. In 1969, he reviewed Townsend's and many other studies of the old in homes for the aged, domiciliaries, and nursing homes and found that they share these characteristics: "Poor adjustment, depression and unhappiness, intellectual ineffectiveness because of increased rigidity and low energy (but not necessarily intellectual incompetence), negative self-image, feelings of personal insignificance and impotency, and a view of self as old."

Other investigators, he reported, found marked increases in psychological breakdown and in mortality rates for aged persons entering institutions. However, after reviewing all this, Lieberman came to a conclusion not unlike the one made by Dr. Blenkner before him:

The stereotype about the destructive influences of institutions on the aged is overdrawn. Many of the supposed psychological effects are really characteristics of an old person *before* he entered the institution and are, in fact, part of the reason for his being there. Lieberman stresses that institutionalization may best be studied as a complex process of several phases. It begins when an old person seriously considers entering one; starts a new critical phase before and perhaps just after entrance; and then goes into the period of long-term residence. The behavior of the old must thus be studied before, immediately after, and then over the long period if the real psychological impact of institutionalization is to be understood.

Lieberman notes that some effects—such as greater feelings of despair and psychological distance from others, as well as a lower future-time perspective—may be the products of an old man's fantasies or dread in advance of entering the institution, not the result of the experience of living in one.

"There appear to be considerably more destructive effects associated with radical environment change—*entrance* into institutions—than with residence in one," he says. His conclusions are tentative because of "methodological biases" in the studies analyzed; the only long-term effect of living in an institution that can be proven, he says, is that on leaving it an old person has great difficulty in re-entering and adapting to the community.

In the course of his work, Lierberman and his associates have come across nine "personality traits" which they use as predictors of how well the old will adapt to life in an institution. They developed the predictors after clinical analysis of 37 persons in three homes for the aged, "old-timers who had made it," men and women who, after three to five years of institutionalization, had weathered its impact and kept functioning at about the same level through it all.

A harsh truth is that personality traits that help a person adapt to life in a special setting may be ineffective—or undesirable—in everyday life in a normal community. Lieberman and his associates recount various studies to make the point: Former criminals who wound up in Nazi concentration camps—particularly those with a predisposition toward psychopathological ruthlessness—had a better chance to survive than the other noncriminal inmates. In Antarctic stations, men who liked social and physical activity—desirable elsewhere —are less able to adapt than those who are "task-oriented" and fulfilled just by doing their jobs. One study found that chronic convicts, who persistently failed at both criminal and noncriminal careers outside of prison, often found themselves more at home, and more comfortable, in prison than anywhere else.

Many of Lieberman's nine traits may be considered undesirable or disagreeable. Still, they are the characteristics that best describe the "old-timers" who successfully adapted to life in the old-age homes. He lists them and explains how they work:

• *Activity-passivity.* The institutional staff rewards residents who are active in institutional functions and penalizes those who are more passive and withdrawn.

• *Aggression.* In a setting in which many residents are incapacitated, an aggressive resident is best able to meet his needs by reaching out assertively for himself.

• *Narcissistic body image.* Physically unattractive residents tend to be avoided by other residents. An attractive appearance is rewarded by overtures and admiration and enhances self-esteem.

• *Authoritarianism.* There is need to differentiate oneself from debilitated residents. Even "helping" other residents confers a dominant position. Identification with strength (and scorn for weakness) may be helpful in getting one's "share" of available resources.

• *Status drive.* The old-timer seeks to identify with staff—which has higher status, controls more rewards and is more attractive— than with other residents. He does this by means of superordination over other residents.

• *Distrust of others.* Old-timers suggest that most other residents should be avoided because interpersonal contacts are likely to involve conflicts. "Stay away from them. They only bring trouble." Distrust may serve a function because debilitated residents may not be able to respond appropriately to friendly overtures; after several such disappointments, the old-timer learns to distrust others.

• *Non-empathy.* The old-timer wants to avoid identification with illness and debilitation, so he shows disinterest or disregard for the viewpoints or problems of others.

• *Extra-punitive.* A tendency to blame others increases engagement with people and focusses staff attention on the self.

• *Non-intrapunitive.* Self-blame diminishes self-esteem and reduces rewards from other residents and staff. Thus the old-timer tends to avoid it.

It appears from this list that the meek, the humble, and the sensitive are least likely to adapt well to life in old-age homes and the most likely to suffer higher death rates because of them. This is tragedy compounded; few of the old want to enter communal homes in the first place. In response to this, many voices have been raised against the present system; the future will see much greater effort to get away from it—to abandon gradually the idea of old-age homes and to cut down on excessive or wasteful use of nursing homes as well.

Peter Townsend speaks out most forcefully against continuation of the present use of old-age homes in England. He notes that they have been separately identified from hospitals and nursing homes as a major instrument of social policy only since World War II and believes they should be treated largely now only as temporary expedients. About 1.5% of the old in England and Wales live in residential homes and institutions. (Another 3% live in mental and other hospitals and nursing homes.) He has already noted the critical effects upon old people of life in old-age homes; the futility and cruelty of the situation is that many of them need not be there at all.

The survey of two hundred residential institutions and homes in England and Wales made this primary point: A large proportion of the old enter homes for the aged mainly because of homelessness and lack of social and financial resources.* About a quarter of the newly admitted had somehow lost homes or been evicted from them; most could not turn to family or friends because they didn't have them or had become separated from them. But they were usually still active people (although, obviously, down on their luck). A large

---

* It must be emphasized that Townsend is not speaking here of nursing homes or hospitals, which, obviously, people enter for different reasons.

proportion of all old people living in homes are capable of being active and of looking after themselves in homes of their own. Why shouldn't they be living in homes of their own? Townsend asks. He found that welfare and social services, available to those living at home, had not been fully utilized. Fewer than a fifth of the old admitted from private households had been receiving home help, meals, or other services. Some had not seen their general practitioners for many months before admission, many sorely needed eyeglasses, hearing aids, or surgical appliances but did not think about getting them or did not know how.

Professional opinion generally is now turning against the idea of keeping many types of patients in institutions for long periods of time; instead it favors giving them every possible chance to live in the community. Why, Townsend asks, cannot England do the same for its active old? He proposes "sheltered housing" as one way of helping people through the transition from "adversity of dependence to an independent home life." Sheltered housing is usually made up of small groups of flatlets or bungalows in which the old or handicapped can live independently but where certain communal services are available and a housekeeper is on call; experiments with it have been under way in several countries for many years.

Above all, he calls for a much richer variety of home services, particularly in health and family help. The old require regular medical visits and examination; health and hospital after-care services also can be provided by medical practitioners in the home or local clinics. A comprehensive local family-help service could knit together the various home services that already exist (though often on a small and improvised scale). This could provide family services to those without families and give "supporting" services to families which carry a heavy burden in caring for the old at home; it would arrange for domestic help, shopping, laundry, meals, occupational therapy, supply household aids such as handrails or wheelchairs, and meet other needs.

The job cannot be done by religious and voluntary bodies, Townsend warns. The help needed is too complex, the number of people needing it too large. "The work should be based on the principle of trained social workers paying regular visits to all aged and handicapped persons in the population to assess their needs," he says, and requires a substantial nucleus of full-time staff with considerable training. However, voluntary bodies could play a major role by developing supplementary services—by friendly visiting and by managing clubs and centers in partnership with local authorities.

Townsend's appeal for the gradual abandonment of old-age homes is also an appeal for an even more enlightened England. While domiciliary services for the aged are much more highly developed in England than in most other countries, he says, "they are nonetheless inadequate and need to be expanded three-, four- or five-fold during the next decade . . . In a prosperous society which is also sensitive to individual freedom as well as individual social security, the need for communal welfare institutions intermediate between home and hospital should be extremely small."

Both need and search for alternatives to institutional care are equally strong in the United States. Helen Kistin and Robert Morris of Brandeis University say that the evidence is "mounting and consistent" that many elderly (and handicapped) persons are placed in nursing homes and other institutions because of a lack of essential services to maintain them at home and in their communities—and not for medical reasons.

They cite a Massachusetts Department of Public Health survey which found that only 37% of the 100,000 patients in licensed nursing homes required full-time, skilled nursing care. Fourteen per cent needed no institutional care; 26% needed a minimum amount of "supervised living"; and 23% needed only limited or periodic nursing care. A study in Buffalo, New York, found that only 27% of nursing home residents needed institutional care. Similar findings have been reported in many large cities.

The inappropriate use of skilled medical facilities is a waste of money and of scarce resources, say Kistin and Morris—to say nothing of what it does to the old who thus lose their home and community ties and find eventual return to normal life difficult or impossible. The two gerontologists find that a wide range of alternative services can be supplied within existing budgets; the average welfare payment for nursing-home care in Massachusetts at the time they wrote their article (1972) was $230 a month more than the maximum basic budget for old-age assistance recipients living at home—"large enough to support a considerable expansion in home care services," they note. In skilled nursing homes, the average all-inclusive cost per client was $512 in December 1970; it cost an average of $198 for those supported at home or in unskilled custodial facilities. They recognize the range of problems which undermine the ability of the old to live independently: unsafe and unsuitable housing, inadequate allowances, difficulty in purchasing and preparing food, isolation and loneliness, the need to travel long distances and sit in clinics for hours to get medical services. Still, on balance, they believe that life at home, in a community, is desirable and that the hazards to the reasonably healthy old may be overcome.

Dr. Morris is head of Brandeis's Levinson Gerontological Policy Institute, Miss Kistin its research associate. The Institute has developed proposals for a program to fill in the gaps in the care of the old and chronically disabled and is aiding in plans and evaluating a pilot program of the Massachusetts Department of Public Welfare for old and handicapped people receiving public assistance. They have studied how, typically, welfare recipients get admitted to nursing homes although many do not need them:

Often, they found, a physician decides to hospitalize a patient because of accident or acute illness. On recovery, complete or partial, the patient is transferred to a chronic hospital or nursing home, again on the doctor's decision. (There is evidence that patients in mental hospitals, ready for discharge, are placed in nursing homes in great numbers, too, when no other suitable living arrangements can be found for them.)

In other cases, relatives or friends will contact a welfare service office because an old person's home situation or condition has deteriorated. The service office may be called on to assist in locating a bed in a nursing home—without evaluating whether the old person needs one.

Once in a nursing home, the elderly welfare patient is rarely discharged. "Usually this occurs only if the patient is difficult (for example, alcoholic) or insists on discharge himself. The decision is made by the physician and the nursing home, and it is possible that self-interest may be a factor," they note acidly. Many elderly clients try desperately to avoid going to nursing homes, even "to the point of endangering their lives," they add.

Among the Institute's proposals, to be tested in Massachusetts, are these:

· The development of a program appropriate to meet the needs of the total population of elderly and disabled.

· A study of the feasibility of diverting some current public assistance expenditures from institution to home and community care.

· The actual provision of needed services in home and community is to be undertaken by an organization under contract with the Massachusetts Department of Public Welfare. The organization (designated as Personal Care Organization) would be a Visiting Nurse Association, a senior citizens' or a health maintenance organization, or some other public or private agency. Some services—such as the "meals on wheels" project or transportation—would be subcontracted. The Personal Care Organization would have freedom to provide a flexible range of needed services.

· There is to be some concentration on supplying more of the less professional services, such as home helpers.

The proposals' sponsors hope they will be eventually tried on a nationwide basis and not limited solely to welfare recipients. In common with Peter Townsend in England, they, too, are seeking ways to free the old from what is often needless confinement, their families and government from needless expense.

One excellent way of doing this is by avoiding institutionalization in the first place. The still relatively new idea of day care centers for the old may serve this among other functions. Dr. Lichtman is hopeful and refreshingly candid—he is, after all, director of a nursing home—about their prospects. "The day care centers can go a long way to solving some of the problems," he says. "They are halfway houses to the institutions. They can keep an old person from going to an old age home—or put off his going there for years."

He reels off some of their basic functions: They provide an essential hot meal; they offer activities and companionship; they can give a bit of medical attention, such as reminding an old man to take his digitalis; they give the old somewhere to go—they need no longer be housebound or, if they do go out during the day, are not a source of anxiety to their families.

These are some of the *basic* functions which, along with several dozen others, are served by the Sirovich Senior Day Center on lower Second Avenue in New York City. Miss Frances King, its director since 1949, bathes its 700 members in love and activity. All are over 60 and their average age is 79; if each took advantage of all the activities at the Sirovich Center they would welcome a rest in a nursing home. Miss King's program, given to all comers, reads: "Mental Health Program—Good Mental Health is Contagious" and then goes on to list no fewer than 55 activities, with "Orchestra, Glee Club, Violin Lesson, Sewing Group, Poetry, French, Beauty-from-the-inside-out, Fashion Show, Exercise Class, Elementary and Advanced English, Journalism, Current Events, Advanced Spanish, Nutrition-Education, Dialogue (Talk), Self-Improvement Clinic, Public Speaking, and Creative Jewelry Making" among them. (After this list is the notation, "If there is anything you would like to do that is not listed here, please let me know and we will see if it can be added.") The services of a public health nurse, nutritionist, and Social Security representative are also available.

Miss King is contagious. She infuses the center with life and good cheer. "It isn't that Frances King can wave a magic wand and banish the housing problems, the muggings, the illnesses and the feelings of neglect that beset [the members] of the Sirovich Day Center," observed a *New York Times* reporter. "It's just that she seems to—by listening so sympathetically and responding so affectionately." She will badger members who phone in saying they are too ill to come to the Center—and they come in anyway and forget about their illnesses. The Center's five floors abound with people learning and doing things: An old woman plays the timpani and tells a visitor, "They taught me how to play the drums and now I'm out of this world." A former restaurateur and painter proudly shows off his latest creation in pottery. A woman takes up sewing for the first time in her life: "If you don't learn something new, the walls close in on you." All the activities are free, except for a low-cost lunch, prepared by members, which is usually preceded by exercises.

Miss King is coauthor, with a medical doctor, of a book called *Golden Age Exercises* and is evangelical on the subject. "Non-strenuous exercises can be fun, can free the body from stiffness and inactivity, can create a more vital response to life, today, tomorrow, and everyday," she says. "Exercise aids respiration, circulation, digestion, and elimination of body wastes." She does insist, however, that members get approval of their doctors before they start.

The Sirovich Day Center is run by the New York City Department of Social Services in cooperation with the William I. Sirovich Memorial Association and the Rose Sirovich Society. The effort to keep people who do not belong there out of nursing homes was one of the recommendations of the 1971 White House Conference on Aging, and the U.S. Congress has since passed Aging Act Title III making federal and state funds available to some types of day centers. In 1972, New York City had 63 senior citizens' centers operated by the city's Department of Social Services; 48 others were privately operated. In the fall of that year, a departmental task force announced that it hoped to double the number, to 231, concentrating in areas of the city with older populations. (About 17% —or 1,375,000—of New York's population is 60 and older, but in some areas of Brooklyn and elsewhere, the old make up 30% or more.)

The Sirovich Day Center, under Miss King's guidance, is a particularly bustling place. This brief recital of its ambitious program should not obscure the basic nature of problems faced by many of New York City's old. Other centers, present and planned, will provide information and referral services for the old. The guidelines of the task force report also call for the employment of the aging whenever possible, with the suggestion that Social Security recipients earn $2.50 an hour for a maximum of twelve hours a week. The report noted that the hot meal—to cost no more than 75 cents— was perhaps the most important part of the program, possibly providing some older persons their first adequate meal in years.

Another type of day care center—perhaps closer to the halfway house concept of Dr. Lichtman—is still in the experimental stage in the United States, with only about a dozen now operating. One is the Bethesda (Maryland) Fellowship House, owned and maintained by Christ Lutheran Church, with funds for its program funneled to it by the Maryland State Commission on Aging under the Aging Act Title III. It was opened in November 1972, with five "guests," ranging in ages from 65 to 96 (although eventually it will accommodate fifteen). "These people don't need the skilled medical care that's available in a nursing home," says the center's director, Goldie Rogers. "They need a pleasant environment and plenty of activities." The center, located in a pleasant white frame house, provides home atmosphere and sociability, as well as activity.

The guests are supervised by two nurses, an occupational therapist, and several volunteers. The day starts at 10 a.m. with snacks and a social period, goes through a period of craft work, 11:30 lunch, rest, then other activities.

It is harder to keep men busy than women, says Mrs. Rogers. "Women will do handwork but men have no hobbies. They've devoted their entire lives to their business and when they retire there's nothing to do . . . If they kept active, they would not deteriorate so rapidly."

None of the guests are ill, but they do have problems. "We try to recognize these problems, such as the need for more fluids and regular bathroom trips to diminish toxicity," she says. "This can reduce their confusion and lack of attention."

The cost for each guest is $7 a day or $30 a week; nursing homes in the area cost between $800 to $1,500 a month for room and board only. Private nursing homes have to make money to survive; the Bethesda Fellowship Center is glad to break even. The personal attention and home atmosphere it gives are virtually impossible to achieve in a big-city day care center.

Ruth Singleterry, occupational therapist of Bethesda, was formerly assistant chief of occupational therapy at the National Institutes of Health. On her retirement, she visited many facilities for the old in England, Denmark, and Sweden—including nursing homes and housing developments—where physical and occupational therapy is used to integrate the elderly. She concluded after the trip that the United States is "about ten years behind the times."

Everywhere there is the search for new ways to avoid institutionalization, to keep spirits and body of the old well enough to stay at home comfortably, without burdening themselves or their families.

"It is now fashionable . . . to seek alternatives to nursing home care," writes Jerome Kaplan, editor-in-chief of *The Gerontologist*.

"Institutional care is one-care system. A second system is home care, including all services allowing for one to remain in home or apartment." He urges that parallel systems of care be recognized, each used as necessary in close interaction, even with the same organization providing both care systems. Instead of the two traditional alternatives—home with minimal and usually inadequate care or institution—he suggests that all feasible choices and combinations be used, with the older person himself having a greater role in deciding how he will live and be cared for.

This idea is echoed by many others, among them Abraham Kostick, director of Baltimore's Levindale Hebrew Geriatric Center and Hospital. "There is a growing theory that aged men and women who require services should be given a range of services from which to select," he says, a concept arising from acceptance of the idea that "older people are persons, with individual feelings, and the right to be involved in decision-making in their own behalf."

Mr. Kostick recently reported on Levindale's experiences in giving greater service to the Baltimore community. Levindale is best known for its 24-hour inpatient service for the sick and disabled old. In 1970, it started a day care program with about twenty old persons being brought in during the 7 a.m. to 3 p.m. shift—the best-staffed shift of the day. All had problems that made it difficult for them to be alone or untended during the day or even to participate in usual day care centers. Some were suffering from stroke, incontinence, mild mental impairments, or Parkinson's Disease. Levindale has 270 beds for its full-time patients, and the day care people were, at first, put among them, in the floor or section best suited to their needs.

There were some adverse reactions to this; regular hospital patients could not accept the fact that people with the same ailments were able to live at home. Some of the hospital staff resented the additional responsibility. The day care people were regarded as outsiders, referred to as the "day campers" (a term given some weight by the fact they are transported to the hospital each morning in a specially equipped camper). Some changes were made; the day care staff organized its own program in a separate area of the hospital, with each old person given individual attention. It is now the responsibility of the day care nurse coordinator to provide medication (although day care people have access to all the facilities of Levindale and services are coordinated with the general hospital staff). As the day care center developed its own program, regular patients and residents of the hospital began to come in, too; there is now a sharing of the "outsiders' " program which enriches all. Within their own area, the day care participants have become a cohesive social group in a busy and companionable setting, but going home each night and not feeling institutionalized or cut off at all.

The name "Hebrew" appears in Levindale's name and, indeed, Jewish philanthropic and self-help groups have been pioneers in establishing institutions for the old in the United States, making them as modern as possible, and—more and more—extending their services to people of all denominations. Jewish tradition insists on respect and care for the old; the tradition is embedded in the Bible, the Talmud, and subsequent teachings. "Cast me not off in the time of old age; when my strength faileth, foresake me not," are the words of the psalmist, the "sweet singer" of ancient Israel. The tradition is very much alive in modern Israel, which has both unique problems and advanced methods in caring for the old.

According to international demographic standards, a population is considered "young" when up to 4% of its people are 65 or over; "mature" when the proportion is from 4% to 7%; "aging" when it is higher than that. (By this definition, Great Britain, the United States, France, Germany, Scandinavia, Canada, and Australia all have "aging" populations.) Israel's over-65 population has increased from 3.8% in 1948 when it was founded, to 6%—close to "aging"—in 1970. Almost from its first years—with the arrival of survivors of Hitler's Europe—Israel developed major programs of rehabilitation and care for the old and disabled. But immigration to Israel is non-selective, open to every Jew who wants to go there, a policy that has brought about an influx of many older citizens of different cultural-social backgrounds.* A high proportion of the new elderly are of Oriental origin, illiterate, and of low economic level. Many are in a state of neglected health, and Israel seeks to give medical care to those who may not know they need it or hesitate to get it.

Dr. I. Margulec, medical director of AJDC-Malben in Israel,

* Migrants seeking freedom or new opportunity tend to be young, generally between 20 and 35. But in Israel's first twenty years of national existence, two-thirds of its citizens over 65 were immigrants—a situation unknown to any other modern society. (Simon Bergman of AJDC-Malben calls this phenomenon "imported old age.")

reports on one effort, a preventive and guidance center for the aged in Jerusalem. The center is located in an area with a population of 15,000, among them 1,200 people over 65. It is directed by a centrally created community agency with the participation of the city's welfare and health departments and AJDC-Malben, concerned mainly with old and handicapped immigrants. The professional team includes a doctor, social worker, public health nurse, physiotherapist, occupational therapist, and chiropodist. First, it established a register of the aged in the area and determined their health, social, and family situation. It dealt at once with their urgent needs through existing community resources, and, in cooperation with family physicians, helped get extended treatment for those who needed it. It also helped family doctors provide care for the old, particularly for the homebound and bedridden living with their families. The center's professional team continues to be very active in the home-care program. Either the rate of illness is high among the old in Israel or the medical authorities are successful in detecting it: In 1969-70, 53% of all the old had illness reported, compared to 30% in Britain and 26% in the United States.

The aged of Oriental origin, more than others, tend to live with their children: 74% of all such widows live with their children compared to 47% of the women of Western origin. The effort, among all the old, is to encourage living at home or with families. Israel has a full-range of institutions—hotel-type pensions, homes for the aged (called "Parents Homes"), nursing homes run by voluntary organizations and private owners, and hospitals. But, says Dr. Margulec, a guiding philosophy is that "the place of the old citizen is in the community, with or near family and friends . . . The institution is the last resort and should be used only for special social and health reasons."

The homes for the aged that Malben does run have a type of "progressive care." Each includes three wings. One is equivalent to the communal home for the healthy aged; another is a nursing home for the "frail-ambulant"; the third is a hospital for the bedridden. The effort is to keep the aged under the same roof as their health status changes, for better or worse, on the assumption that each person prefers a familiar environment, even in an institution, and that displacements are shattering. Malben also recommends small institutions with no more than 150 beds, and preferably only 100. Fewer beds, says Dr. Margulec, help create "a home-like environment, and allow better and more flexible staffing patterns and progressive care."

Respect for the individual and the need for "home-like environment" or, better yet, home itself were not always tenets of those concerned with the old. We've come a long way in approach to the problem, although, obviously, there is enormous lag between aims and reality. In partial explanation of its achievements, Dr. Margulec notes that "Israel strives to become a welfare state," a term which to this day chills the bones of many political conservatives. Still, most progress in care of the elderly has been made in those nations whose governments have assumed responsibility for the welfare of its citizens; private or voluntary aid alone is never adequate in the "aging" societies of the West. (Communist countries do not at all represent the ideal, although their economies are run according to an overall plan that includes old-age policy, not subject to interference, or help, by private interests. "Old people's lives should be better looked after in these states than they are in capitalist countries," says Simone de Beauvoir. "But unhappily it seems that this is not always the case.")

Still, with the best of intentions—and England is as well-motivated as any western nation in this field—mistakes and horrors occur. In *On Our Conscience,* his study of the old in Sheffield, Jack Shaw makes the point that good intentions are not enough. Three large blocks of buildings were erected in Sheffield containing more than 1,000 apartments for the old. Partly because of the hilly nature of the land, partly, it seems, because of the architect's lack of foresight, each tenant has to climb thirteen steps to reach his apartment. Elevators, when they exist, are frequently out of order and often the old simply cannot mount the thirteen steps. As a result, many of the apartments have become virtual prisons for the old.

The case is not exceptional or characteristic of England alone. Many architects are reluctant to take on public housing projects. Governments, even if wealthy, are not often generous; contracts tend to go to the lowest bidder, sometimes without regard to the quality or aptness of design. The prominent American architectural firm of

Hirshen and Partners has gotten around this, through ingenuity and some dedication to the idea of designing useful public dwellings for the old. On the island of Maui in Hawaii, Hirshen designed homes for retired sugar-cane workers, mostly of Japanese extraction. The homes are staggered to provide a sense of privacy. The architects, on their own, thought of putting in a community center. The building was ignored at first, but soon the residents started using it for social gatherings, for classes in the crafts, and—most noteworthy—for Oriental group exercises, an aspect of their heritage that had been lost to them when they lived in scattered shanties.

Hirshen and Partners have also designed public dwellings in Pleasanton, California. Before doing so, a Hirshen team interviewed prospective tenants to find out what they wanted. Among their findings: Most old people want a sense of privacy and personal ownership; safety and easy maintenance; a porch and a garden shaded part of the day; a living room big enough to entertain grandchildren; a functional kitchen; a bathroom with fixtures for drying handwashed clothes; and lots of storage room for the accumulations of a lifetime. They did not want—often feared—such things as slippery floors, low fences or walls to stumble over; cabinets that jut out (they prefer cabinets with sliding doors); or winding paths—hazardous and annoying to an old person with a cane who wants to get where he is going as directly and easily as possible.

They also wanted a separate bedroom or, at least, a sleeping alcove that could be screened off; most were accustomed to them and could also use them for painting or sewing without disturbing a neat living room. The bedroom was considered far more desirable than a separate dining room; most of the old said they eat in front of a television set in the living room.

Watching television, the study found, was a major occupation of the old; it had been for years, and their way of life generally had given them little opportunity to meet new people. They didn't seem to care about a community building. Still, Hirshen is going to include one in Pleasanton, too, hoping it will bring the old together as it did in Hawaii. "It takes time setting up new activities," explained a Hirshen partner, "but it's well worth the effort."

Equally ambitious and suitably designed for the middle-income elderly—although located in an urban setting—is Kittay House, sponsored by the Jewish Home and Hospital for the Aged. Made up of 294 efficiency and one-bedroom apartments in a new twelve-story building in The Bronx, New York City, Kittay House includes all safety features imaginable for the reasonably healthy old: emergency buzzers, grab-bars in bathrooms, door sills and other such hazards eliminated. Each apartment has a kitchenette for snacks or breakfasts; the tenants eat lunch and supper in a communal dining room. The facilities include lounges, areas for crafts and recreation, an exercise-and-health club, a library, and an auditorium for movies, lectures, and theatricals. A doctor and nurse are available for emergency services; a doctor's office is maintained in the building. Aside from the communal dining room, tenants may be as independent as they wish. They furnish their own apartments and can live completely private lives.

Retirement communities in town, suburb, and country; retirement hotels; trailer courts and mobile-home parks primarily for older persons—there is a variety to suit the taste of the old who can afford them.* Their value, however, is often questioned by gerontologists who believe that age integration is desirable and that retirement communities isolate the generations. The old, particularly the healthy old, may not like being bunched together in projects planned exclusively for them. Nor may it be desirable, or conducive to the good long life—unless, somehow, their lives are closely entwined with those of the young.

The immediate and practical value of the age-segregated community cannot be overlooked. Clark Tibbitts, of the Administration on Aging, says that it serves a useful social and psychological function for some of the old. After retirement, he notes, many people live in the general community without status or role. "But the minute you set up a retirement village, there is a new society. There are all kinds of organizations developed within it . . . They begin

---

* Buying a mobile home is an increasingly popular way of realizing the dream of "getting away from it all"—although mobile homes usually move only once, to the site where they're to be occupied. More than 600,000 mobile homes were manufactured in the United States in 1972; major buyers were young married couples or retirees. The United States now has more than 22,000 mobile-home parks or communities, many of which are equipped with special facilities and services for the elderly.

to make assignments of positions, or status, and people develop roles" they would not have elsewhere.

But the more general view is offered by Nathan W. Shock of the National Health Institute: "Maybe there are people who would like to have only people of their own age group around them. I don't happen to be one of them," he says. "To encourage it, and in many instances to enforce it, by building large blocks of apartments and whatnot containing nothing but elderly people, seems to me to be a mistake, both from the standpoint of the individual and certainly from the standpoint of society."

Bernice L. Neugarten, of the University of Chicago, takes it a step further: The old have as much right as anyone to live where they want—and to change their minds if they want. "First of all, there are very few proportionately [among the old] who choose to live in a retirement community," she says. "Some people may enjoy segregated living, some don't. Liking is variable. It changes rapidly too. People want one thing at 65 and do not want it at 70 or 75." The answer, she says, is "to provide lots of possibilities for change . . . to increase freedom of movement."

Freedom of movement—and access to people of all ages—is as vital to the old as to the young. The evidence is that multigeneration living is much closer to the ideal. Somehow, the old get older quicker when they are deprived of cross-generational views; James E. Trela points out that even in senior centers, when the old associate only with other old, they increasingly adopt age as their reference point to interpret social and political processes—and everyone suffers accordingly. Certainly there is new life and stimulation for the old in seeing and sharing even casual experiences with the young. Aneurin Bevan, British Labour leader and minister of health, once said that old people sometimes want to see perambulators, not just the funerals of their friends. The age-segregated society, no matter how practical or attractive, tends to become in time a ghetto of mind and spirit.*

---

* A theme picked up in a recent *New Yorker* cartoon showing a group of men and women lined up, playing shuffleboard, in a retirement community called "Leisure Haven." A man is whispering over his shoulder to his neighbor. The caption reads: "The break is set for eleven. Pass it on."

A foremost program to desegregate the old is the city-run effort in Grenoble, France. Now in operation for almost a decade, it aims to integrate people of "the third age"—primarily the retired—into the first and second ages, the young and the working adults. (There is a "fourth age," too, in France—the handicapped old—also involved in the program.) Instead of age-segregated retirement villages, the Grenoble plan calls for integrated living with one of every ten apartments in new buildings reserved for people over 62; included in the buildings are dining rooms where everyone eats together, at small tables and at low cost. The Grenoble plan includes organized activities, exercises, a counseling service, a free mobile health clinic for the elderly, and much more. The program is a sensitive one of great depth. Conceived by a medical doctor, Robert Hugonot, and a philosopher, Michel Philibert, and administered by the Grenoble Office of Aged Persons, it combats the easy acceptance of the "infirmities" of old age by people who can still enjoy and participate in life.

More than 6,000 of Grenoble's elderly meet in "vitality clubs"— *clubs d'animation*—in age-integrated houses or centers to plan classes, activities, excursions. There is a third-age travel agency, with trips outside of France at modest prices. Dr. Hugonot advises an old person obsessed with his problems to "go out into a forest and breathe deeply. You'll find your memory returning, your handwriting steadier." Philosopher Philibert preaches education for the old—and continuous education throughout the life cycle—as one good way to avoid atrophy. Grenoble's old, some of them more than 90, have responded to the program with zest and become part of the city's mainstream.

There is nothing as ambitious yet undertaken in the United States or Great Britain for age-integrated living. The best alternative often mentioned is the two- or three-story garden-apartment development, with the old living on the ground floor, younger people above them. Sadly enough, objections to this rise quickly; many young people simply don't want to see or pass through a ring of old people, not even related to them, each time they come home. To say nothing of having to haul those baby carriages up the steps.

The problem is a serious one, still to be solved. The Grenoble plan is experimental and being carefully observed. But we've come a long way from the almshouse.

12 DEATH AND DYING

To a writer, "Immortality evidently means being loved by many unknown people," Sigmund Freud wrote to Marie Bonaparte, his patient, student, and friend, in 1937. "I know I shall not mourn your death, for you will long survive me. And I hope you will soon console yourself over my death and let me go on living in your friendly recollections—the only kind of limited immortality I recognize."

He was to die two years later, at the age of 83, after sixteen years of increasing agony from cancer of the palate and jaw. Until almost the very end, he would take little but aspirin to relieve his pain: "I prefer to think in torment than not to be able to think clearly," he said. A friend called on him two months before his death to take his last leave; he was struck by the fact that Freud, despite all, showed no signs of irritability or complaint and that he was still vitally interested in personalities and developments in psychoanalytical circles. In his final days, Freud could hardly eat. The last book he read was Balzac's *La Peau de Chagrin,* which, he said with some humor, was "the right book for me to read. It deals with shrinking and starvation." (Many years earlier, in 1896, Freud had written of his dying father, "He is steadily shrinking . . . toward a fateful date.")

His friend and biographer, Ernest Jones, who came to say good-bye, called him by name as he dozed. "He opened his eyes, recognized me, and waved his hand, then dropped it with a highly expressive gesture that conveyed a wealth of meaning: Greetings, farewell, resignation."

Later, Freud took the hand of Max Schur, his personal doctor for the past eleven years, and said: "My dear Schur. You certainly remember our first talk. You promised then not to foresake me when my time comes. Now it's nothing but torture and makes no sense any more."

Schur recounts in *Freud: Living and Dying:* "I indicated that I had not forgotten my promise. He sighed with relief, held my hand for a moment longer, and said, 'I thank you,' and after a moment of hesitation he added, 'Tell Anna [Freud's daughter] about this.' All this was said without a trace of emotionality or self-pity, and with full consciousness of reality.

"I informed Anna of our conversation, as Freud had asked. When he was again in agony, I gave him a hypodermic of two centigrams of morphine. He soon felt relief and fell into a peaceful sleep. The expression of pain and suffering was gone. I repeated this dose after about twelve hours. Freud was obviously so close to the end of his reserves that he lapsed into a coma and did not wake up again. He died at 3 a.m. on September 23, 1939."

His body was cremated a few days later in the presence of a large number of mourners. His ashes were placed in one of his favorite Grecian urns.

Eleanor Roosevelt had already written out her instructions for her funeral and burial before she went to the hospital in 1962 with a rare bone-marrow tuberculosis: She wanted a plain wooden coffin, covered with pine boughs from her woods, no embalming, and she wanted her veins cut because she had an "irrational fear" of waking up with earth piled on top of her.* She had told her doctor, David

---

* "Irrational" according to her biographer, Joseph P. Lash, but hardly an uncommon fear. It is now understood that "clinical death"—the absence of a specific set of signs of life—and real and final death may not be the same thing. Further, imitation of death, or psychological death, is well known among animals, a prime example being the opossum who "plays 'possum" by transforming himself into a dead-looking ball of fur when in terror. (Scientists have determined through electroencephalographic readings from an opossum's skull that he is then really in an alert cortical stage.) There have been many reports in medical and

Gurewitsch, that if her illness flared up again, she expected him to save her from a long agonizing death. But when the time came, he was unable to comply with her wishes, according to Joseph P. Lash in *Eleanor: The Years Alone*. Mr. Lash's wife, Trude, wrote to a friend that in the last few months of Mrs. Roosevelt's life "there was only suffering . . . There was no moment of serenity. There was only anger, helpless anger at the doctors and nurses and the world who tried to keep her alive . . . She was not afraid of death at all. She welcomed it. She was so weary and infinitely exhausted, it seemed as though she had to suffer every human indignity, every weakness, every failure that she had resisted and conquered so daringly during her whole life."

Mrs. Roosevelt pleaded with the doctors to let her go home and "rejoin the human race." They finally did, but newspaper photographers had been alerted, and she, "who had such dignity and pride of bearing, was shown to the world stretcher-borne, her face puffy, her white hair straggly, her head sagging," Mr. Lash writes. She was still meticulous in her concern for others, ordering a children's party to be held at her home while she was in the hospital, on her return making sure that the stretcher-bearers were properly tipped.

She told her nurse she wished to die, and the nurse said that the Lord who put her here would take her away when she had finished the job for which she was in the world. "Utter nonsense," Mrs. Roosevelt said, looking about at the needle punctures in her arm, the oxygen tank, and other medical equipment being used to keep her alive.

Mr. Lash describes Eleanor Roosevelt's final battle: ". . . often in a semicoma, her determination to die alone was steady and iron-willed. She rejected pills, clenched her teeth to keep her nurse from administering them, spat them out if the nurse was successful, and becoming more wily, secreted them in the recesses of her mouth . . ."

---

popular literature through the years of people who have been mistaken for dead and processed for burial. These led, half a century ago, to the sale of coffins with a chain to be placed in the hand of the "corpse"; if he came to life after burial he was to pull it to signal by bell above ground that he wanted to be let out. Some scientists believe that there probably were a substantial number of premature burials in the past and, perhaps, still are.

"There are so many indignities to being sick and helpless . . . I find myself praying that whatever is the very best for her happens quickly," her daughter said at the time.

Mrs. Roosevelt finally died on November 7, 1962, at the age of 78. Doctors who examined her body said she had the brain of a young person.

About ten years earlier, she had expressed her view on life after death in the book *This I Believe*. "I believe that all you go through must have some value, therefore there must be some *reason*. And there must be some 'going on' . . . There is a future—that I'm sure of. But how, that I don't know. And I came to feel that it didn't really matter very much because whatever the future held you'd have to face it when you came to it . . . And the important thing was that you never let down doing the best you were able to do . . ."

Attitudes toward death and dying reveal the intimate core of personality. In the face of death, Freud and Eleanor Roosevelt—two remarkable but dissimilar people—were alike in many ways. Neither feared death and both had asked for an end to prolonged suffering. Both had a unique, unconventional faith to sustain them and a special view of immortality. Until close to the end, they were consistently themselves, aware of the world about them, compassionate, not at all pessimistic. This does not mean, however, that they—or anyone else—could have anticipated their reactions in their final days: "There is almost no relationship between what people think they think about death and how they really feel when they face it," says psychologist Robert Kastenbaum of the University of Massachusetts in Boston.

Both Freud and Eleanor Roosevelt, with their vitality and special gifts, escaped one problem common to most of humanity—the disengagement that begins as we reach the last part of life. Aside from that, these brief accounts of their deaths raise many of the issues, as they concern everyone, that go into the study now usually called "Death Education" or "Death and Dying."

There is nothing particularly lugubrious or morbid about the field or the attitudes of those who work in it: physicians, psychologists, psychiatrists, clergymen, nurses, and others. And the literature in the field, except for some undue reliance on poetry to help its authors over bad moments,* is among the most insightful and clearly written in any of the sciences. In recent years, Herman Feifel's compendium *The Meaning of Death* and Elisabeth Kübler-Ross's *On Death and Dying: What the Dying Have to Teach Doctors, Nurses, Clergy, and Their Own Families* are generally considered watershed works, although there are dozens of other specialists whose works are of equal value, if not renown. Many are active advocates in the cause of death education; they feel, as Rollo May wrote in *Love and Will,* that "the ways we repress death and its symbolism are amazingly like the ways the Victorians repressed sex."

"Death is obscene, unmentionable, pornographic; if sex was nasty, death is a nasty mistake [May wrote]. Death is not to be talked of in front of the children, nor talked about at all if we can help it. We dress death up in grotesquely colorful caskets in the same way Victorian women camouflaged their bodies by means of voluminous dresses. We throw flowers on the casket to make death smell better. With make-believe funerals and burial ceremonies and fancy tombs we act as though the deceased had somehow not died; and we preach a psycho-religious gospel that says the less grief the better . . ."

Death does seem, in some ways, to have replaced sex as the pornography of the late-20th-century mind, and advocates of death education are fighting the same fight that advocates of sex education have now largely won. If any further proof were needed that repression kindles interest, a survey of readers of a magazine of popular psychology recently disclosed that death, not sex, was now the subject they most wanted to read about.

Death used to be a less hidden and more intimate family affair. An old man would die in bed, at home, as a patriarch surrounded by his family. Most likely his body would be prepared for burial there, too. Today death is "bureaucratized," and an old man is more likely to die in an institution, a curtain around his bed, few if any

---

* A practice that British scientist J. B. S. Haldane tried to put an end to. He wrote with outrageous humor about the ailment that was soon to kill him:

> My final word, before I'm done
> Is cancer can be rather fun.
> I know that cancer often kills
> But so do cars and sleeping pills.

members of his family with him at the final moments. More than 55% of all deaths now occur in hospitals which manage "the crisis of dying." The mortuary industry—the term "funeral parlor" or "funeral home" nods to lost tradition—prepares the body and makes most of the arrangements. In urban centers, more than 90% of funerals start out from a mortuary, not a home. Thus the dying and the dead are segregated, placed in the hands of relatively impersonal specialists; "Neither their presence while alive nor as corpses interfere greatly with the mainstream of life," notes sociologist Robert Blauner.

The ascendancy of the funeral home is one sign of the bureaucratization of dying. It is easy to poke fun at or deplore the mortuary industry for its abuses: taking advantage of grief and bewilderment, overselling, making up a corpse so that "he never looked better in his life." "Mortuary science" is taught at colleges, and one of its professors, Robert Slater of the University of Minnesota, explains that most people are ripe for plucking, even demand it, whether or not the undertaker oversells. Professor Slater told a seminar that "it is tied in with identity notions . . . In most instances, the higher a person is on the income scale, the less expensive funeral [his family] buys proportionately. A $1,000 funeral for a wage earner in the $10,000 bracket would be looked upon by most people as a good or better than average funeral. The man with $100,000 income might be more likely to have the $400 or $500 one . . . When he dies the family doesn't feel that he needs one last attempt to say, 'Look who I am.'"

Nor do the likes of Freud, with his cremation, or Eleanor Roosevelt, in plain wooden coffin covered with pine boughs from her woods, have the need to say, "Look who I am."

*   *   *

"The feeling of health is only acquired by sickness. . . . When old age sets in, the state of being unwell becomes a sort of health, and we no longer notice that we are ill. Did not the recollection of the past remain, we should hardly be aware of the change. For this reason, I believe that it is only in our eyes that animals grow old. A squirrel that on its death day leads the life of an oyster is not unhappier than the oyster. Man, however, who lives in triplicate—in

the past, in the present, and in the future—may be rendered unhappy by but one of the three being amiss. Religion has even added
a fourth—eternity."

So Georg Christoph Lichtenberg explained how man alone is
aware, with increasing age, of changes in body and mind. The fear
of death, too, is not elemental or basic or primitive. Animals have no
such fear, nor do small children, at least not in the same sense that
adults do. At four, children may be terrified of dragons, the dark,
or thunder, but they perceive death differently, as a form of punish-
ment in some cases, or as the natural province of grown-ups (like
marriage or divorce) or of the old (and the old, in a child's mind,
have always been old; that is their station in life). Or as something
not quite permanent: "We buried our dog in the backyard. He's going
to come back in the spring." Mainly their views are shaped by
their parents—what they say within a child's hearing or how they
react to a death. From nine or ten on, a child will recognize that
death is final and inevitable. But fear of death itself, of being no
more, is not a child's persistent fear. A young man may feel that
he will never die; certainly he feels less threatened by the idea of
death than an older man. It is in the middle years, somewhere between 40 and 55, that the fear of death is strongest. It is a newly
developed fear made worse by every intimation of mortality, graying
hair, loss of physical stamina, the advent of wrinkles, aches, and ailments that most likely will never go away. The fear is often combined with anger or a sense of outrage that what a man or woman
has spent a lifetime building will some day collapse, that all is
wasted in the inevitability of death. The fear may become obsessive.
Older people have made the adjustment and are not particularly
afraid of dying; only about 10% expressed strong or marked fear
of death in a study of men and women between the ages of 50 and
86 made by the Gerontology Center of the University of Southern
California.

When an adult, young or old, learns that he is dying his responses
fall into a pattern. For her book *On Death and Dying,* Elisabeth
Kübler-Ross interviewed 500 hospital patients who had been told
or somehow became aware that they were hopelessly ill. She formulated five phases in the process of dying. Some overlap, some may
be skipped, but all are usually identifiable. The first stage is *denial.*
The patient may first react with shock. As the numbness wears off,

the feeling becomes, "No. It cannot be me." In the unconscious mind we are all immortal, death inconceivable. In this stage, a patient may demand more tests, change doctors, fight for a more promising prognosis.

When denial no longer works, the second stage begins: _anger._ "Why me? Why not somebody else?" The third stage is _bargaining,_ usually with God for a little more time in exchange for services rendered—"I will dedicate my life to God (or in the service of the church, or science)." The fourth stage is _depression,_ the point at which the case of the dying person becomes more difficult and family, medical personnel—and the patient—become more disengaged. The final stage is _acceptance,_ neither anger nor depression but "the final rest before the long voyage," one patient said. It is neither a happy nor an unhappy stage, but one almost void of feeling.

According to Kübler-Ross, most terminally ill patients know they are dying, whether they have been told or not. Cicely Saunders, medical director of St. Christopher's Hospice in London, says that 50% of her patients not only knew they were dying but talked about it with her. "Of the remaining 50%, there were some who were senile, some who had cerebral tumors, and some who were just not able to have insight," she says. Her feeling is akin to that of Kübler-Ross: "The real question is not 'What do you tell your patients?' but rather, 'What do you let your patients tell you?' Learn to hear what they are saying; what they are not saying; what is hidden underneath; what _is_ going on," Dr. Saunders says.

This is unquestionably sane and psychologically sound advice. Her hospital is exemplary; unfortunately, many urban hospitals do not have adequate facilities or personnel—psychologists, therapists, counselors—to treat the dying with such care and unhurriedly. It is not unknown, in some New York City hospitals for example, for a dying person to have most of his serious conversations about the meaning of life and death with a hospital orderly or cleaning woman and to find out that he is dying from the inadvertent remarks of a night nurse who thought the patient already knew, or did not have the time or wit to be politic.*

---

* A nurse who wittingly breaks the rules and informs a patient that he is dying will probably lose her job or her place in the referral system.

There is a doctor's joke about what to tell a patient who has been found to be incurably ill:

Patient: "Doctor, am I going to die?"

Doctor: "My dear fellow. That's the *last* thing you're going to do."

The ambiguity is not at all uncommon. About 80% of physicians in the United States do not believe in telling their patients the truth in such cases, according to a number of studies. Most say that "clinical experience" indicates that telling a patient will make him fall apart, and that it is cruel or sadistic to tell a patient something he does not want to know, and to deprive him of the hope necessary in a fight for life. But a sampling of sixty patients reported by Herman Feifel, a psychiatrist at the University of Southern California, showed that 82% wanted to be informed of their condition and to make their plans accordingly. (The figure of 80% or more has been substantiated by other studies.) It is quite possible, says Anselm L. Strauss, professor of sociology at the San Francisco Medical Center, that physicians, like others, "shy away from the embarrassment and brutality of making direct reference to another person about his impending death" as well as from the scene that is likely to follow.

Actually, the patient has the right to know and—as U.S. courts have ruled—the right to die without further medical therapy if he has no prognosis for recovery. The fact that a "patient has the right to withhold his consent to life-saving treatment" was made known to doctors by the American Medical Association's legal department in 1961; it was reaffirmed by the American Hospital Association early in 1973 in its Bill of Rights for hospital patients, approved by the AHA's board of trustees and consumer representatives after a three-year study. The 7,000 member hospitals of the association are expected to make copies available to all patients. Three of the twelve points say that a patient has the right:

- to obtain from his physician complete current information concerning his diagnosis, treatment, and prognosis in terms the patient can be reasonably expected to understand
- to receive from his physician information necessary to give informed consent prior to the start of any procedure and/or treatment, including the specific procedure, the risks, and probable duration of incapacitation

• to refuse treatment to the extent permitted by law, and to be informed of the medical consequences of his action

Still, practice has been contrary to this policy which has been urged upon hospitals by various associations for many years. Professor Strauss points out that "hospitals are admirably arranged, both by accident and design, to hide medical information from patients. Records are kept out of reach. Staff is skilled at withholding information. . . . Staff members are trained to discuss with patients only the surface aspects of their illnesses, and . . . are accustomed to acting collusively around patients so as not to disclose medical secrets."

One result is a serious undermining of the doctor-patient relationship since the patient is uncertain about how much or how honestly the doctor is reporting to him. This is not to indict the doctor: it is, to a large extent, through the advances of medical science that people now live longer and die more slowly. But one result, says medical historian Morris H. Saffron, is that "the general physician —formerly the great comforter—is now more than ever overwhelmed with the problem of the 'living dead.' " And, since the doctor himself has no secure philosophy of death and dying, "he finds it as difficult as any man to accept 'the death of myself.' "

The problem is greater still when the doctor is faced with the death of someone close to him personally; his wisdom and strength must be extraordinary. One man who coped with the problem admirably—and surmounted it—is a Los Angeles neurologist who, with his incurably ill wife, spent her last year together in therapy. "She was learning how to die; I was learning how to live without her," he said. "I think we both would have been the poorer if she had not been told she was going to die. It was a terrible year, of course, but it was also a year of great love and closeness. If I may use the term, it was a year of greatest beauty."

*   *   *

In the language of the medical profession, positive euthanasia involves "the institution of therapies that are hoped to promote death sooner than otherwise might occur in terminally ill patients." Negative euthanasia is "the planned omission of therapies that would prolong life in terminally ill patients." Freud had an understanding with his doctor and, when the time came, he was helped over his agony, his death presumably hastened—positive euthanasia. Eleanor Roosevelt's doctor, according to Joseph P. Lash, felt that "his duty as a doctor prevented him" from complying with her wishes and, apparently, she was denied either type. Hence her desperate efforts to avoid taking life-sustaining pills.

An overwhelmingly dramatic example of self-destruction to end the pain and indignities of terminal illness was that of Charles Wertenbaker, a former editor of *Time* magazine who lived with his wife and children in a Basque village in France. His wife, Lael Wertenbaker, tells the story in her book *Death of a Man* (later made into a play, *A Gift of Time*). Their French doctor had gone far beyond regulations in providing them with morphine derivatives but the doctor also believed, "truly and profoundly, that it was his duty, at any price, to prolong life as long as he could." Wertenbaker, at the age of 53, had reconciled himself to death from cancer and chose to die at a time and place of his own choosing. His last few days, as recounted by his wife, were ones of intense love, humor, and appreciation for the life they had known together. They were also days of pain, frantic phone calls to Paris to get more morphine, and abortive efforts to die from overdoses of it. Finally, with the help of his wife, Wertenbaker took his freshly stropped razor, cut his wrists, letting the blood flow into red casseroles so it would not spill onto bed and floor. The morphine and the razor took effect, even as his wife was saying, "I love you I love you I love you please die."

Former President Harry Truman, at 88, was kept alive for 22 days through intensive, extreme medical care; most hospital patients of his age and his condition would probably have been dead within a few days. Duke University's Dr. William Poe, who opposes keeping the incurably ill alive by extraordinary means, commented that "had I been in President Truman's place and had my wits about me, I would have said, 'Please spare me the anguish. Please don't pour life into me, don't treat me like a machine.' " But Dr. Poe also concedes that it is likely that there would be "natural pressures" from Truman's wife and daughter to keep him alive as long as possible. And there was the pressure, in the glare of public attention, to do everything possible to fight for the life of the former President.

The doctor's dilemma stems from the fact that the Hippocratic oath requires him to preserve life—and to relieve suffering; the two requirements are sometimes in conflict. The problem is compounded by the debates on the subject among lawyers, theologians, and doctors and by the fact that no one knows just who has the right to make the decision—patient, family, or doctor—and when? Despite all, euthanasia and suicide in the face of terminal illness are not uncommon, as doctors know very well. At a Hamline University symposium on death education, Dr. Zigfrids Stelmachers, professor of clinical psychology and director of a suicide prevention center in Minneapolis, was asked whether he considered self-destruction an irrational act. His response was "not necessarily, since many of the things that happen in people's lives give them rational reasons for ending them." A nurse said that a terminal cancer patient of hers had slashed his wrists; she asked the doctor: "Did anyone really have the right to stitch them back up?" His answer shows another side of the doctor's dilemma:

"A doctor is responsible to more than one set of ethics. It would make a pretty crude report if he were to write on the chart: 'I didn't stitch this patient because I decided he would be better off dead.' But obviously the circumstances do affect our ways of reacting to suicidal intent. Nurses and doctors may ignore or look the other way, when patients refuse treatment or remove some of their life-saving apparatus . . ."

Thus, the issue of euthanasia is considerably less controversial than it sometimes seems, and both euthanasia and "looking the other way" while terminally ill patients seek death probably occur quite often. The Roman Catholic Church, with its relatively rigid position against abortion on behalf of the sanctity of unborn life, has a milder view about the prolongation of life *in extremis*. In 1957, Pope Pius XII issued a pronouncement arguing that "normally one is held only to use *ordinary* means according to the circumstances of persons, places, times, and cultures, that is to say, means that do not involve any great burden for one's self or another." Dr. Robert Veatch, in interpreting the pronouncement from a Catholic point of view, says that a procedure is "extraordinary or ordinary depending on the condition of the patient . . . It would be considered extraordinary if it is exceptionally costly, unusual, painful, or dangerous considering the condition of the patient. An example would be the use of a kidney machine. In technological terms it is an extraordinary procedure. Yet if the kidney machine returned the person to many years of reasonably normal and productive life, you might want to call it an ordinary procedure. On the other hand, if the kidney machine patient found himself to be a slave to the machine, found that the machine made life inhuman, found that life was meaningless and its maintenance extremely painful and costly, then the procedure might be seen as extraordinary."

However, Dr. Veatch makes clear that positive euthanasia, taking action to hasten death, is against Catholic ethical teaching—as, of course, is suicide, "which interrupts the process of living."

"Refusing to prolong the dying process is radically different from ending the living process," he writes. "What is crucial is the patient's right to control the ethical choice . . . [But] there is no moral imperative to preserve life at all costs or to prolong the dying with useless remedies . . ."

Euphemisms seem to be in order when the subject is so disagreeable a matter as death or, as in this case, negative euthanasia. A recent issue of the *AARP News Bulletin* (of the American Association of Retired Persons) featured an article on "Death with Dignity" ("The desire to die with dignity and not to be kept alive by heroic means when there is no chance to recover," was the *News Bulletin* definition). Opposed to this was an argument for "maximum care," calling for the use of all resources of medical science to the last breath and, possibly, beyond. The publication reported that it had received 250 letters in response to the feature; only 35 letter-writers supported "maximum care," while 215, many of whom "had seen a loved one's life prolonged when death was imminent," endorsed the idea of "death with dignity." The letters against negative euthanasia usually mentioned the responsibility of a doctor to his Hippocratic oath and the idea that where there's life there's hope. Those in favor of it cited the pain, futility, expense, and emotional drain on a family in prolonging life when a condition was clearly terminal and the conviction that, given the unalterable facts, a patient has a right to his choice in the matter.

The doctor's responsibility is staggering; all decisions stem from his professional appraisal of the inevitability of death. Many doctors accept it without the compunctions of Mrs. Roosevelt's physician. Dying patients and their families often request or implore doctors to stop treatment; a study reported in the *Journal of the American Medical Association* in 1970 found that 38% of the doctors questioned had received requests for negative euthanasia from patients; 54% had received them from patients' relatives. In 1969, Dr. Robert H. Williams reported a survey of doctors showing that 87% favored negative euthanasia and that, indeed, 80% of them had practiced it. (Fifteen per cent of them said that they were in favor of positive euthanasia as well.) Dr. Williams said that both patient and family "probably desire negative euthanasia far more often than this is practiced by the physician."

The relatives of dying patients, to judge from some of the letters to the AARP *News Bulletin,* often believe that doctors will not let a patient die because doctors and hospitals make more money by keeping them alive to the bitter or painful end. This is probably rarely, if ever, the case; even if a doctor calculates that way, there is not much profit in prolonging dying, and hospital facilities everywhere are taxed. It is the weight of social convention and "morality" that inhibit doctors from practicing euthanasia more than they do. Positive euthanasia is rejected in traditional Christian belief chiefly because it appears to conflict with the prohibition of murder in the Sixth Commandment; Socrates, Plato, and the Stoics considered it morally permissible. Switzerland, since 1937, has given direct sanction to a form of euthanasia; a Swiss physician may provide, but not administer, a lethal drug at the request of a suffering patient. The Swiss federal code says that lending assistance with a view to suicide is punishable only if the assister was impelled by selfish motives. Both the United States and Great Britain have had societies to legalize euthanasia since the 1930s but have had only limited success.*

A panel of the British Medical Association in 1970 pointed up the disadvantages of legislation and gave sharp focus to the

---

* A standard euphemism for euthanasia—"mercy killing"—is itself a hindrance to their success. When pet animals are relieved of their misery, the term is a more gentle and acceptable one—"putting to sleep."

issue: What is needed, the doctors said, is not legislation for euthanasia but more resources for the care of the elderly and the chronic sick and a change in attitude toward them. They said that no doctor or nurse should be asked to assume the responsibility for administering euthanasia.

The British doctors said that there was no way that euthanasia legislation could provide adequate safeguards and that if euthanasia were permitted, the relationship between doctor and patients would be placed in jeopardy. "To be a trusted physician is one thing, to appear as a potential executioner is quite another," they said. This is the conservative position and the public one. Meanwhile, there is little doubt that many doctors do, indeed, exercise their private options.

Much of the professional literature on the subject seems to favor euthanasia for patients who are clearly dying. Favoring euthanasia is a "psychologically desirable attitude toward life and death," David Cappon concluded a decade ago in an article in the *Canadian Medical Association Journal*. He also found that the majority of the dying "want some control over the time and manner of their deaths."

This concerns dying people of all ages. Stewart Alsop once said, while he was fighting leukemia, "when you feel sick enough, you don't much fear death, and even half welcome it. In such ways, God tempers the wind to the shorn lamb." But how do old people, not yet facing death, feel about euthanasia? Dr. Williams and an associate recently reported on a study of 35 women and 65 men with a mean age of 72 and an age range from 60 to 95 years. They all lived in a publicly supported home for the aged or in a private nursing home. Two-thirds of them said they felt well at the time of their interviews and were not particularly concerned about their health; a majority of the total—like most people no matter what their age—rejected the stereotype of being old. In the course of their interviews they were confronted with hypothetical conditions of great distress, heavy medical expenses, and fatal illness. Almost half wanted life at any cost. About a quarter said, in effect, "Let me die but don't kill me." And about a third said, "Let me die or help me die." The evidence that the subjects did indeed have such preferences was unequivocal, the authors of the report said.

"Toward the actual person who has died we adopt a special attitude; something like admiration for someone who has accomplished a very difficult task," Sigmund Freud wrote in *Thoughts for the Times on War and Death*. The attitudes of the living (and the dying themselves) toward that "difficult task" are influenced mainly by age, more than by other circumstances of death or religious faith.

Indeed, religion appears to be less and less a factor in shaping views toward death. Both Freud and Eleanor Roosevelt were sustained by other than conventional faiths. A study reported in Feifel's *The Meaning of Death* suggests that religious orientation, in western societies at least, has only limited bearing upon a person's anxieties about death. There may be a greater degree of religiosity in later life but, unless one has the faith of a zealot—a Joan of Arc or a John Brown—it is not necessarily sustaining in the face of death. Church activities and Bible reading give many older people the comfort of a return to earlier habits, the counsel of a minister, and a highly acceptable widening of what might otherwise be an utterly drab social life. But even though a person may believe that his religion offers salvation or a hereafter, he may also feel that he is inadequately prepared for it or be guilt-ridden or suspect that he is not in a state of grace and does not truly deserve it. A 1958 study of the "sociology of death" reported that "emotional responses suggesting either fear of death or of the dead were more frequent among spiritually oriented than among temporally oriented individuals." The alternatives of heaven or hell seem to frighten more than to give courage.

Age is the determinant. Death means one thing at 20, something else at 40, something else again at 60. And after 70, most people have come to face the idea of death with a reasonable amount of equanimity.* They have seen too·many friends and family members

* Unless a person feels so strongly about tasks undone and creativity unspent or the life force remains dominant for other reasons. Even the personal milestones of life are enough to keep a person, no matter how old or sick, fighting to stay alive. A study of death rates of famous Americans noted that death was least likely to occur in the months preceding a birthday. Other studies show that an old person will manage to keep alive until, for example, a fiftieth wedding anniversary party, or the birth of a new grandchild, or the wedding of an older one.

die; what seemed unjust in middle age has come to seem merely inevitable. One study of 35 geriatric patients found that 21 had made positive references to dying, accepting the idea of their own deaths calmly; 11 made neutral references; only 3 expressed alarm, fear, or apprehension.

The society about them also accepts the death of older persons with greater equanimity. Psychiatrist Sidney Levin cites the experience of a newspaper reporter assigned, as a cub, to writing obituaries. He said he could tell the age of the deceased without asking for it or looking it up but just by the attitudes of the people he telephoned in the course of writing a story. The writer describing this said that "when young people die, even when there has been some warning, there is devastation; old people leave a composed sadness. It was not, [the reporter] felt, because there was less love but because there is 'a time for living and a time for dying.' "

Dr. Levin says that most likely there is less grief over the death of an old person because libidinal attachments have already been weakened or severed. Long before death, the doctor suggests, an aged person feels this withdrawal of libido and "intuitively perceives that others are not only waiting for his death but also wishing for it."

Disengagement—"the decreased interaction between the aging person and others"—is particularly marked among people who are in institutions of one sort or another; there is evidence that far from fearing death they are the ones who await it, sometimes expectantly, as their lot and their release. It is probably better, some psychiatrists have said, for a hospital room or ward for the very old or dying *not* to be absolutely silent but to be reasonably noisy, with the comings and goings of well people and other sounds of life. Even young and healthy people, when they are sealed off in silence, without human communication, tend to lose normal perceptions and balance and, if isolated long enough, go mad. It is no different for the old.

The old and sick have another problem, uniquely their own, particularly if an old person is to die in an institution. Now disengagement is almost complete. His time has run out, and so has the patience of those who will survive him. The family, un-

consciously or not, would like it all to be over; there has been
too much expense in time and money, too much intrusion in their
lives—no matter what their protestations of love, no matter how
much sorrow they will express after the death.

When a geriatric patient wants to talk about his impending death,
the family will pretend and protest, "Shh. Don't talk that way."
Many old patients have a compelling need to talk about themselves,
their lives, and their deaths. Doctors and nurses too—perhaps 95%
of them—will shun the topic. But talking about death is not a
matter of personal distress for the dying old patient. Besides, if he
is very old, he will tend to lose much of his self-concept; in talking
about death he may blur the distinction between his death and that
of others. All are being carried away in the river of time.

Psychotherapists, too—as understanding as they may try to be—
often avoid contact or conversation with the geriatric patient.
There is pain in it for them, says Robert Kastenbaum, because "the
old patient's anguish may well be a forecast and foretaste of the
clinician's own future dilemma. To share over and over again the
anguish that old age can bring is not a prospect that most therapists
are likely to find appealing."

There is also the bleak outlook for satisfaction. Many psychotherapists feel that since old people do not have much time to live,
"it is just not worthwhile to put in so much effort for so little return,"
Kastenbaum says. Furthermore, the clinician probably anticipates
a joyless relationship with an aged patient. The stereotype is that
love and pleasure are the province of the young and that depression
in a young man in unnatural and may be treated and cured. But
depression in the old, a psychotherapist may feel, is normal and
untreatable, the situation to be shunned. The clinician is wrong,
but he is also human.

Both Freud and Eleanor Roosevelt were mentally alert long
after terminal illness had set in, Freud almost to the final moment
of consciousness. Ernest Jones mentioned that the dying Freud
communicated with him at their last meeting with a look and wave
of the hand. Much of the communication with a dying person is
nonverbal: a look or touch to show support or understanding.* But

---

* Dr. Charles A. Leale, tending the mortally wounded Abraham
Lincoln in the house across the street from Ford's Theater, carried this

often the healthy person does not even try to communicate. There is a common assumption that the old are in poor mental contact as they are dying; it is not unusual for family and friends to talk in the presence of a dying old man as though he were no longer there, or to ignore him, assuming that his mind is as ravaged by age and sickness as his body.

Dr. Kastenbaum once tested this assumption through the use of "psychological autopsies"—the study of the mental life of dying geriatric patients through interviews with the doctors, nurses, social workers, chaplains, therapists, and psychologists who had treated them. They were asked to evaluate the mental condition of people they had come to know well—61 men and women, with an age span of 69 to 96 years, who had been hospital patients for at least two years.

The study found that almost half—49%—of the dying old patients were "consistently in clear contact until death," 26% "fluctuated between clear contact and confusion," and 22% were "consistently in partial contact." Only two of the 61 patients were "consistently out of contact" during the last days of their lives.

These findings, his study concludes, give no credence at all to the notion that the thinking processes of the typical aged and dying person are massively impaired. Yet the notion is a common one and in it rests the ultimate horror of being old: being cut off from life while the mind is still active and the emotions still pleading for love and response—indeed, of being "buried alive."

---

to the extreme. He wrote of that long night: "Knowledge that frequently just before departure recognition and reason return to those who have been unconscious caused me for several hours to hold his right hand firmly within my grasp to let him in his blindness know, if possible, that he was in touch with humanity and had a friend."

13 AGE AND ACHIEVEMENT

How long can we continue to be creative?

The answer is, to the end of our years. Just as memory and intelligence may be sustained all through the process of growing old, so, too, may creativity. But the key to the question is the word "continue." The greater our intelligence in youth, the more apt we are to increase and sustain our intelligence in old age. The more creative we are in youth, the greater chance we have to be creative as we age, even striking out into new, unexplored fields of endeavor and achievement.

It is comforting, as one grows older, to look at the examples of remarkable men of 70, 80, or more who have created masterpieces, made great scientific discoveries, or somehow shaped and moved the world. The list is long, memorable, and extends throughout history:

- Konrad Adenauer (*"der Alte"*), who became chancellor of West Germany at the age of 73, leading the remarkable reconstruction of that country for 14 years
- Sophocles writing *Oedipus Rex* at 75
- John XXIII, elected pope at 77, going on to bring new, modern concepts to Roman Catholicism
- Gandhi serving as the moving force behind his people's drive for freedom and reform until cut down at 78
- Voltaire, when past 80, leading his country's struggle for greater respect for the rights of man

243

- Goethe completing the last part of his *Faust* shortly before his death at 83
- Sigmund Freud writing *Moses and Monotheism* at 83
- Verdi composing his tragic masterpiece *Otello* at 73, completing *Falstaff* at 80, *Te Deum* at 85
- Michelangelo, architect of St. Peter's, working on his sculpture virtually until the day of his death at 89
- Bertrand Russell, who died at 97, choosing to enter prison at the age of 89 to dramatize his quest for universal freedom from the terror of nuclear weapons
- Pablo Picasso continuing to paint prolifically until his death at 91
- Pablo Casals, who for three-quarters of a century was considered the greatest cellist of all time, continuing to play, conduct, and teach master classes up to his death at 96

The list may be extended indefinitely—Einstein and Schweitzer, Tolstoy and Shaw, Toscanini and Stravinsky—and everyone seems to have his favorite great and illustrious man or woman, to serve as a model and a hope.

The list is comforting to the extent that it shows how vitality, intelligence, and creativity may be sustained into advanced old age. But it must be read carefully if we are to have realistic expectations for ourselves.

Many people feel, "I just haven't got started yet. Some day soon, when I'm 50 or 60, I, too, am going to write that book (or paint that masterpiece, or make the great invention, or find fame and fortune somehow)." But we are, really, the same persons at 50, 60, or 80 that we were at 30. We flourish and mature and gain greater skills and wisdom, but the chances for being creative in old age are immeasurably enhanced if we have been creative in youth and middle age. None of the men on the list were, in any sense, late bloomers. All had made considerable impact in their worlds—or showed their genius—long before they reached old age and, indeed, usually before middle age. For better or worse, it appears that a man's thirties are his golden age for creative achievement.

For many years, Harvey C. Lehman, professor of psychology at

Ohio University in Athens, Ohio, studied the relationships between chronological age and outstanding creative achievement in science, medicine, art, literature, philosophy, invention, athletics, entertainment, politics, religion, business, and other fields of endeavor. He started writing on the subject in 1928 and twenty-five years later published *Age and Achievement,* a book studded with facts, statistics, and tables confirming that in the most creative activities, in literature, the arts and sciences, the most creative years, when the most durable work of finest quality is done, are 30 to 39—and sometimes younger.

Lehman was somewhat obsessed with his subject and, after a while, tended to get defensive about his findings. In 1962, he reported that he had, for the first time, undertaken a study of living scientists, compared them to scientists in the past, and had come to the same conclusion: "Both past and present generation scientists have produced more than their proportionate share of high quality research *not later than* at ages 30 to 39 and it is as useless to bemoan this fact as to deny it."

Lehman's methodology has withstood criticism. His system was simple and laborious. He would select the evidence of outstanding achievements from source and reference books and original documents, cross-referencing when possible, without considering the ages of the achievers. He would then classify them according to the age when produced, and compute the average production per age interval. A large enough sample of achievements permitted reliable comparisons to be made between different age groups.

He depended upon specialists, more qualified than he, to judge the quality of an achievement. In chemistry, for example, he pored through Hilditch's *A Concise History of Chemistry,* which tells when nearly 250 noted chemists first published accounts of what later proved to be outstanding contributions. Nearly 1,000 contributions were tabulated. The highest proportion of these occurred when the contributors were in the 30-34 age group; two-thirds of all contributions were made before 40, only 3% after 60.

He then asked three colleagues, chemists, to select the 100 most important contributions of the 1,000. They agreed on 52; these were then considered "high quality" contributions. The age distribution for them is revealing: They began when the chemists were in their early twenties, and the rate of output increased rapidly up to the ages 25-29. This early peak was followed by a sharp decline which ended completely by the age of 60. Lehman concluded, from this and other studies, that highest-quality achievement occurs earlier in life than achievement of lesser merit and that it declines more rapidly. While the "total output" of a sample of authors fell off slowly with age, the rate of output for an author's one "best book" —using that as a measure of quality—fell off steeply after the middle thirties. A study of poets showed an early peak period, 25-29, an abrupt decline to ages 35-39, then a very gradual decline up to the age of 90.

Criticism of Lehman's work usually concerns the validity of the choice of "best work," although he carefully selected specialists to make the selection, without reference to age. Then there are differences affecting performance within each creative field which have nothing to do with age or intelligence: An historian may have to wait later in life to do his best work, after he has gained time for research and, perhaps, the use of a research staff.* But a poet is unalterably alone, has no such needs, and does his best work much earlier. (The evidence is that there are few great poets who did not show signs of their greatness by the age of 15.)

The age trends fluctuated somewhat in the creative fields, but the general picture was consistent. However, when Lehman got into business and government, the age groups for achievement were much higher. Recalling that his findings were published in 1953, "Receivers of 'earned' annual incomes of $50,000 or more" were in the 60-to-64 age group; outstanding commercial and industrial leaders, 65 to 69; presidents of American colleges and universities, 50 to 54; presidents of the U.S. prior to Harry Truman, 55 to 59; men in charge of the U.S. Army from 1925 to 1945, 60 to 64; speakers of the U.S. House of Representatives from 1900 to 1940, 70 to 74; popes, 82 to 92.

* The principle applies in many fields. For example, architect Edward Durell Stone says that his is not a young man's profession since people hesitate to entrust huge sums of money to an architect until he has built up an organization. "As a rule of thumb," he says, "an architect only tools up for his life's work when he's about 50—so it pays to keep his health and live forever if he wants to get that life's work done."

A glance at the average ages of recent presidents of the United States from Harry S Truman to Richard M. Nixon shows that they are no younger than presidents of the past. (Theodore Roosevelt, not John F. Kennedy, was the youngest man ever to become president.) That is also true for leadership of European and Asian countries; today's legislative, judicial, diplomatic, religious, educational, and military leaders are as old as or older than those of past years and centuries. It is only the "creative" achievers who tend to be younger and younger.

Gerontologist Dennis B. Bromley of the University of Liverpool explains why leadership skills occur much later in life than scientific and artistic ones—and why this fact presents a peril:

Becoming a leader requires more than a balance of intelligence and experience. It also requires access to the levers of power. "The membership of older people on committees, councils, and other bodies puts into their hands the machinery of social control," Dr. Bromley says, "and their familiarity with this machinery—rules, procedures, rituals, ways and means, sources of information and the like—enables them to use their experience where a young man's greater intelligence might avail him little."

A nation's or a community's leaders are masters of the social skills, the last to develop in the life cycle, and their achievement usually represents a slow building up of power and prestige, the manipulation and assistance of many techniques and forces. Bromley sees the hazard in this: The divorce of leadership skill from intellectual ability means that older people in influential positions cling to "older, familiar attitudes and methods and resist the introduction of social reforms—for example in penology, education, and the armed forces—which they may be unable to understand." The clash of age and viewpoint is, of course, frequently and violently heard; the "revolution" of May 1968 in Paris and campus eruptions throughout the United States are clear examples.

Lehman did not intend, in any way, to debunk great old men and their achievements. To avoid that suggestion, he carefully included in his book chapters of almost identical length on "Young Thinkers and Great Achievements" and on "Older Thinkers and Great Achievements." He did not put Thomas Alva Edison in either category, probably because Lehman thought of him as a practical inventor, not as a thinker. Edison took out his last patent in 1928, three years before his death at the age of 84. But Lehman disposes of him—and goes on to make his primary point—with the use of a chart showing the ages at which Edison's lifetime total of 1,086 patents were granted. The chart shows that 35 was Edison's most productive age. Between the ages of 33 to 36, he took out a total of 312 U.S. patents—more than a fourth of all the U.S. patents he applied for during his inventive career of over sixty years.

Lehman's chapter on "Young Thinkers and Great Achievements" shows how creative people get started early. Among its facts: Jane Austen wrote *Pride and Prejudice* when she was 20 (although it was not published until sixteen years later).* William Cullen Bryant finished writing "Thanatopsis" when he was 18. Samuel Colt was 18 when he sent a description of a "multi-shot firearm of the revolving barrel type" to the U.S. Patent Office. John Keats wrote "On First Looking into Chapman's Homer" at 20. Guglielmo Marconi transmitted signals one mile without wires at 20. Felix Mendelssohn's overture to "A Midsummer Night's Dream" was performed when he was 17. Giambattista della Porta first described the *camera obscura,* pinhole and all, when he was 15. Justus von Liebig discovered fulminic acid when he was 16. (Lehman was then solely concerned with thinkers already dead, otherwise he might have included Albert Einstein who, in 1905, at age 26, produced four papers each containing a great discovery in physics, one of them the creation of the special theory of relativity.)

* Women live longer than men, a type of superiority in itself, and specialists in aging are hardly the ones to hold prejudiced notions about them. Still, women occupy little space in Lehman's book on age and achievement throughout history. The reason why is made clear in Lewis M. Terman's study of about 1,500 intellectually superior elementary and high school children with a mean intelligence quotient of 150. Dr. Terman reviewed their development and achievements over an eighteen-year period and noted that although "the women equal or excel the men in school achievement from the first grade through college, after school days are over the great majority cease to compete with men in the world's work . . . The woman who is a potential poet, novelist, lawyer, physician, or scientist usually gives up any professional ambition she may have had and devotes herself to home, husband, and children. The exclusive devotion of women to domestic pursuits robs the arts and sciences of a large fraction of the genius that might otherwise be dedicated to them."

In citing these cases, Lehman warned that an early start at one's life work will not implant potential talent where no talent previously existed. But sometimes, talent is thrown away by delay in using it: "when potential ability is present but remains undeveloped for too long a time, subsequent efforts to develop it may be less successful than earlier efforts would have been."

The ages for peak achievement among "most highly successful athletes" are surprisingly close to the age for peak intellectual achievement—a harsh fact to an athlete whose career is much shorter and may be over just after he reaches that peak. Among Lehman's examples: professional football players, 22 to 26; professional prize fighters, 25 to 26; professional baseball players, 27 to 28; professional tennis players, 25 to 29; both professional golfers and "winners of important bowling championships," 31 to 36. He found that leading contestants at chess were between the ages of 29 and 33; a scientist commenting on this said that "it appears almost as difficult to win a chess championship after 50 as it is to win a tennis championship." (Boris Spassky, at 34, did sometimes seem like a burnt-out case in the "chess match of the century" won by Bobby Fischer, then 29.)

Lehman also studied the careers of film stars and found that actresses tend to rise to fame at an earlier age and to reach the peak of their fortunes earlier than actors—25 to 29 years compared to 30 to 34. Their decline was found to be faster than that of men, too. And, as in intellectual achievement, the higher the level of a film star's achievement, the faster the rate of decline with age after the peak years. (This offers logical explanation for some of the frenzy and desperation in the entertainment world.)

This is a further sampling of Lehman's ages for "maximum average rate of highly superior production" in various creative fields:

- Ages 30 to 34: mathematics, physics, electronics, practical inventions, botany; composition of vocal solos and symphonies; writing of short stories and satiric poetry
- Ages 35 to 39: geology, astronomy, physiology, medical discoveries; composition of chamber music, orchestral music, and grand opera; writing of books on logic, ethics, esthetics, and general philosophy; contributions to educational theory and economics; American sculpture

- Ages 40 to 44: composition of cantatas, light opera, and musical comedy; writing of best sellers; modern architecture

Lehman suggested why the best creative years in the arts and sciences start and end so early in life. As we age, he said, several or all of the following factors are most likely to contribute to the decline in achievement of any one person:

- Physical vigor, energy, and resistance to fatigue may start to decline even before the age of 40.
- A diminution in sensory and motor capacities (including impaired vision or hearing)
- Poor physical or mental health
- Glandular change and metabolic deficiencies
- Personal maladjustment and related problems which worsen with age
- Older persons—after 35 or 40—tend to become preoccupied with practical concerns, earning a living and getting ahead, and become more "realistic," often losing the capacity to experiment or take chances.
- A man who was successful early in life may no longer try as hard; he already has some prestige and recognition, which may have been his primary motivation. And too easy, too great, or too early fame may breed complacency.
- An older person may be deadened by nonrecognition, by destructive criticism, or by his inability to "make it."
- Increased apathy or passivity with age
- Younger persons tend to have better formal education, may have grown to maturity in a more stimulating social and cultural milieu—and may have had less time to forget what they've learned.

Other writers on the subject face up to the same reality. It's best to get started early. There is some self-deception in clinging, uncritically, to that list of great old men and their achievements. Benjamin Franklin *did* invent bifocals in 1784 at the age of 78 but, in the course of his varied and splendid careers, he had long since proven himself an inventive genius with far more daring or difficult discoveries to his credit, including his experiments with electricity and the development of the Franklin stove more than forty years earlier. Sigmund Freud felt that in his last great work *Moses and Monotheism* he was going over old ground, and he said of it, "An old man no longer discovers new ideas. All that is left to him is repetition." Art historian and critic Bernard Berenson, who died at 94, felt that "what a man writes after 60 is worth little more than tea continually made from the same leaves."

Winston Churchill died at 91 and seems to appear on everyone's list of great old men although his decline had set in by the time he reached 70. Churchill was a late bloomer in one sense only: He became prime minister of a Britain at war in 1940 at the age of 66, old for a man who had been famous for so long. But Churchill was also an exceptional *young* man, always in a hurry. (He was even born prematurely.) By 1898, at the age of 24, he earned his first fame as an author for his dispatches from India, where he served with the Malakand field forces. He was first elected to Parliament at the age of 26 to become a major and controversial force in his nation's life during the forty years before he became prime minister. Churchill's physical decline apparently started in 1943, and he was never the same man again. He needed considerable help in the writing of his World War II memoirs. In 1949, he had a stroke; his memory weakened, and he became deaf. Occasionally he roused himself to show glints of his old greatness, but the notes of his doctor, Lord Moran, are a record of a long pathetic struggle against physical and mental decay. In the last sixteen years of his life, he was fading rapidly and was often a source of acute embarrassment to his colleagues in public life.

The list *does* wind down. Igor Stravinsky may—or may not—have written all the articles and books or made all the recordings attributed to him in his later years; the suspicion is raised by Lillian Libman, his personal manager for the twelve years preceding his death at 89 in 1971. Albert Schweitzer, philosopher and humanitarian among other things, spent half a century in Gabon and, until his death at 90, had the same limited view of Africans as when he first arrived; they were to be treated as children, to be scolded and punished as he, their Alsatian grandfather, decided. Professor Lehman was too kind a man to bolster his case by mentioning that Thomas Edison, in his later years, doggedly fought against the introduction of alternating current.

Still, the greater fact is not that some of the men on the roster of the creative and great old had foibles or that they lost some of their energy of youth. It is that all of them continued to function, create, and contribute to the world long past the usual time of retirement.

Most of them lived in times when life was much harder than it is today. That alone makes their acts of creativity all the more remarkable. The everyday needs of survival often choked off creativity in the past. Given today's signs, there is good chance that the old will have much greater opportunity to use their creative impulses in the future. With new leisure, greater independence and security, they will be able to turn even unsuspected talents to use. Many of the reasons Lehman gave for the falling off of creative energy will lose their validity. The health of the old will be better, the best-functioning years prolonged by medical science. And their greater security will allow the aging and old to have more of the freedom of thought and expression needed to be creative.

Even today, examples of creativity unleashed in old age abound. Newspapers frequently report—as news—the stories of a man going back to college at 73 to get the degree he didn't complete fifty years earlier because he had to support his family; of a grandmother of 68 who takes up flying to help a doctor reach remote towns in the Canadian wilderness; of a man of 82 entering politics—to become president of a town council; of a woman who turns from photography to painting at 55, then starts sculpting at 70. In fact, there are so many instances of this kind that what is more remarkable is that newspapers still treat them as phenomena.*

---

* It is easier to understand why newspapers treat *negative* achievement among the old as a phenomenon. The following story fully warrants the attention given to it by the Associated Press:
Woman, 90, Held As Drug Pusher
Philadelphia, June 12, 1973.—Police have a 90-year-old woman narcotics suspect on their hands.
Police said Mrs. Francis Kelly was arrested Saturday night after several women complained that she was selling narcotics. The arresting officer said he chased her a short distance and caught her when she failed in an attempt to climb a wall. Police said the woman dropped three glazed packets containing a white powder believed to be heroin. A neighbor said she had noticed teen-agers going in an out of Mrs. Kelly's home lately.

Examples taken from four different fields show how creativity may develop in old age, either in new guise or as a continuation of earlier work:

• In painting: Grandma Moses, past manual labor at 75, turned to her new career with an energy and skill that can hardly be explained, and spent the last twenty-five years of her life earning fame and considerable fortune. Hers is a rare case; until 75, she had given no indication of her extraordinary talent to recapture, in primitive style, the scenes of her childhood. (A retired Israeli diamond cutter—Shalom of Safed—started painting in his seventies and now, in his mid-eighties, has achieved nationwide and some international renown. He is often referred to, naturally, as Grandpa Moses.)

• In literature: William de Morgan was an English ceramic artist whose works are still on display at the Victoria and Albert Museum in London. Retiring as an artist at the age of 66 in 1905, he took up writing. In the remaining twelve years of his life he wrote *Joseph Vance, Alice for Short,* and seven other novels (two published posthumously) which earned him money, distinction and a reputation as "the modern Dickens." No less remarkable was the great novelist Thomas Hardy, who began writing lyrical poetry in his late sixties and produced a sizable body of fine verse until his death at 88.

• In education and social action: Ethel Percy Andrus was a retired high school principal when she founded the National Retired Teachers Association in 1957. Eleven years later—at age 74—she established the American Association of Retired Persons to help the old attain "goals of personal dignity and social usefulness by recognizing their individual worth." She was a joyous, energetic woman—with great leadership qualities barely evident in her teaching years—until her death in 1967 at 83.

• In making use of retirement: Lillian Martin retired from Stanford University to become a counsellor to the aged. She learned to drive a car at 76, traveled up the Amazon River at 88, and undertook the running of a 50-acre farm at 99 (with four 60-year-old women to help her). Dr. Martin summed up the prospects for the rest of us when she said about age and achievement: Life can be reclaimed by making good use of mental processes long disused, and "normal human beings learn to grow at any age."

14 THE GOOD LONG LIFE

Man dreads old age and its disfigurements, death and its darkness, and has dreamed a thousand ways to avoid them or keep them at bay.

Elixirs and potions and fountains of youth. Brewer's yeast, organic foods, yogurt, and yoga. Handball, water skiing, and new "passions" every seven years. Hot baths, Couéism, face lifts, and "scientific exercises."

In the brandy district of Cognac, there are more centenarians than anywhere else in France, suggesting one prescription for the good long life. Konrad Adenauer believed that standing erect whenever possible was a good way to fight infirmities of age. (He died at 91.) U.S. billionaire H. L. Hunt, at 83, announced that creeping on all fours several times a day keeps him fit and young. "The Hunzakuts of the Himalayas live to play polo in their 100's," he said. "I can do that." Body and food cultist Bernarr MacFadden lived to 87 and, according to his wife, kept his virility right up to his death. Her prescription for the good long life, offered at age 66, is vegetables, wheat germ, and bicycle riding, "but I believe the best exercise is sex."

Sex, or at least the rejuvenation of reproductive organs, has been a preoccupation for centuries among men trying to stay the inevitable. The elders of ancient India and China, 3,000 years ago, are supposed to have eaten the sexual organs of wild animals to improve their vigor and offset decline. The servants of a King David "stricken in years" urged that he be brought the fairest virgin in Israel to "let her lie in thy bosom, that my lord the king may get heat." (Abishag became companion to the king and ministered to him, but David "knew her not.") Within the past hundred years, particularly in Europe, doctors and surgeons have acquired fame and notoriety for experiments with injections or transplants of testicular material from healthy young animals in older animals or humans to bring about "new enjoyment of life." Among the doctors are Charles Edouard Brown-Sequard, Jürgen W. Harms, Eugen Steinach, and Serge Voronoff, with the last, perhaps, the best known for his transplants of monkey glands in men. (None of these procedures has withstood the test of time very well. There is no evidence that aging of the body as a whole depends on the activity or failure of the sexual glands *per se*.)

Some people look to the deep-freezing of a now incurably sick body, to be unfrozen at some future date when a cure for the sickness will have been found.* Others, much more realistically, look to the lessons to be learned from the Abkhasians and other Caucasian peasants of the USSR who have a disproportionate number of centenarians among them. In Abkhasia in 1954, the last year overall figures were available, 2.58% of the population was over 90—a percentage twenty-five times higher than in the Soviet Union generally and six times higher than in the United States. The Abkhasians themselves attribute their longevity to their practices in work (retirement is unknown), in sex (30 is considered the right age for a man to begin regular sexual relations), and in diet. (Eat slowly, chew carefully; little meat, much corn meal mush; a variety of fresh fruits and vegetables, plus pickled vegetables, buttermilk, and abundant but low-alcohol wine; day-old food is considered unhealthful.)

Can we successfully adopt any of these lessons to increase our life span? The answer is yes and no. Some are valid, none are valid—depending on how we define "life span" and what we expect. D. Chebotarev of the USSR Academy of Medical Sciences, Institute of Gerontology of Kiev, tells us that 100 years is about the life expectancy of man as a biological species. But few people live that

* The science of cryonics. Average cost: $20,000 a person.

long; even in the Soviet Union there are but 21,000 centenarians in a population of 240 million. An average life expectancy in the Western world in this century is from 70 to 75 years; this may improve gradually, along with improvements in standards of living, to around 80, he believes. "It is quite probable that when we learn to influence man's genetic material, we will be able to improve his life span," he adds.

Academician Chebotarev is impatient with unrealistic hopes. "Rejuvenation" is a term used frequently by popular writers, and he says that "if anyone thinks it is possible, in any way, to grow younger, I must answer him with a categorical no."

'A person of 40 who looks 70 must have grown prematurely old for a number of reasons," he explains. "If geriatric therapy is *completely* successful, we may make our patient look his age —40. Can this be called rejuvenation? If a miracle worker could turn him into a 30-year-old, perhaps that would be rejuvenation. This never happens in real life."

He feels that newspaper articles that hold out the promise of rejuvenation and the prolongation of life expectancy to 300 years are harmful because they distract from the real task of gerontology today which, he says, is the fight against premature old age. "And there are still so many mysteries about arteriosclerosis, cancer, and hypertension," says Dr. Chebotarev.

The elimination of these three may add about seven years to man's present average expectation of life of 70 to 75 years, he believes. Getting rid of unfavorable environmental factors—measures to improve everyday life and reduce emotional wear and tear—may add another seven or eight years. (He is not at all sure this is possible in today's society.) Other "biological methods"—the use of vitamins, hormones, adaptagens, and the like—may also help man to reach a biological life span of 100.

Beyond that? Well, "healthy old age, marked by wisdom, is not distressing at all and need not be fought. It is a natural process in the human organism," he says.

To a large extent, the longevity of each individual is determined at birth. Every important study ever made on the subject, said Stephen Jewett, an American gerontologist and psychiatrist, sup ports the fact that heredity is the most important of all the components that determine the potential life span of a person—the longest period that he may be expected to live. Dr. Jewett asked—and answered—two highly relevant questions:

"Can an individual, by giving thought, add even *one week* to his potential life span?" Can diet, work habits, exercise, state of mind add to a man's potential life span? His answer was an unequivocal "no"—we have no control over the genes of heredity.

His second question has a more satisfying answer to anyone actively seeking the good life:

"Can one, by giving thought, help one's life span to reach its potential?" Or, "by not giving thought, prevent it?" His answer is "Yes—to a certain degree." *

Dr. Jewett did not find any short cuts, special devices, or means or nostrums to help people live to their longest and fullest. Instead, he found something far more basic: a "longevity syndrome"— the common characteristics, traits, habit patterns, and heredity factors that go into the good long life. Dr. Jewett, who died in 1971 at the age of 87, was a prime example of the longevity syndrome, and he wrote the paper describing his interviews and findings in the last year of his life.

His interest in the subject was quickened in 1951 by a newspaper article headed "A 'Second Prime of Life' after Seventy" which described "nimble nonagenarians" who showed unusual characteristics and behavior. He began to interview people of 85 or over who were in excellent health, with a feeling of well-being and mentally alert, creative, and enjoying their lives. (He was then 67.) The project languished because of other pressures. In 1956 he was impressed by an article by Flanders Dunbar, "Immunity to Afflictions of Old Age," which used the term "longevity syndrome" and which talked of people with the same "personality profile" he had found in his interviews five years before. Finally, in 1968, after discussion with a colleague, Dr. Alexander Gralnick, he decided to interview more old people and write his impressions. In all, he studied 79 men and women ranging in age from 87 to 103.

---

* Dr. Jewett had still a third question "Can a man, by giving thought, increase the potential life span of his progeny?" His answer, based on the use of computer methods and newer knowledge of genetics: "Possibly but not likely in our day."

In his usual work, Dr. Jewett had seen many old people suffering devastating effects of disease. But now he was looking for something entirely different: healthy, functioning old men and women enjoying life—the kind, he said, that "rarely are seen in physicians' offices, never in nursing homes, and seldom in homes for the aged or retirement areas." Such people, because of their varied interests, almost never stay in one place in retirement, and he had to find them far afield, often in the course of his travels. He found one octogenarian, for example, in the Alhambra in Granada, traveling alone gathering material for an article on Moorish culture. He found another subject, a woman of 90 traveling with her 87-year-old sister and 86-year-old friend, in the British cemetery of Funchal in the Madeira Islands. She was searching among the tombstones, trying to reconstruct her genealogy.

These are the common characteristics that Dr. Jewett found to make up the longevity syndrome:

Heredity. Some of Dr. Jewett's long-lived men and women lived in the New England area and had records that went back twelve generations. "All of them were able to give proof that many of their progenitors had lived to advanced ages," he said. "So it seems safe to write that the hereditary factor in their longevity is a very important one, for it was common to all." High immunity to illness is an obvious part of the longevity syndrome. In escaping or surviving the diseases of mid-life and the geriatric diseases particularly prevalent in the years 65 to 75, people are likely to have "an excellent chance of living out a good part of their potential life spans laid down in their germ plasms."

Sex and marriage. Benjamin Rush, a famous U.S. physician and medical educator, said in 1805, "I have met only one person beyond the age of 80 who had never been married." Marriage favors longer life spans and there are many reasons why people with potentially long life spans seek marriage, Dr. Jewett said. He saw a relationship between the sex drive and long life. Noting that others had reported that 60% of couples between the ages of 60 and 74 remain sexually active, Dr. Jewett—who was about 86 while writing this—said that the idea that sex is harmful in old age is a myth, "yet that belief is a problem among younger people."

"This is not to be interpreted as saying that the sex drive is suddenly resurrected in their eighties, but rather that many people who live that long and remain well are originally endowed with greater vitality," he said. He quoted, with much approval, the words of a 16th-century rabbi, Joseph Caro: "Whosoever lives without a wife lives without joy, without goodness, without shelter, without peace. He cannot even be considered a man. Whosoever does not engage in begetting children is like one who sheds blood." And Dr. Jewett noted that Rabbi Caro begot his sixth child, Judah, when he was 83.

In his group of 79 healthy men and women between the ages of 87 and 103, Dr. Jewett found that "all either had been married or were still married. Several reported continued sexual activity."

Physical characteristics. Giants and dwarfs always die at a fairly early age, Dr. Jewett said, and all the people in his group were of average size and body structure. Average height of the males was 5 feet 7½ inches, of the females, 5 feet 2 inches. (These were good average heights for people born when they were, about the third quarter of the 19th century. Improved nutrition has brought about taller averages since.) None was over- or underweight. Their weights barely varied throughout their adult lives and were about the same as when they were 25 years old.

Their reflexes and reaction times had not slowed down to the norms established for their age. Common characteristics were good muscle tone, lack of atrophic changes in the skin, and good grips. All those who owned cars still drove them. Some still rode horseback and many indulged in physical activities long since abandoned by others in their sixties and seventies.

Intelligence and efficiency. Dr. Jewett's group bore out the studies which show that neither intelligence nor efficiency necessarily decrease with age. Judging by their backgrounds and achievements, the men and women in his group had superior native intelligence. Little or none of their capacities was lost; they retained a good general fund of information, keen interest and knowledge of current events, and engaged in lively conversation. They also had excellent memory of both recent and remote pasts and kept up varied intellectual interests. Some were taking up new languages with facility. "All had obviously passed through the dangerous age of senescence without show of scar."

Anxiety. Dr. Jewett defined the term: "Conscious and reportable experiences of inner dread and foreboding . . . usually derived from internal psychological problems . . . and chronically present, leading to more serious and long-lasting somatic and psychological changes."

His group didn't experience anxiety. Some 60% of the ailments that entail visits to or by doctors, he noted, are of emotional origin. If freedom from psychosomatic manifestations can be taken as a fair index of freedom from anxiety, he said, then an absence or minimal amount of anxiety was a common characteristic of the people he interviewed. Neither their histories nor present activities gave any evidence of a problem of anxiety.

He checked back in their memories to see how much time they had spent ill in bed or ill away from work or other pursuits. They averaged less than a total of two weeks each for the full period of fifty years and more. (The average for the population at large is greater than this *every single year.*) Even the common cold was scarcely known among them. And they had taken fewer pills in their lifetimes than many people take in one week.

Being accident prone is a matter of emotions and anxiety, too. Dr. Jewett's group had a history of very few accidents. They were simply not prone to worry. All were deeply concerned about problems but took things in their stride, usually with other projects in the offing to give them new interests. Dr. Jewett noticed another tendency: The type of work they did allowed them to take short vacations periodically, which helped to keep them in a state of equilibrium.

Vocations. There was a common denominator here, too. In their younger years, all the octogenarians, nonagenarians, and centenarians gravitated to work that let them be their own bosses or let them maintain a great amount of independence of choice and action. Thus they were able to avoid many on-the-job frustrations. They were active in a variety of fields: The majority were in small businesses of their own (and, in a few cases, very large ones); in law, medicine, and architecture; and in farming and related fields, such as the nursery business. But always they had the freedom of action usually denied the organization man. Retirement was never forced upon them, and many remained active long beyond 65. They did not, could not, evade the hardships of their times; many had to start rebuilding their lives while in their fifties or sixties when stricken by the great depression of the 1930s. They did so successfully.

Of great importance was the fact that they all kept their ambitions within reasonable bounds. Living each day happily was more important to them than ceaselessly driving to the top. "No doubt," comments Dr. Jewett, "this was one factor which enabled them to escape the catastrophic diseases of mid-life."

Joie de vivre. Another common denominator was their capacity to enjoy life, without artificial stimulation. All were optimists with an unusual sense of humor, and boredom was unknown to them. Life seems to have been a great adventure and, in common, they had a highly developed capacity for observation of beauty and nature. All were capable of finding amusement and recreation for themselves, with no one having to create it for them. "Whether this trait of joy-in-living was genetically derived, or sprang entirely from the reservoir of constructive factors in their childhood, I have no dogmatic answer," added Dr. Jewett.

Response to change. Great adaptability was a common characteristic. They treasured many past good things and cherished many childhood memories—but none wished to return to the past. All preferred to live in the present, with all its changes. They showed little sign of the generation gap that seems to exist between many adults and today's youth and were understanding of youth and its problems.

One of the changes the old must adjust to is the idea of death. This group was remarkably free of preoccupation with the subject. Their philosophy of life and death was epitomized by one of them, a man who said (in the original Latin): "I do not wish to die, but I will not care when I am dead."

Religious beliefs. None had been inflicted with religiosity or extreme orthodoxy but all were religious in the broad sense of the word. Their backgrounds happened to be Judaic-Christian, with different faiths represented, but all had respect for other beliefs. "Like the octogenarian Thomas Jefferson," said Dr. Jewett, "each 'never told of his religion or scrutinized that of another!' "

Eating habits. The way we eat is on index of our emotional maturity, Dr. Jewett said. In adults, a wide range of eating habits is also an indication of a person's capacity to change, to venture into unexplored fields. Dr. Jewett's 79 healthy old people were all moderate eaters but extremely willing to try new and unusual dishes. The only common denominator in the food they ate was that it was usually high in protein and low in fats. Since their weight varied only within narrow limits, none had recourse to any special diets. They had no add aversions to foods nor were any of them compulsive eaters.

Sleeping habits. None had ever been accustomed to sleeping long hours. All were early risers. They averaged between six and seven hours of sleep a night, but many rested in bed another hour as well. A few napped half an hour or so after lunch, but not as a matter of routine or when it might interfere with something more important or gratifying.

Alcohol, tobacco, coffee. None of them said that total abstinence is the secret of long life. In this case, there was no uniformity among them. Some drank alcohol, some said they had drunk too much on occasion, some never drank. Smoking habits, too, were varied: Some had smoked moderately but given it up long ago, a few were still inveterate pipe smokers, some had never smoked. Most drank coffee but were not tied to its use.

Dr. Jewett, in summing up, added one other conclusion to his personality profile of the healthy old: Their common set of characteristics had existed when they were young, as far back as their adolescence. A healthy adolescence is forerunner and harbinger of a healthy old age.

Dr. Jewett's findings about the longevity syndrome are confirmed, in different ways, by many others, both in detailed studies and popular prescription. However, because it was limited to 79 people, his study has its sketchy aspects. Many gerontologists are much more concerned about smoking than he was, both for the psychological implications of what it means to be a smoker and for the deadly effects of cigarettes. Some say that cigarette smoking has caused a "demographic perturbation" in the United States; because men started smoking earlier and more heavily than women, there are

now more widows and fewer widowers than anticipated in demographic projections made a decade or more ago. And, because of
the limited sample, Dr. Jewett's study does not accurately tell which
professions are most conducive to long life.

A study reported in the Metropolitan Life *Statistical Bulletin* in
1968 goes much further. Based upon an analysis of *Who's Who in
America* and the mortality rates of prominent men over 45, it shows
these relative positions for the vocations analyzed:

The best record for longevity was held by scientists, with mortality
rates about 20% below the average for all men in the study. College
professors and administrators as well as clergymen came next, 10%
to 15% below the average. Military officials and artists, illustrators,
and sculptors had mortality rates just below the average.

The worst longevity record—with mortality rates twice as high
as all the rest—was held by correspondents and journalists. Editors,
authors, writers, critics, and historians were not as bad, but their
mortality rate, as a group, was about 30% higher than the average.
Government officials were nearly 20% higher than the average;
physicians and surgeons had a death rate about 10% higher; business
executives and lawyers were close to average.

It was anthropologist Sula Benet of Hunter College, New York,
who noted that Abkhasians themselves attribute their long lives to
their practices in sex, work, and diet. She has lived among them and
studied their ways and has developed a more scientific conclusion.
Most likely as many live as long as they do—to 120 years or more
—because of the extraordinary cultural factors that structure their
existence and group behavior, the unbroken continuum of life's
activities: the same games, the same work, the same food, the same
self-imposed and socially perceived needs, and the increasing prestige
that comes with increasing age and makes a long life gratifying.

The Novosti Press Agency prepared a report, in 1970, for *The
Gerontologist* on the subject of very old people in the USSR. The
oldest man in the country at that time was 165-year-old Shirali
Mislimov from Azerbaidzhan, a deputy to his village soviet, a man
who "never gets angry and laughs at the mischief of his great-grandchildren and great-great-grandchildren." The article went on to say
that "his pulse is normal—72 beats a minute. His blood pressure is

that of a healthy young man, and his weight is 136 pounds." * The oldest woman was reported to be Ashura Omarova, 195 years old. One couple, living in the village of Sanakari, was reported to have celebrated its one hundredth wedding anniversay, the husband at 127, the wife at 125. The Soviet agency stated that the characteristics of the long-lived people in the Caucasus and the Pamir regions were that they "were thin and proportionately built. The men's average height was 5 feet 4.6 inches, the women's 4 feet 11.6 inches; respective weight was 139 and 103.5 pounds.

"Long life is apparently related to various factors which exist in Daghestan. The geographical and climatic conditions of the mountainous part of that republic; the simple dairy, vegetable, and meat food; life-long physical work (farming) in which the residents are engaged; adequate rest; activity (physical exercises, sports, various amusements and dancing); meaningful cultural traditions and customs transmitted from generation to generation; satisfying family life; humor and a "strong" nervous system; well-developed folk medicine; good heredity; and the constant improvement of the population's material and cultural standards with special emphasis on all-inclusive health services, all appear to have varying effect," the report said.

The last item, true or not, has the ring of government propaganda. Much of the rest conforms—in astonishing detail—to the findings of anthropologist Benet in her work among the Abkhasians and to the longevity syndrome of Dr. Jewett, working primarily among Americans.

Not matter where we live—and especially in industrialized societies —gerontologists have a good idea of what goes into longevity. From a person's earliest years, a fair prediction may be made of how long he will live. By the time he has reached middle age, the prediction can be made with remarkable accuracy: how long he will live, how good an old age he will have. Countless unforeseen things may hap-

---

* Mislimov lived in the Caucasus, which has the reputation of being the region with the highest longevity rate in the world: 84 persons over 100 for every 100,000 inhabitants. He died in September 1973, at the age of 168, according to Soviet officials, who considered him to be the oldest person in the world. He had no records to prove his age, however, and the claim is disputed by Western gerontologists.

pen, of course. Health, economic and social position may change drastically; accidents and catastrophe happen all the time. Barring these, the predictors of longevity are sound and accurate. The Duke University Center for the Study of Aging and Human Development has done much research in this field. Some of its findings were published in 1971 in a small volume, *Prediction of Life Span,* edited by Erdman Palmore and Frances C. Jeffers. Some of its conclusions are interpreted here:

Physiological predictors. It is certain that the maximum life span for the member of a given species is set by the nature of the DNA (deoxyribonucleic acid) that species contains. (DNA is the key molecule of life which enables living things to reproduce and which transmits heredity.) From those insects which live for only a few happy reproductive hours, to man (and some birds) which can last for over a century, to trees which can live for thousands of years, the maximum length of life is determined by genetic factors. In the case of humans, members of some families are bound to short life spans because of DNA defects which bring about certain diseases; members of other families may have, predictably, a greater-than-average life span because of a good DNA factor.

Thus the facetious remark "If you want to live long, choose your parents carefully" is grounded in fact. And even more so because parents and their lot in life establish the environment in which a child grows. Longevity is influenced by nongenetic factors, too. It is difficult, however, to gauge the importance of hereditary factors compared to environmental ones; people with similiar heredity tend to have similar environments.

There is some evidence that longevity on the mother's side may have more influence than longevity on the father's. It also seems likely that, to live longer, it is better to be born of young parents than old ones.

For the sake of a few more years of life, it is better to have been born female at this moment in history. Women live longer than men in industrialized societies. But this has not always been true, particularly when there were more deaths in childbirth. The fact that women live longer than men today may be due entirely to differences in environment, roles, and life styles between the two sexes. Women generally have more protected environments, less dangerous occupations, fewer violent deaths, accidents, and suicides. To the present, at least, they also suffer less from the consequences of smoking and lung cancer. A 1970 study, in fact, concluded that men's greater mortality could be accounted for, in toto, by their more extensive smoking.

"Keep your weight down, keep physically active, and cut down on cigarettes" is standard advice of doctors to middle-aged patients. The wisdom of the advice is thoroughly borne out by the Duke studies. Sudden death from arteriosclerosis and heart diseases is much less frequent among the middle aged who are physically active, maintain moderate weight, and avoid cigarette smoking completely. Cigarette smoking is not a debatable subject among gerontologists; it is unquestionably bad and a predictor of mortality. The risk of sudden, unexpected death may be as much as five times higher among smokers than nonsmokers. The only good news about cigarette smoking has to do with giving it up: Death from coronary disease is clearly increased with the *number* of cigarettes smoked daily, but not tied to the duration of the smoking habit. When a person gives up cigarettes, his risk of coronary disease appears to be reduced to the lower level of those who have never smoked.

Among the normal aged who live at home, physical activity, weight control, and no smoking also contribute to longevity and less illness. Among the aged in institutions, the strongest predictors of mortality are physical disability, incontinence, and chronic brain syndrome.

Psychological predictors. All studies indicate that good intelligence and sustained interest—the keener the better—in one's activities are predictors of longevity. Among the normal aged, higher intelligence or mental status continues to be a good predictor of a longer life. A sudden and marked decline in the thinking functions of an old person predicts that he is likely to die within one to five years.

Social predictors. Higher social class and occupation predict greater longevity. This is simply because a person with more money can presumably eat better, live better, get better medical care. Poverty shortens life. Among the normal aged, higher financial status, more social activity, and more life satisfaction are significant predictors of the number of years remaining. For men, satisfaction with their work (or whatever their organized behavior) is the single best predictor of longevity. For women, it is how happy they are.

Dr. Palmore closes on a tentative note: "Hope and will-to-live may be predictors of survival, especially among hospital patients." Other gerontologists are much more emphatic about this than he. They believe that hope and will-to-live, as expressions of an attitude toward life, are basic to successful aging. Dr. Jewett spoke of *joie de vivre* as part of a longevity syndrome. Edward Bortz, a former president of the American Medical Association, embraced the same idea in his four rules for the good long life: Keep a sense of humor; control your emotions (or, at least, don't allow them to overwhelm you)—excessive emotional tension leads to personal ineffectiveness; seek good companionship among family and friends; and keep an open mind, with zest for change and challenge. In sum, keep growing all your life.

Implicit in all such formulas are the essentials for the good long life discussed earlier: good health and financial security. The two often go together. Poverty destroys men physically and psychologically. Poor health stifles energy and will to achieve—and breeds poverty. Fortunately, it is in just these two areas—health and finances—that much progress has been made in Western society in our time. Science has performed gigantic feats in keeping people healthy and restoring health. And social welfare legislation and pension systems—designed to shield people from the worst aspects of poverty—are infinitely more advanced than they were fifty years ago, even in such "retarded" countries as the United States.* Certainly, problem areas and inequities abound. But today's old have better health and greater financial independence—and the greater dignity that goes with them—than ever before.

There is another predictor of long life which neither science nor governments nor organizations can do much about. Marriage is a somewhat battered institution these days but more important than ever in the eyes of the gerontologist. Dr. Jewett noted that "marriage

---

* This is the long, cosmic view. Many of today's old, with one life to live, have a much grimmer perspective. See Appendix II, *A Note on Gerontology,* for an appraisal of the immediate situation.

favors longer life spans" without giving much evidence. The evidence exists: Married people have greater life expectancy at all ages (except for women aged 20 to 24).* One of the two reasons for this—of lesser importance because they are doomed to shorter lives in any event—is that people in poor health and of "unfavorable temperament" are less likely to marry because they choose not to or because they are passed by. Thus people with poorer prospects for long life are screened out in advance by the requirements of marriage.

The other reason is that married people live in an environment more favorable to longevity. In a normal marriage, each partner has the advantages of more emotional support and comfort, better nutrition, and better chance for care in times of illness. And marriage gives each person a rhythm and stronger base in life, higher status, the chance for a sustained and satisfactory sex life, and the enormous gratifications—despite the crises and frustrations—of seeing children grow.

Life expectancy figures show that married people, both men and women, live longer than single, widowed, or divorced ones. This is supported by mortality rates which, in one study, showed that the death rate was 29% higher for single men than it was for married men, 42% higher for widowed men, and 54% higher for divorced men. The figures were not quite as high for women who, presumably, can take better care of themselves by themselves. Their death rate was 15% higher for single women than for married ones, 26% higher for widows, and 43% higher for divorced women. Any basic change of status has an effect on mortality; divorce, being a less accepted status than widowhood, cuts down on the prospects for a longer life.

The studies do not go into breakdowns of the quality of marriages, whether they are good or bad, made in heaven or hell. It is just that, overall, the state of being married helps fill vital emotional needs, gives greater creature comforts—and helps people live longer. Living outside of marriage tends to kill; among single men, for example, the incidence of death by violence is much greater than among married men.

This small voice extolling the benefits of marriage may not be

* Presumably because of the risks of pregnancy and childbirth.

heard in a day when marriage seems somewhat out of style. Unless we naturally possess Dr. Jewett's longevity syndrome, we may know *all* the predictors of the good long life and, individually, not be able to do a thing about them. No matter how good our heredity, few of us have the power or self-control to do the things necessary to live as long as possible (or to abstain from the things that kill us).

But growing old, being old, is no longer the solitary matter it once was; together we are beneficiary to the vast new knowledge about aging, in all its forms. We have seen how this knowledge is being put to use and the greater fact is that man, collectively, is doing a great deal about improving the length and quality of life. The quiet revolution—the conquest of age as we have known and feared it—is a natural development at this time. Today's science and society—and the instinct for survival—are producing it and no force can stay it. It has had its terrible setbacks, but the human race, instead of going out of fashion, seems determined to live longer and better than in the past.

APPENDIX I
EXTRAORDINARY OLD
PEOPLE

This is not a collection of the accumulated wisdom of the distinguished or celebrated aging and old, just some of their thoughts, often in passing, on growing old, being old, or on how they face the future. All are more or less contemporary, very much alive or having died in the recent past. A few are dour, more are exuberant. To that extent, this is an accurate reflection, overall, of the feelings of the successful and old: Most are happy people.

Albert Schweitzer (1875–1965) was a doctor, theologian, musician, and philosopher who developed the theory of reverence for life, all life. When asked who would replace him as head of his jungle hospital at Lambaréné in Gabon:

"I am always asked that question. I still have much to do. I will never retire and am not yet dead. Please, have a little reverence for *my* life."

(at age 86)

Archibald MacLeish, born in 1892, is poet, playwright, and former Librarian of Congress.

"Yeats became a great poet, as distinguished from a gifted Irishman with poetic gifts, when he was close to 60, and his greatest work was done later . . . I am just senile enough to be persuaded that I am writing far better now than at 30, 40, or 50 . . . At 80 you have to begin to look ahead. What will be left when they carry you off?"

Charles Chaplin, cinema actor and director born in 1889, married Oona O'Neill in 1943. He was then 54, she barely 20. They have since raised a family of eight and live in Switzerland.

"My life is more thrilling today than it ever was. I am in good health and still creative and have plans to produce more pictures— perhaps not with myself, but to write and direct them for members of my family—some of whom have quite an aptitude for the theater. I am still very ambitious; I could never retire. There are many things I want to do; besides having a few unfinished cinema scripts, I should like to write a play and an opera—if time will allow. . . . For the last twenty years I have known what happiness means. I have the good fortune to be married to a wonderful wife. I wish I could write more about this, but it involves love, and perfect love is the most beautiful of all frustrations because it is more than one can express."

(at age 75)

Bertrand Russell (1872–1970), English philosopher and champion of individual liberty, influenced his times as profoundly as did Voltaire in the 18th century and John Stuart Mill in the 19th. Two of his works, The Principles of Mathematics, *published when he was 31, and* Principia Mathematica *(with Alfred North Whitehead), published ten years later, helped determine the direction of modern philosophy. He was awarded the Nobel Prize for Literature in 1950.*

"Psychologically, there are two dangers to be guarded against in old age. One of these is undue absorption with the past. It does not do to live in memories, in regrets for the good old days, or in sadness about friends who are dead. One's thoughts must be directed to the future and to things about which there is something to be done. The other thing to be avoided is clinging to youth in the hope of sucking vigor from vitality. . . .

"The best way to overcome it—so at least it seems to me—is to make your interests gradually wider and more impersonal, until bit by bit the walls of the ego recede, and your life becomes increasingly merged in the universal life. An individual human existence should be like a river—small at first, narrowly contained within its banks, and rushing passionately past boulders and over waterfalls. Gradually, the river grows wider, the banks recede, the waters flow more quietly, and in the end, without any visible break, they become merged in the sea and painlessly lose their individual being."

(at age 80)

Pablo Picasso (1881–1973), founder of cubism, was the foremost artist of his time.

"It takes a long time to become young."

(at age 86)

Picasso and Janet Flanner, The New Yorker's Genet who has chronicled Paris life for fifty years, had often sat at separate tables at the Café de Flore at night, watching the passing scene. But they had never met or spoken to each other. This description by Miss Flanner when, finally, they were introduced:

"Picasso turned to me with his hand outstretched in greeting, and then, with a loud cry of astonishment, shouted, 'You! Why didn't you ever speak to me in the old days at the Flore? For years we saw each other and never spoke until now. Are you just the same as you were? You look it!' By this time he had his arms around me and was thumping me enthusiastically on the shoulders. 'You look fine, not a day older,' and I said, 'Nor do you,' and he said, 'That's true, that's the way you and I are. We don't get older, we just get riper. Do you still love life the way you used to, and love people the way you did? I watched you and always wanted to know what you were thinking . . . Tell me, do you still love the human race, especially your best friends? Do you still love love?' 'I do,' I said, astonished at the turn the monologue was taking. 'And so do I,' he shouted, laughing. 'Oh, we're the greatest ones for that, you and I. Isn't love the greatest refreshment in life?' And he embraced me with his strong arms, in farewell."

(Picasso at age 90, Miss Flanner at about 80)

Edmund Wilson (1895–1972), critic and historian, author, and scholar, was America's foremost man of letters of his time.

"The knowledge that death is not so far away, that my mind and emotions and vitality will soon disappear like a puff of smoke, has the effect of making earthly affairs seem unimportant and human beings more and more ignoble. It is harder to take human life seriously, including one's own efforts and achievements and passions."

(at age 68)

Arthur Rubinstein, born in 1886, on being told that he was playing the piano better than ever:

"I think so . . . I am 80. Isn't that so? So now I take chances I never took before. You see, the stakes are not so high. I can afford it. I used to be so much more careful. No wrong notes. Not too bold ideas. Watch tempi. Now I let go and enjoy myself and to hell with everything except the music!"

Pearl S. Buck (1892–1972), novelist and biographer, author of 84 books, was awarded the Nobel Prize for Literature in 1938.

"Life is a continuing process. This much I am sure of and this much I must state on a fine sunny morning as I reflect that I have begun to live the eightieth year of my life. It is an enjoyable year. I am in good health, I have much work to do, and I enjoy myself and what I do. . . .

"Young and old are for me meaningless words except as we use them to denote where we are in this process of this stage of being. Would I wish to be 'young' again? No, for I have learned too much to wish to lose it. It would be like failing to pass a grade in school. I have reached an honorable position in life, because I am old and no longer young. I am a far more valuable person today than I was 50 years ago, or 40 years ago, or 30, 20, or even 10. I have learned so much since I was 70! I believe I can honestly say that I have learned more in the last ten years than I learned in any previous decade. This, I suppose, is because I have perfected my techniques, so that I no longer waste time in learning how to do what I have to do, which is what I also want to do."

Havergal Brian (1876–1973), British composer, wrote twenty-two symphonies after reaching the age of 80. He had lived in obscurity most of his life and first heard one of his thirty-two symphonies played in 1954, when he was 78. In 1966, a capacity audience in the Royal Albert Hall in London cheered Sir Adrian Boult's performance of Brian's "Gothic" Symphony.

"You know, the amazing thing isn't me having written the work, it's Boult being up there conducting. He's over 70."

André Maurois (1885–1967), French writer best known for his biographies of 19th-century literary and political titans, wrote his masterwork, Prometheus: The Life of Balzac, *at 80.*

"I don't like being old; it's unpleasant. I hope there are not too many more years for me."

(at age 81)

Margaret Kuhn, born in 1904, is leader of the Gray Panthers, dedicated to the idea that America give its older members an active role in society:

"The problem is that we last too damned long. But aging is natural, and the changes in us are natural. My wrinkles and my arthritis are a part of my testimony of change."

(at age 68)

René Dubos, born in 1901, is a scientist whose work has aided in development of antibiotics and penicillin. He was awarded a Pulitzer Prize in 1969 for So Human an Animal: How We Are Shaped by Surroundings and Events, *one of his many books.*

"I don't see more happiness—total or indiivdual—but on the whole I see less suffering [than when I was young] . . . I think the greatest danger is that we will continue to accept worsening conditions without realizing that little by little we are spoiling the very quality of life . . . What we need is for more and more people to take a stand against this toleration of conditions, for the development of a stimulating and diversified human environment free of pollution, the restoration of the pleasantness of life . . . This sense of awareness that one must *not* accept these conditions but must take a stand against them —this I think is our greatest hope.

"[People] should retain as long as possible the ability to experience many kinds of situations—to discover what they like and what makes them productive and happy. They should not become prisoners of their past too early in life . . . Young people must fight to maintain a diversity of situations to give them options of choice—this is the essential of freedom. . . . If the options exist but you can't take advantage of them, you will be a very unhappy person."

(at age 71)

Albert Einstein (1879–1955), the great theoretical physicist, in a letter to a friend a few months before his death, wrote:

". . . to one bent by age, death will come as a release; I feel this quite strongly now that I have grown old myself and have come to regard death like an old debt, at long last to be discharged. Still, instinctively one does everything possible to delay this last fulfillment."

(at age 76)

Arnold Toynbee, born in 1889, is best known for his monumental multivolume Study of History.

"As one grows older, the temptation to dwell on the past and to avert one's eyes from the future grows. If one were to fall into this backward-looking stance, one would be as good (I mean as bad) as dead before physical death had overtaken us . . . Our minds, so long as they keep their cutting edge, are not bound by our physical limits; they can range over time and space into infinity. To be human is to be capable of transcending oneself."

(at age 81)

Norman Thomas (1884–1968)—American socialist leader, six times a presidential candidate, and constant fighter for humanitarian ideals—was given a mammoth party in New York in 1964 on his eightieth birthday. Thousands cheered the veteran crusader, now deaf and almost blind. As he was leaving, a reporter asked, "What are you going to do now?"

"The same thing I've always done."

Robert Frost (1874–1963), one of the world's great poets, was 87 when he undertook, with the endorsement of President John F.

*Kennedy, a meeting with Premier Nikita Khrushchev in Moscow.
The year was 1962, the purpose of the meeting to explore mutual
Russian-American fears, hopes, and ideals at the time the Cuban
missile crisis was developing. Frost said soon after his return:*

"The only trouble with dying is not knowing how it will all turn
out."

(at age 88)

*Karl Jaspers (1883–1969) was a philosopher and father of German
existentialism. Forced to give up his post at Heidelberg by the Nazis,
he passed most of the rest of his life as professor of philosophy at
the University of Basel, in Switzerland.*

"In my mind I am still very young. My writings sound young,
according to others . . . [but] it is only when you are old that you
know what life is about. It is splendid to be old because I have seen
so much. I feel that I have witnessed 1,000 years of history. I have
seen the world undergo many changes. I have watched the world
develop during the time of Bismarck, the Kaiser, and now. My grandparents were farmers. In my youth I saw a way of farm life which is
now seen only in Africa.

"I have a Utopian theory about life. Most people think they cannot
influence world history. I believe they can. Every person is important
and should influence history—by living fully, and by being sincere,
faithful and true. Follow your conscience and instincts. Feel everything you do has a definite purpose. Always have that in mind in
daily decisions.

"Wisdom is never fully attainable but there are ways of getting at
it. Do what is important. Avoid trivial daily tasks. Mere industrious-
ness is not enough. It is particularly important to have regular hours,
regular study, regular sleep, proper exercise, and avoid trivia."

*Eleanor Roosevelt (1884–1962) was a tireless campaigner for
human rights.*

"Where do I get my energy? Part of it is in not getting too self-
absorbed. And this becomes more important as one gets older.
Inevitably, there are aches and pains, more and more, and if you pay
attention to them, the first thing you know you're an invalid."

(at age 75)

Gabrielle (Coco) Chanel, famous French couturière, on being asked her age by a reporter:

"I will tell you that my age varies according to the day and the people I happen to be with . . . When I'm bored, I feel vary old, and since I'm extremely bored with you, I'm going to be a thousand years old in five minutes if you don't get the hell out of here at once."

(about age 86)

Will Durant, born in 1885, is author of The Story of Philosophy and, with his wife Ariel, the ten-volume The Story of Civilization. *These works have sold in the millions and have established him as a foremost popularizer of the subjects.*

"When I was a young man, I used to talk about the bondage of tradition. But now, as an older man, I distrust the fetishness of novelty. We exaggerate the value of newness in both ideas and things. It is much easier to be original than wise. We would do well to remember that the customs, traditions, conventions, and creeds of mankind are the harvest of trial and error. History demonstrates that it is unlikely that any individual, even the cleverest, can come up within one lifetime to such a breadth of knowledge and understanding as to sit in sound judgment on ancient ways. . . .

"I am not depressed [about the future]. Let us admit half the terrible pictures that have been drawn of humanity, and let us agree that in every generation of man's history we find superstition, hypocrisy, cruelty, crime and war. But place all these against the roster and production of poets, composers, artists, scientists, historians, philosophers and saints. Let us remember in our gloomier moments that man wrote the plays of Shakespeare, the music of Handel and Bach, the odes of Keats, the *Republic* of Plato, the *Principia* of Newton."

(at age 87)

Arthur Fiedler, born in 1893, has conducted the Pops Concerts at Boston's Symphony Hall since 1930.

"I know older people don't think too much of modern music. It sounds terrible to them. But they must remember that 25 years from now a lot of today's unpleasant music will be considered 'old favorites'. . . . We all remember the songs we used to sing when we were younger. The same thing will be true of the modern generation. And they'll probably be upset by all that weird music their children and grandchildren are playing."

(at age 77)

Helen Hayes, born in 1900, is a distinguished American actress. She made this comment a few years after the death of her husband, playwright Charles MacArthur.

"There is beauty in sincere and honest aging. I guess people who concentrate on themselves are most afraid of age. If they would think of the purpose of our being here, they wouldn't stop to worry if their teeth were crumbling or if a bit of gray appeared in their hair. I believe we are all here to help each other. It took a great tragedy to make me fully aware of it. I found comfort and help and sympathy when I needed it most. To be helpful to others makes the world so much brighter, keeps one youthful and active . . . There is simply no time to worry about growing old. It's such a wasted effort to try to turn back the clock when there's so much to be done."

(at age 60)

Averell Harriman, born in 1891, is a statesman, diplomat, and former governor of New York State. He served under three presidents as ambassador to the Soviet Union or ambassador at large.

"It is true that our culture discriminates against age . . . The most important computer is the human brain. Good judgment comes from years and years of that brain's storing up millions and millions of important impressions. A wise decision comes when a man who has lived a long time is able to dig deep into that brain. To throw away people who have developed such magnificent mental computers is a great waste.

"I'm afraid our country, as a whole, hasn't made much headway in preparing people for retirement . . . I do know that you cannot sweep away the problem by isolating older people into apartments built only for older people. I think that keeping older people in the general community may serve to remind younger people that they must psychologically prepare for old age, as well as making economic preparations. That's one great strength of the Russian people. The

Russian family is a tightly packed unit comprising all ages—babies, parents, grandparents. The Soviets have never been able to destroy the Russian family. As a result, the family is a great, joyful part of Russian life."

(at age 80)

Maurice Goudeket, born in 1889, is a French writer and husband of Colette.

"There is a shortness of breath, a slowness of movement, a back that will not bend so easily, to be sure, but these are things for our bodies to cope with. The immaterial being that gives our threatened building all its life does not show a single wrinkle, nor will it ever do so."

(at age 75)

James A. Farley, born in 1888, was an American political leader and government official under President Franklin D. Roosevelt and, more recently, an international business executive.

"I don't know that I follow any regular program but my philosophy, if you will, could break down into five points. The first might be: exercise regularly . . . I also keep fit by following my rule number two: keep busy at what interests you . . . My point three: seek recreation you enjoy . . . My fourth point: live by a buoyant philosophy. My fifth and final point: to look to the future."

(at age 83)

Baroness Mary Stocks, born in 1891, is a British author, broadcaster, and educator, and former general secretary of the London Council of Social Service.

"I thought [old age] attractive because old people were interesting and experienced and, sometimes, since character has shaped the lines on their faces, very beautiful. Sybil Thorndike at the age of 89 is to my mind incomparably more beautiful than the entrants of 'Miss World' beauty contests, who seem to me to all look the same."

(at age 80)

Dame Sybil Thorndike, born in 1882, is the first lady of the British stage.

"I don't feel 90 in my head, but I feel 180 in my body. It's such a nuisance."

(on her ninetieth birthday)

Karl Menninger, born in 1894, is a founder of the Menninger Clinic and Foundation in Topeka, Kansas, an internationally known center for the treatment of mental illness.

"We all have a tendency towards this existential fear of death that creeps out in the things we say and do. More important is our attitude towards ourselves. It isn't 'mature' to give up and flop. I see people my own age surrendering prematurely to the feeling they're not needed any more. They think in terms of 'What use is there for me? The younger people can get along without me.' To some extent that's true. Sure they can, but not as well.

"Some people tend to resign—to retire or to withdraw too early. Others may not recognize the necessity of switching their function to one that is less active and more advisory. I don't believe in retiring from life. Retirement from business is an artificial, technical thing, simply from a certain responsibility to a certain group. It s true that some older people become too inflexible, too habituated to certain ruts and reaction they can't get out of. But then there some people of 40 to whom this also happens and some to whom it does not happen even at 80. . . .

"There are a lot of things older people can do. Feeling it's too late, or we can't do it any more, can become an alibi for not doing the things we could do. I cannot ride vigorous horses with safety as I once could. I can't stay up as late as I used to. But it's easy to exaggerate one's weaknesses. We should not pity ourselves or indulge ourselves in thinking, 'Well, I can't do that, I'm too old—I'm too weak!'

"I don't think about age, don't believe in getting old. . . . If I were told tomorrow, 'Your jobs have all run out, your committees have all fired you, your consultant jobs have expired, no patients want to have appointments—there is nothing for you to do but quit everything,' I'd say 'Well, I've got my writing.' And if they said, 'Your writing is no good. You can't write anymore.' Then I'd still say there is chess, bridge, and reading and painting. I'd reclassify my books. Every few years I have a new notion on how my books should be

reclassified. Then, doing that, I'd run across books I had forgotten
to read and I'd tear into them . . ."

(at age 77)

*Pablo Casals (1876–1973), master cellist and humanitarian, con-
tinued to teach and conduct until his 79th year. A physician, after
watching him vigorously rehearse an orchestra in a Haydn symphony,
told Casals that his energy seemed to be that of a man of 40. Casals's
eyes widened and he snapped:*

"Twenty! I am old, but in music I am very young."

*On being asked "What is the 'secret' of your good old age?," Casals
replied:*

"I live. Very few people live."

*Jacques Lipchitz (1891–1973), born in Lithuania in 1891, was one
of the world's best-known and prolific sculptors.*

"I still need more time, lots of time. I want to create a new breed
of monster whose visual language would not make nature blush."

(at age 81)

*Gertrude Stein (1874–1946), poet, novelist, and literary innovator,
awakened from an operation the day of her death to ask:*
"What is the answer?"
No one at her bedside responded.
"In that case, what is the question?"

(at age 72)

APPENDIX II
A NOTE ON
GERONTOLOGY

The subject of aging and old age has interested man in all times and all societies. Attitudes toward the aged have always been a complex and intimate part of a tribe's or society's mores. "Thou shalt rise up before the hoary head, and honor the face of the old man" in Leviticus is a basic expression of Judeo-Christian intent. (The fact that it had to be put in commandment form, and repeatedly, is in itself revealing.)

Of the tracts and essays on aging written throughout history, Cicero's *De Senectute* is among the earliest and certainly is the best known (for its highly quotable observations, such as "Old age has no fixed term, and one may fitly live in it so long as he can observe and discharge the duties of his station"). But scientifically valid works have proliferated only in our time, starting with *Senescence: The Last Half of Life,* by G. Stanley Hall, published in 1922. Research on the psychological aspects of aging began seriously wtih the work of Walter R. and Catherine Miles about 1932. Although a few biologists had earlier reported on their research in aging, E. V. Cowdry's *Problems of Ageing,* published in 1939, was the first major compendium on the subject. Interest in the organization of professional services for the old also grew greatly after World War II.

Gerontology—the scientific study of the phenomenon of aging and problems of the aged—started to bloom about the same time. It has grown mightily since, along with the world population increase, much greater life expectancy, and the fact that there are now more old people than ever before. It is hard to tell where the science of gerontology starts and ends since it involves so many areas and levels of life. Gerontologists sometimes discuss the highly academic point: Is theirs a multidisciplinary or interdisciplinary science? The professional tendency is to break gerontology down into four major categories: (*1*) social and economic problems raised by the increasing number of old people in the population; (2) psychological aspects, including intellectual performance and personal adjustment; (*3*) physiological bases of aging, along with pathological deviations and disease processes; and (*4*) general biological aspects of aging in all animals. Geriatrics is the branch of medical science dealing with prevention and treatment of diseases in old people, a part of the broader field.

Membership of the Gerontological Society of the United States, formed in 1940, is organized by "biological sciences," "clinical medicine," "psychological and social sciences," and "social research, planning, and practice." This means that the members may come from any of a dozen departments within a university, a variety of public and private institutions, civic or social welfare groups, government agencies, business or labor organizations. Either of its two publications, *The Journal of Gerontology* or *The Gerontologist,* may include reports on research in such disparate subjects as: the reminiscences and memory of centenarians; the extent of petty theft in old age homes; "Leisure Time Pursuits Among Retired Blacks by Social Status"; aspects of postmenopausal behavior; analyses of pension plan systems; how to get along without a car after 70; or an inspired discussion—without a trace of cant or gibberish—on what it is really like to be old in a society which appears to venerate youth. And either may cite articles in other journals with such titles as "The Prolongation of the Life Span of Kokanee Salmon (*onoorhynchus nerka kennerlyi*) by Castration before the Beginning of Gonad Development" (actual title).

These are only slightly more inter- or multidisciplinary than the work of the International Center of Social Gerontology, which has its headquarters in Paris. Despite use of the word "social" in its title, the Center's publications may include "The Importance of the Locomotor System in Gerophylaxis," by the head of the German Association of Gerontology; an article by a member of the University of

Milan's medical faculty on medicine and social implications in gero-psychiatry; and an international symposium on the philosophical meaning of death. There is a crowding of ideas in gerontology and sometimes—in each specialist's zeal and concern with his area—a crowding out. At a London meeting of gerontologists, for example, a nutritional expert, who had spent years developing low-cost, scientifically valid meals for the old, was told off testily by a psychologist: "Eating is a social event to the old, not just a matter of satisfying physiologic needs. What's more important is not what they eat but with whom they eat. Your diets are meaningless because they're without a context." (To which the nutritional expert retorted: "I'm talking about primary function. There are no vitamins in table talk.")

The people working in gerontology include not only the usual professionals—social scientists, doctors, nurses, social administrators and workers, and the like. There are also lawyers, economists, historians, politicians, publicists, lobbyists, government officials, trade unionists, and others. There are complicated reasons why all are attracted to a field which, like being old itself, has had relatively low status.

Many other professionals in problems of emotions and behavior—psychiatrists, for example—tend to shun the old. For them, treating the old lacks many of the gratifications usually present in helping to heal and is a relationship made worse by the possibility that an old person will not live long enough to pay back a therapist's investment in time and skill. Indeed, the professionals who work in gerontology and geriatrics seem to be singularly compassionate and dedicated. "The only thing we seem to have in common," said one gerontologist-psychiatrist, "is that as children we all must have been in love with our grandmothers."

This book was researched in Paris, London, Washington and elsewhere in the United States, and is also based upon material received from and correspondence with professional workers in many European countries, Israel, and Japan. Throughout, the emphasis is on studies and new findings made in the United States, simply because in gerontological research—as in a number of other fields of scientific endeavor—the United States leads the world. This is not to minimize the gifted research done elsewhere—for example, in England under the auspices of the Nuffield Foundation; in the gerontology centers of the USSR; in Israel, which for its size has had massive problems and come up with truly innovative solutions; increasingly in almost every European country. Nor is this to say that the United States treats its old better than they are treated elsewhere. The United States is organized, in a massive way, to support a panoply of scientific programs, but it is not as well organized to apply the programs that scientific research may indicate are essential. Older Americans, in fact, are relatively worse off than older people in some West European countries where the standard of living is lower.

A look at the directory of U.S. *National Organizations With Programs in the Field of Aging,* a 100-page document listing some 250 organizations and prepared under U.S. government grant by the National Council on Aging—or a reading of the massive documents emanating from White House Conferences on Aging—gives the appearance that Americans are passionately doing something about their old. In fact, they are not doing very much, despite the advanced state of gerontology as a science in the United States. The statement that "older Americans are relatively worse off than older people in some Western European countries" comes from a report edited by an official of the Administration on Aging of the U.S. Department of Health, Education, and Welfare with a highly critical view of America's treatment of its old. For all of the American aged, he says, "it is a struggle against being pushed out of the mainstream into a subculture of poverty and social uselessness." In the United States, the old—persons 65 years of age or older, by government definition—make up 10% of the total population but 20% of the poor. "The size of the aged's share [of current production of goods and services] is determined by how much purchasing power is transferred to them," he says. "In the end, it comes down to the younger group's willingness to share—in other words, on the ordering of their total national priorities."

"The younger group" has not been very willing. Getting children to pay for the support of their parents has *always* been a problem. To be old in the United States, land of the young and the affluent, is like being poor in the United States—somewhat worse by contrast and more demeaning than it is in Europe. And "old" and "poor" have often, still do, go together.

This sad reality can hardly be ignored. One consolation is the fact that the old are less poor than in the past, with better chance for an adequate minimum income. But the economics of aging, along with the ordering of national priorities, has been and remains an essential concern of the very busy, very multidisciplined science of gerontology.

APPENDIX III
SOURCES
OF INFORMATION

Information about many of the specific problems that face people in retirement—where to live, how to budget, how to start a second career or find a job, how to take advantage of the many benefits and opportunities now available—is easily obtainable, and often in gratifying detail, at nominal or no charge from the following sources:

- *Superintendent of Documents, Government Printing Office, Washington, D.C. 20402*

Many excellent publications—often with highly practical advice— prepared by various government departments, agencies, and committees. The easiest way to find out what's available is to write to the above address for "Price List 78—Social Services." This is free and includes descriptions and prices of current publications in the field of aging, family planning, handicapped, Medicare, nursing homes, pensions and retirement, poverty, social security, and social welfare. For overall news on trends, new programs and publications in aging—governmental and nongovernmental—the single most comprehensive publication is *Aging,* published monthly by the Administration of Aging of HEW. Subscriptions are available from the Government Printing Office at $2.50 a year.

287

- *American Association of Retired Persons / National Retired Teachers Association, 1909 K Street, N.W., Washington, D.C. 20006*

The two are sister organizations and, as in the case of their fine "Better Retirement" booklets, sometimes co-publishers. Annual membership in either organization is $2 and carries with it subscriptions to either *Modern Maturity* or *NRTA Journal* and news bulletins (as well as participation in money-saving services such as the purchase of medicines and prescription items, group travel plans, and group health insurance plans). The magazines' articles range from the inspirational to the hard fact and are consistently helpful. The "Better Retirement" booklets are free and individually cover such subjects as food, jobs, hobbies, moving, safety, health, pets, or most any area of life of interest to retirees.

- *National Council of Senior Citizens, 1511 K Street, N.W., Washington, D.C. 20005*

The National Council comes out of the trade union movement and still has a "Waiting for Lefty" flavor which I, for one, relish. Organized in 1961, its first job—in its own words—was to take on "one of the most powerful political lobbying organizations, the American Medical Association, in a David-Goliath struggle for health insurance for the elderly under Social Security (Medicare)." It now represents about 3 million members of more than 2,700 affiliated senior citizens clubs. Members of the clubs pay dues of $2.50 a year and share in a prescription drug program, a Medicare supplemental health insurance plan, and group travel arrangements. The monthly *Senior Citizens News* offers items about council and club events throughout the country and keeps a careful watch on legislative developments and the doings of legislators concerning the elderly.

- *The National Council on the Aging, 1828 L Street, N.W., Washington, D.C. 20036*

A voluntary nonprofit agency that provides leadership services and materials for organizations and individuals concerned with aid to the aging. Most of its publications are addressed to professionals and paraprofessionals, but its annual "Publications" lists many items on retirement and virtually all other aspects of aging of interest to the general reader, too. Some—like *Tender Loving Care: A Model Community Action Program to Employ Older People as Aides to Work with Very Young Children,* prepared by NCOA under contract to the Office of Economic Opportunity—are, indeed, models of their kind.

Various states of the Union have bureaus concerned solely with retirement prospects and opportunities. (There is, for example, the Florida Department of Commerce Retirement Department, Collins Building, Tallahassee, Fla. 32304.) They will be able to supply information about tax advantages, weather, life expectancy, companionship (over-65's make up almost 15% of Florida's total population), housing accommodations, and living costs. Information can be obtained by writing to the respective state capitals, usually to the Department of Commerce.

• *Department of National Health and Welfare, Brooke Claxton Building, Ottawa, Canada K1A 0K9,* is the most reliable source of Canadian information regarding pensions, income tax exemptions, and other beneficial legislation for older persons.

• *Office of Aging, Ministry of Community and Social Services, 5th Floor, Hepburn Building, Queens Park, Toronto, Ontario M7A 1E9,* distributes free literature about the various services of the Ministry, homes for the aged, and welfare centers, and has a large staff which provides information on request.

• *The National Pensioners and Senior Citizens Federation, 105 Fourth Street, Toronto, Ontario M8V 2Y4,* a voluntary nonprofit organization operated by and for the older people of Canada, published a small quarterly periodical, studies new pertinent legislation, is in the process of establishing a governmental lobby regarding problems of older persons, and maintains a limited information and referral service.

• *Community Information Center of Metropolitan Toronto, Box 595, Station Q, Toronto, Ontario M4T 2N4,* is a good source of information and distributes, at a small charge, booklets on available services and rights of older persons.

NOTES AND SOURCES

INTRODUCTION

The quotation from J. B. Priestley appears in *Time*, September 24, 1973.

Now in its fourth edition, *The Care of the Geriatric Patient*, edited by E. V. Cowdry and Franz U. Steinberg (St. Louis, Mo.: Mosby, 1971), is addressed to the internist, but much of it is comprehensible to anyone who wants to keep his doctor on his toes.

CHAPTER 1, THE PROMISE OF AGE

"The young voice" quotation comes from the mystery story *The China Governess*, by Margery Allingham (New York: Manor Books, 1971), the other from a *New York Times Book Review*, but such references abound.

Dr. Maslow was chairman of the psychology department of Brandeis University, a president of the American Psychological Association and—in the words of Joyce Carol Oates—"a tough-minded philosopher whose books give us the vocabulary for a new assessment of the world." The quotation used here appears in *Death Education: Preparation for Living*, proceedings of a symposium sponsored by Hamline University, St. Paul, Minnesota, edited by Betty R. Green and Donald P. Irish (Cambridge, Mass.: Schenkman, 1971).

The study "Factors in Age Awareness," by Ewald W. Busse, Frances C. Jeffers, and Walter D. Christ, was a project of the Duke University Center for Aging and Human Development. It is described in *Normal Aging: Reports from the Duke Longitudinal Study, 1955–1969*, edited by Erdman Palmore (Durham, N.C.: Duke University Press, 1970).

Wilma T. Donahue's remarks appear in *46 National Leaders Speak Out on Options for Older Americans*, prepared for the 1971 White House Conference on Aging by the National Retired Teachers Association and the American Association of Retired Persons (Washington, D.C., 1971).

The description of the singing career of 90-year-old Elizabeth Gilfillan appears in *Modern Maturity*, February-March 1971.

The figures for retirement ages in various countries of the world come from *Vie et Santé: Chronique du 3e âge* (Paris), October 1971.

The quest for better age descriptions for workers is described by Norman Sprague, director of the National Institute of Industrial Gerontology, in "A Note on Terminology," *The Gerontologist*, Spring 1968.

The set of maximum life spans appears in the *Encyclopaedia Britannica*, 1967 edition; other sources give somewhat different figures.

Dr. James E. Birren is a leading American gerontologist and editor-in-chief of *Journal of Gerontology*. The center he heads is now called the Ethel Percy Andrus Gerontology Center at the University of Southern California, dedicated in 1973 in honor of the late founder of the American Association of Retired Persons and the National Retired Teachers Association. Dr. Birren's basic ideas are given in his chapter, "Principles of Research and Aging," in *Handbook of Aging and the Individual*, edited by James E. Birren (Chicago and London: University of Chicago Press, 1960).

Dr. Bromley can be held responsible only for the first two of the observations about growing old. They appear, along with much useful information, in his book *The Psychology of Human Ageing* (Harmondsworth and Baltimore, Md.: Penguin, 1966).

CHAPTER 2, OUR WORLD GROWS OLDER

Population statistics and figures on the aged in the United States come from a variety of sources, notably *Statistical Abstract of the United States*, 1971, 92d edition (Washington, D.C.: Bureau of the Census, 1972); the monthly *Statistical Bulletin* of the Metropolitan Life Insurance Company, New York; and specialized publications such as *The Older Population: Some Facts We Should Know*, prepared by Herman Brotman (Washington, D.C.: Administration on Aging, 1971). Worldwide figures come from the *United Nations Demographic Yearbook*, 1970, or the *United Nations Statistical Yearbook*, 1972, from various publications of the World Bank or of demographic bureaus of the respective countries.

Ethel Shanas is professor of sociology, University of Illinois in Chicago; Bernice L. Neugarten is a psychologist and chairman, Committee on Human Development, University of Chicago, and past president of the Gerontological Society. Their comments—and others used in this book—appear in *46 National Leaders Speak Out* (cited in Chapter 1). Marguerite L. Buser's views appear in *Age Concern Today*, a quarterly publication of the National Old People's Welfare Council, London. Gray Pantherlady Margaret Kuhn is now making news with her insistence that old people are "getting the shaft" (her term) and is quoted from *The New York Times, Washington Post*, and elsewhere.

The reference to Sheffield as a geriatric slum appears in *On Our Conscience: The Plight of the Elderly*, by Jack Shaw (Harmondsworth and Baltimore, Md.: Penguin, 1971). Mr. Shaw was head of a team of five Sheffield *Star* journalists which found more than 1,300 examples of old people living neglected and miserable lives in the heart of the thriving city.

Baroness Stocks's reflections appear in *Age Concern Today*, Spring 1972.

Cheyne's advice appears in "George Cheyne's Essay on Health and Long Life," by Trevor H. Howell, *The Gerontologist*, Autumn 1969.

The Duke University research is reported in "Wives and Retirement: A Pilot Study," by Dorothy K. Heyman and Frances C. Jeffers, *Journal of Gerontology*, October 1968.

The quotation from Dr. Nathan W. Shock comes from *46 National Leaders Speak Out on Options for Older Americans* (cited in Chapter 1). Dr. Shock is chief of the Gerontology Research Center, National Institute of Child Health and Human Development, Baltimore, Maryland.

The statements by Nobel Laureates Northrop and Thomson appear in *Extended Youth: The Promise of Gerontology*, by Robert W. Prehoda (New York: Putnam, 1968).

Kenneth Boulding's remark appeared in an article he contributed to *The Careless Technology: Ecology and International Development*, edited by M. Taghi Farvar and John P. Milton (London: Stacey, 1973).

The speech by Sir Richard Doll, Regius professor of medicine at Oxford, was reported in *The Daily Telegraph* (London), June 28, 1973. The following day, the newspaper reported reactions under the heading " 'Prepare for death' plea angers pensioners" and editorialized: ". . . it is surely going too far to suggest that people of 65 and over have some sort of 'social responsibility' to 'live dangerously.' This comes close to saying that it is their duty to get out of the way as soon as they decently can in order to make room for younger people. Perhaps Sir Richard was joking. Even so, his jest has worrying implications."

Dr. Harry Sobel's note appeared in "The Control of Longevity," *The Gerontologist*, September 1966, based upon a lecture delivered in the University of California, Los Angeles, Human Agenda series. Dr. Sobel was then visiting professor-in-residence at UCLA and chief of aging research, Veterans Administration Hospital, Sepulveda, California.

Edwin Kaskowitz, in conversation with the author, October 31, 1973.

Harvey Wheeler's highly original image of the future appears in his article "The Rise of the Elders," *Saturday Review*, December 5, 1970.

Robert J. Havighurst is internationally renowned for his contributions to gerontological thought and progress. This statement on the quality of life after 60 comes from his article "Body, Self and Society," *Sociology and Social Research*, April 1965.

CHAPTER 3, THE COURSE OF LIFE

Erik H. Erikson's theory appears in his book *Childhood and Society* (New York: Norton; London: Hogarth Press, 1950) and is discussed in "Erikson's Eight Stages of Man," by David Elkind, *The New York Times Magazine*, January 18, 1970.

Professor Havighurst's "Dominant Concerns in the Life Cycle" appears in *Festschrift für Charlotte Bühler: Gegenwartsprobleme der Entwicklungspsychologie* (Göttingen: Verlag für Psychologie; Dr. C. J. Hogrete, 1963). It is used here with permission of the author and publisher. The title of this chapter, "The Course of Life," is suggested by Professor Havighurst, who notes that, although not as familiar in English as "life cycle," it is a better translation of the German *Lebenslauf* as used by Charlotte Bühler.

Havighurst's Searle Award Address was given at the Twentieth Annual Meeting of the Gerontological Society, November 10, 1967, and appears in *The Gerontologist,* Summer 1968.

Among G. Stanley Hall's pertinent works are "The Contents of Children's Minds," *Princeton Review,* 1883, and *Senescence: The Last Half of Life* (New York: Appleton, 1922).

James E. Birren's comment appears in his article "Aging: Psychological Aspects," *The International Encyclopaedia of the Social Sciences* (New York: Macmillan and Free Press, 1968), Vol. 1, pp. 176–86.

The comment of John G. Taylor, professor of applied mathematics, Kings College, University of London, appeared in *The Times Literary Supplement* (London), June 23, 1972.

The remarks by Theodore Lidz appear in his book *The Person: His Development Through the Life Cycle* (New York: Basic Books, 1968).

The material cited here from Bernice L. Neugarten comes from her chapter, "The Awareness of Middle Age," in *Middle Age and Aging: A Reader in Social Psychology,* edited by Dr. Neugarten (Chicago and London: University of Chicago Press, 1968). It is based on a study carried out in collaboration with Dr. Ruth J. Kraines, lecturer in human development, University of Chicago, and James E. Birren.

Dr. Looft's statement appears in his article "Reflections on Intervention in Old Age: Motives, Goals, and Assumptions," *The Gerontologist,* Spring 1973. Dr. Looft is associate professor of human development, College of Human Development, Pennsylvania State University.

A fuller description of the Townsend Plan appears in *Since Yesterday: The Nineteen-Thirties in America,* by Frederick Lewis Allen (New York: Harper, 1940).

Margaret Kuhn's remarks appear in "An Eminent Gray Panther," by Phil Casey, *Washington Post,* July 22, 1973.

The Cornell and Purdue studies are reported in "Are the Aged a Minority Group?" by Gordon F. Streib, in *Middle Age and Aging,* edited by Bernice L. Neugarten, *op. cit.*

Information about American elections appears in *The Real Majority: An Extraordinary Examination of the American Electorate,* by Richard M. Scammon and Ben J. Wattenberg (New York: Coward, McCann, 1970).

John Schmidhauser's remarks appear in his article "The Political Influence of the Aged," *The Gerontologist,* Spring 1968. Dr. Schmidhauser is professor of political science, University of Iowa.

Angus Campbell's remarks appear in his article "Politics through the Life Cycle," *The Gerontologist,* Summer 1971.

M. Warner Schaie's remarks appear in his article "Intervention Toward an Ageless Society?," *The Gerontologist,* Spring 1973.

The Nashville study is reported in "Interracial Attitudes Among the Old," by Jeanne M. Thune, Celia Webb, and Leland E. Thune, *The Gerontologist,* Winter 1971, Part I.

CHAPTER 4, WHY WE MUST GROW OLD

Biologists—including cell and molecular biologists, biophysicists and biochemists, immunologists and theoretical biologists—have made enormous progress in the past quarter-century in revealing and translating the genetic code. Their reports are voluminous, detailed, and highly complex, and I have sought here to simplify greatly. These are some of the sources for material in this chapter.

Articles:

Isaac Asimov, "Why We Must Grow Old," *Science Digest,* December 1970.

"Aspects of Aging," *Oasis* (The Social Security Administration, Washington, D.C.), February 1972.

Charles H. Barrows, Jr., "The Challenge—Mechanisms of Biological Aging," *The Gerontologist,* Spring 1971, Part I. Dr. Barrows is with the Gerontology Research Center, National Institute of Child Health and Human Development, Baltimore, Md.

"Can Aging Be Cured?," *Newsweek,* April 16, 1973.

Howard J. Curtis, "A Composite Theory of Aging," *The Gerontologist,* September 1966, Part I.

Albert Damon, Carl C. Seltzer, Herbert W. Stoudt, and Benjamin Bell, "Age and Physique in Healthy White Veterans in Boston," *Journal of Gerontology,* April 1972. Drawn from the Normative Aging Study, Boston Outpatient Clinic, Veterans Administration, Boston, Mass.

Alfred H. Lawton, "Characteristics of the Geriatric Person," *The Gerontologist,* Summer 1968. Dr. Lawton is dean of the College of Medicine, University of South Florida.

"Programmed Biological Obsolescence," *The Johns Hopkins Magazine,* Spring 1968.

Morris Rockstein, "The Biological Aspects of Aging," *The Gerontologist,* Summer 1968. Dr. Rockstein is professor of Physiology, School of Medicine, University of Miami.

Alvin Rosenfeld, "The Longevity Seekers," *Saturday Review—Science,* March 1973.

Nathan W. Shock, "Age with a Future," *The Gerontologist,* Autumn 1968, Part I.

E. V. Cowdry and Franz U. Steinberg (eds.), *The Care of the Geriatric Patient,* 4th ed. (St. Louis, Mo.: Mosby, 1971).

Books:

Carl Eisdorfer, "Background and Theories of Aging," in *The Future of Aging and the Aged,* edited by George L. Maddox (Atlanta, Ga.: Southern Newspaper Publishers Association Foundation, 1971). Dr. Eisdorfer is now chairman, Department of Psychiatry, School of Medicine, University of Washington, Seattle.

Leo Gitman, *Endocrines and Aging* (Springfield, Ill.: Thomas, 1967).

Robert W. Prehoda, *Extended Youth: The Promise of Gerontology* (New York: Putnam, 1968).

Nathan W. Shock, "The Beginning of Deterioration," in *The Art of Predictive Medicine,* by Webster L. Marxer and George R. Cowgill (Springfield, Ill.: Thomas, 1966).

Nathan W. Shock and Neil Solomon, "Physiology of Aging," in *Dentistry for the Special Patient,* by Arthur Davidoff *et al.* (Philadelphia: Saunders, 1972).

Statistics on life expectancy are drawn from "Health Characteristics of the Elderly" (August 1968) and "American Longevity" (August 1970), articles in the *Statistical Bulletin* of the Metropolitan Life Insurance Company, New York.

CHAPTER 5, AGE AND NUTRITION

Two basic works on nutrition provide many of the insights in this chapter. One is the section "Nutrition," by Henry A. Schroeder, in *The Care of the Geriatric Patient,* edited by E. V. Cowdry and Franz U. Steinberg, 4th ed. (St. Louis, Mo.: Mosby, 1971). Dr. Schroeder is professor of physiology, Trace Element Laboratory, Dartmouth Medical School. Much of his work is completely suitable for the lay reader, and its tables on dietary intake, vitamins, and elements are helpful to persons interested in their own nutritional problems.

The other is a special issue of *The Gerontologist* (Autumn 1969) called "Nutrition and Aging: A Monograph for Practitioners," edited by Sandra C. Howell and Martin B. Loeb. Dr. Howell was then with the Department of Community Medicine, St. Louis University School of Medicine, and projects director of the Gerontological Society; Dr. Loeb is director of the School of Social Welfare, University of Wisconsin. The monograph, made possible through a grant from the Administration on Aging, is a treasury of fundamental and practical information, and its appendixes make it fun as well. A table, "Calories Expended During Various Physical Activities," discloses that "Caring for Young children (feeding, dressing, etc.)" uses up more calories per minute (.06 C/kg./min.) than does "Marching or playing in band" (.05) and the same number as Golf, with caddy." "Making up beds" consumes more calories (.06) than does "Cycling" (.05). "Shopping for groceries" (.05) uses up twice as many calories as "Waiting while wife shops for groceries" (.025). "Unspecified or miscellaneous housework" takes up .05, while "Active sitting (writing, talking, etc.)"—which could describe many men at their jobs—takes up only .027. No one says so, but this gives the idea that, unless the man is a manual worker, a woman expends more energy than her husband, therefore is presumably thinner, and, as we all know, lives longer.

Among the excellent publications of the U.S. Department of Agriculture on many aspects of food and nutrition is *Food Guide for Older Folks,* an inexpensive 24-page booklet of practical information and recipes prepared especially for budget-conscious older people. (Home and Garden Bulletin No. 17—stock number 0100–1515, revised February 1972, obtainable from the Superintendent of Documents, Washington, D.C. 20402).

The National Academy of Sciences comment on vitamin E was widely reported by the Associated Press on September 11, 1973.

Dr. Jean Mayer's views appear in an interview, "Diet and Aging," by Arthur S. Freese, in *Modern Maturity,* April-May 1973.

The conclusion that detection of malnutrition in the old is "nearly always worthwhile" is made by A. N. Exton-Smith in his article "Nutrition Surveys and the Problems of Detection of Malnutrition in the Elderly," *Nutrition* (London), Vol. 24, 1970.

Jack Weinberg's remarks appear in "Psychologic Implications of the Nutritional Needs of the Elderly," *Journal of the American Dietetic Association,* April 1972. Dr. Weinberg is clinical director of the Illinois State Psychiatric Institute and professor of psychiatry, University of Illinois College of Medicine.

The quotation from Dr. Shock appears in *Newsweek,* April 16, 1973.

Dr. Montoye's comment comes from the book *Golden Age Exercises,* by Frances King and William F. Herzig (New York: Gramercy, 1968). The book's jacket bears the subtitle "A proven system of physical conditioning for the health and well-being of men and women over 60," and the book offers just that: gentle and realistic exercises which are done daily and with much joy by the old people who come to New York's Sirovich Day Center, run by Miss King.

Dr. Peyton's calculations come from his book *Practical Nutrition,* 2d edition (Philadelphia: Lippincott, 1962).

Some of the experiments of Dr. de Vries and his associates are described in "Comparison of Exercise Responses in Old and Young Men," two articles by Herbert A. de Vries and Gene M. Adams, *Journal of Gerontology,* July 1972. The authors are with the Gerontology Center and Department of Physiology, University of Southern California.

The study of rats on a treadmill is reported by Dee W. Eddington, Arthur C. Cosmas, and William B. McCafferty in "Exercise and Longevity: Evidence for a Threshold Age," *Journal of Gerontology,* July 1972.

The salt-free cure for insomnia is reported by Otto Wolfgang in his article "How Aging Affects Sleep," *Modern Maturity,* December 1970-January 1971. The doctor who tested it is M. M. Miller of Washington, D.C. The findings about the changed effects of barbiturates and coffee on the old is reported by Alfred H. Lawton in "Characteristics of the Geriatric Person," *The Gerontologist,* Summer 1968.

Dr. Shock presents the dilemma in "Physiologic Aspects of Aging," *Journal of the American Dietetic Association,* June 1970.

W. Ferguson Anderson is professor of geriatric medicine, University of Glasgow. His question comes from *The British Encyclopaedia of Medical Practice—Medical Progress, 1971–72* (London: Butterworths, 1972).

Dr. Horwitt's remarkable statement is reported in *The New York Times,* September 30, 1973.

CHAPTER 6, MIND, MEMORY, AND TIME

Frances M. Carp's findings are reported in "Senility or Garden Variety Maladjustment?," *Journal of Gerontology,* April 1969.

The senility label is discussed in "A Social Role Analysis of Senility," by Michael Baizerman and David L. Ellison, of the Graduate School of Public Health, University of Pittsburgh, in *The Gerontologist,* Summer 1971, Part I. After mentioning how the old are sometimes institutionalized on specious grounds of senility, Drs. Baizerman and Ellison close with the question: "Several Eskimo tribes were considered barbaric in the white world because of their social institution in which older people 'went to the ice to die, alone.' Are we really that progressive?"

"Sensory Training Puts Patients in Touch" is a good description of a program at the White Plains (New York) Center for Nursing Care. Written by high-school senior Beth Heidell from her own experience, it tells how the brain-damaged old may be helped to regain use of their senses. *Modern Nursing Home,* June 1972.

Dr. William A. Nolen is quoted from "Senility and How You Can Avoid It," McCall's, October 1971.

Dr. Henry J. Mark is associate professor of environmental medicine, The Johns Hopkins School of Medicine. His remarks appear in "The Good Life and the Aging Brain," *The Johns Hopkins Magazine,* Spring 1968.

Robert N. Butler's quotation comes from his chapter, "The Life Review: An Interpretation of Reminiscence in the Aged," in *New Thoughts on Old Age,* edited by Robert Kastenbaum (New York: Springer, 1964). See also "An Explanatory Study of Reminiscence," by Robert J. Havighurst and Richard Glazer, *Journal of Gerontology,* April 1972; and "Reminiscing and Self-Concept in Old Age," by Charles N. Lewis, *Journal of Gerontology,* April 1971.

Dr. Belle Boone Beard is director of centenarian research, Sweet Briar College, Virginia. References here come from her articles, "Some Characteristics of Recent Memory of Centenarians," *Journal of Gerontology,* January 1968, and "Social and Psychological Correlates of Residual Memory in Centenarians," *The Gerontologist,* June 1967, Part I.

Dr. Jon Kangas is director of the Testing and Counseling Services,

University of Santa Clara, California, and the author of "Intelligence at Middle Age: A Thirty-Eight-Year Follow-Up," *Developmental Psychology,* Vol. 5, No. 2, 1971.

Drs. Blum and Jarvik also serve with the Department of Psychiatry, College of Physicians and Surgeons, Columbia University. Some aspects of the New York State Psychiatric Institute longitudinal study are reported in "Intellectual Change and Sex Differences in Octogenarians," by June E. Blum, James L. Fosshage, and Lissy F. Jarvik, *Developmental Psychology,* Vol. 7, No. 2, 1972. Others are covered in "Genetic Components and Intellectual Functioning During Senescence: A 20-Year Study of Aging Twins," by Lissy F. Jarvik, June E. Blum, and Andre O. Varna, *Behavior Genetics,* Vol. 2, No. 2/3, 1972; and "Rate of Change on Selective Tests of Intelligence: A 20-Year Longitudinal Study of Aging," by June E. Blum, Lissy F. Jarvik, and Edward T. Clark, *Journal of Gerontology,* July 1970.

Dr. Birren's statement is made in "Toward an Experimental Psychology of Aging," *American Psychologist,* Vol. 25, 1970.

Professor Alan T. Welford tells about characteristics of the old in intelligence tests in "Psychometer Performance," in *Handbook of Aging and the Individual,* edited by James E. Birren (Chicago and London: University of Chicago Press, 1960).

Jeanne Gilbert's remark appears in "Patterns of Declining Memory," *Journal of Gerontology,* January 1971.

Some of the references to Dr. Birren's views used here come from "Psychological Aspects of Aging: Intellectual Functioning," *The Gerontologist,* Spring 1968, Part II, and from "Does Your Mind Age?" by James A. Peterson, in which Dr. Birren is interviewed. *Modern Maturity,* October-November 1971.

Dr. Bromley's statement appears in "Studies of Intellectual Function in Relation to Age and Their Significance for Professional and Managerial Functions," *Interdisciplinary Topics in Gerontology* (Basel and New York), Vol. 4, 1969. Dr. Bromley is president of the British Society of Social and Behavioural Gerontology and author of *The Psychology of Human Ageing* (Harmondsworth and Baltimore, Md.: Penguin, 1966), among other works. Another specialist in the field of problem solving is Dr. Marguerite L. Young of the National Institute of Mental Health; an example of her work is "Age and Sex Differences in Problem Solving," *Journal of Gerontology,* October 1971.

Disorders of Memory and Learning, by George A. Talland (Harmondsworth and Baltimore, Md.: Penquin, 1968), has excellent but highly scientific material on the subject of aging.

Uncle Antonin is a character in *The Second Face,* by Marcel Aymé (New York: Harper, 1951).

The emotional reaction to time is mentioned in "The Place of Time and Aging in the Natural Sciences and Scientific Philosophy," by Maria Reichenbach and Ruth Anna Mathers, in *Handbook of Aging and the Individual,* edited by James E. Birren, *op. cit.*

Alvin Toffler's remark appears in *Future Shock* (New York: Random House, 1970). Material about the various types of biological clocks comes from the *Encyclopaedia Britannica,* 1967 edition; *Extended Youth,* by Robert W. Prehoda (New York: Putnam, 1968); "Biological Periodicities, Mathematical Biology, and Aging," by Herbert D. Landahl, in *Handbook of Aging and the Individual, op. cit.;* and *Mathematical Biology,* by V. A. Kostitzin (London: Harrap, 1939).

Dr. Robert E. Ornstein, research psychologist, Langley-Porter Neuropsychiatric Institute, San Francisco, California, is the author of *On the Experience of Time* (Harmondsworth and Baltimore, Md.: Penguin, 1969).

CHAPTER 7, WHAT IT'S LIKE TO BE OLD

Dr. Frances M. Carp's study (which was supported by the Hogg Foundation for Mental Health, University of Texas, Austin) is described in "Attitudes of Old Persons Toward Themselves and Toward Others," *Journal of Gerontology,* July 1967.

Andrew Hendrickson, visiting professor of adult education, Florida State University, Tallahassee, is the author of "A Geriatric Autobiographical Sketch," *The Gerontologist,* Spring 1973, which was written in response to an editorial request for autogerontology made in the Autumn 1972 issue of *The Gerontologist.* The fact that Professor Hendrickson is having a uniquely successful old age may account for his writing about it; I have seen no other responses in the publication.

"The Old Man in the Bronx," by Herb Goro, appears in *New York,* January 10, 1972.

Philip Wylie's article, "Our Old People: Part of Their Lonely Exile Is Their Own Fault," appears in *Today's Health,* August 1971.

John Kenneth Galbraith's comment appears in his article "Eleanor and Franklin Revisited," *The New York Times Book Review,* March 19, 1972.

"How Does It Feel to Grow Old?" by Robert J. Havighurst, appears in *The Gerontologist,* September 1966. The responses of five men and six women were the substance of the article "How Does It Feel to Grow Old—Eleven Essayists Answer," by Jean L. Roberts and Larry R. Kimsey, *The Gerontologist,* Winter 1972. Dr. Roberts and Dr. Kimsey are with the Department of Psychiatry, University of Texas Southwestern Medical School.

The analysis of the "Forget Me Not" television program appears in "A Ninety-Minute Inquiry: The Expressed Needs of the Elderly," by Elaine M. Brody and Stanley J. Brody, *The Gerontologist,* Summer 1970.

The "living on an island" response appears in *The Johns Hopkins Magazine,* Spring 1968.

Old People in Three Industrial Societies is by Ethel Shanas, Peter Townsend, Dorothy Wedderburn, Henning Friis, Poul Milhøj, and Jan Stehouwer (London: Routledge & Kegan Paul; Chicago: Aldine-Atherton,

1968). This major cross-national survey arose out of discussions of the Social Research Committee of the International Gerontological Association.

Dr. Marjorie Lowenthal's study of the relationship of loneliness and mental health was made under the auspices of the Langley-Porter-Institute, San Francisco, California. The findings reported here, and subsequent comments by James Peterson, come from Dr. Peterson's article "Loneliness in the Later Years," *Modern Maturity,* August-September 1972. Dr. Peterson, a foremost interpreter of new research in the field of aging, is director of liaison for the American Association of Retired Persons and the Andrus Gerontology Center at the University of Southern California.

Dr. Theodore Lidz's story about preconceptions is told in his book *The Person: His Development Through the Life Cycle* (New York: Basic Books, 1968).

The story of Mr. and Mrs. Johns appears in "Basic Knowledge for Work with the Aging," by Naomi Brill, *The Gerontologist,* Autumn 1969. Miss Brill is on the faculty of the Graduate School of Social Work, University of Nebraska, Lincoln.

"Psychological Developments in the Second Half of Life," by Robert Peck, appears in *Psychological Aspects of Aging,* edited by John E. Anderson (Washington, D.C.: American Psychological Association, 1956).

The study by Elaine Cumming and Mary Lou Parlegreco, which they made in Kansas City, Missouri, is described in "The Very Old," in *Growing Old: The Process of Disengagement,* by Elaine Cumming and William E. Henry (New York: Basic Books, 1961).

The statement by Dr. Henry Betts appears in "Let the Handicapped in Our Buildings," by Harold A. Katz, *Today's Health,* May 1972.

The American city studied was New Orleans. The study's author, H. E. Bracey, notes in his book *In Retirement* (Baton Rouge, La.: Louisiana State University Press, 1966) that in the United States, particularly, the ability to drive a car is so important that without it "you may be literally marooned in your own house."

Cyril F. Brickfield's remarks appear in "Getting There Is Half the Problem," *NRTA Journal,* July-August 1972.

Let's End Isolation is Administration on Aging Publication No. 129 (Washington, D.C.: U.S. Government Printing Office, 1972).

Interesting, useful material is contained in *The Multi-Purpose Senior Center: A Model Community Action Program,* prepared by the National Council on the Aging for the Office of Economic Opportunity, June 1972 (revised).

The statement about the eventual role of senior centers in the lives of the old was made by John B. Martin, commissioner, Administration on Aging.

Hayward McDonald's comments appear in "Let the Handicapped in Our Buildings," by Harold A. Katz, *Today's Health,* May 1972.

The "trivial proportion" statement is made by Frances M. Carp. Together with supporting facts, it appears in "Retired People as Automobile Passengers," *The Gerontologist,* Spring 1972. San Antonio, Texas, is the city studied. Dr. Carp adds that generally the old would rather drive with someone from a community agency. When they have to rely on a relative or friend, they feel a loss of independence and that they are "being a burden."

CHAPTER 8, THE OLD IN THEIR FAMILIES

A primary source of statistical material and much insight into the ways of life and behavior of the elderly appear in *Old People in Three Industrial Societies* (cited in Chapter 7). This cross-national survey of the old in Denmark, Great Britain, and the United States developed out of discussions held under the auspices of the Social Research Committee of the International Gerontological Association and now stands as a uniquely successful exercise in international research cooperation. Some of the facts in this chapter comparing American and British conditions and attitudes—and some of the fresh views of family life—stem from this work. Another publication of great value in this field is "Aging and the Family," a special issue (January 1972) of *The Family Coordinator: Journal of Education, Counseling, and Service,* published quarterly by the National Council on Family Relations, Minneapolis, Minnesota. The special issue is edited by Felix M. Berardo of the University of Florida. A good general discussion of the family life of the old appears in *The Aged, the Family, and the Community,* by Minna Field (New York and London: Columbia University Press, 1972).

The estimate of the amount of time spent by the old at home is made by Gary D. Hansen in *Housing Issues: Proceedings of the Fifth Annual Meeting, American Association of Housing Educators,* University of Nebraska, 1971.

Simone de Beauvoir looks at the past in *Old Age* (London: Deutsch and Weidenfeld & Nicolson, 1972; issued in the United States as *The Coming of Age,* New York: Putnam, 1972).

Lewis Mumford's description appears in *The City in History: Its Origins, Its Transformations, and Its Prospects* (New York: Harcourt, Brace & World, 1961).

The percentages on where the old live come from *Aging in Society,* Vol. 1: *An Inventory of Research Findings,* by Matilda W. Riley and Anne Foner (New York: Russell Sage Foundation, 1968).

The quotation from Sussman and Burchinal appears in their article "Kin Family Network," *Marriage and Family Living,* August 1962.

The account of Nelba Chavez appears in *A Different Woman,* by Jane Howard (New York: Dutton, 1973).

Comparative figures for ages at time of marriage and bearing of children and some of their implications for future generations appear in *Old People in Three Industrial Societies, op. cit.*

The quotations on discipline and affection in the family come from the chapter "The Old Person in a Family Context," by Gordon F. Streib and Wayne E. Thompson, in *Handbook of Social Gerontology: Societal Aspects of Aging,* edited by Clark Tibbitts (Chicago and London: University of Chicago Press, 1960).

Dr. Simos's study, "Relations of Adults with Aging Parents," is reported in *The Gerontologist,* Summer 1970.

Freud's view is quoted in "On Loneliness," by Henry D. Von Witzleben, in *Psychiatry,* Vol. 21, 1958.

Some of the differences between becoming a widow and becoming a widower are pointed up in a most original study, "Reactions to Widowhood in the Elderly," presented at the 1972 annual meeting of the American Psychiatric Association by Dorothy K. Heyman and Daniel T. Gianturco, both of the Duke University Medical Center. It is popularly assumed that a man is bewildered and inept around the house after his wife dies. That may be true but Professors Heyman and Gianturco found it is women who are less happy after widowhood. Particularly if they have been primarily homemakers all their married lives. Widows suffer a loss of role central to their "self esteem and gratification" and feel useless. They suffer further because they no longer have anyone to share their thoughts with. In psychiatric ratings, it is widows who report an increase in "depressive feelings," even though they remain somewhat more active than widowers.

The processes of widowhood are described in "Widowhood and Preventive Intervention," by Phyllis R. Silverman, *The Family Coordinator,* January 1972. Dr. Silverman is with the Department of Psychiatry, Harvard Medical School.

The study of old people in working-class London is *The Family Life of Old People,* by Peter Townsend (London: Routledge & Kegan Paul, 1957; abridged edition, with a new postscript, Harmondsworth and Baltimore, Md.: Penguin, 1963).

Margaret Mead is quoted in the article "Grandparents Who 'Cop Out,'" by Lillian G. Genn, *Modern Maturity,* April-May 1973.

Joseph Weinreb's warning and the dos and don'ts for gandparents that follow come from the article "Ten Tips for Grandparents," by Lillian G. Genn, *Modern Maturity,* August-September 1972.

Gordon F. Streib of Cornell University is here quoted from his article "Older Families and Their Troubles: Familial and Social Responses," *The Family Coordinator,* January 1972.

CHAPTER 9, SEX AND MARRIAGE

Some gerontologists may be exhausting the subject; the introduction to a recent article in a scientific journal—based upon a study of "4,200 persons ranging in age from 8 to 99"—announces as a finding that "it appears that persons in our culture exhibit sexuality in their mental processes to a greater degree than in their actions." If this means what I think it does—that people think about sex more than they do anything about it—it is a finding I made by myself in early adolescence. The following references have more original things to say.

Erdman Palmore is associate professor of medical sociology, Center for the Study of Aging and Human Development, Duke University. Dr. Palmore's "Attitudes Toward Aging as Shown by Humor" appears in *The Gerontologist,* August 1971, Part I.

Degas's remark appears in *My Life and Loves,* by Frank Harris (New York: Grove, 1963).

Other jokes about old age appear in *Rationale of the Dirty Joke,* by G. Legman (New York: Grove, 1968; London: Cape, 1969).

The myths about the old are discussed in James A. Peterson's article "Marriage and Sex and the Older Man and Woman," *Modern Maturity,* December 1970–January, 1971.

Human Sexual Response (Boston: Little, Brown, 1966) and *Human Sexual Inadequacy* (Boston: Little, Brown, 1970), by William H. Masters and Virginia E. Johnson, will answer many questions that come to mind on the subject of sex and aging.

The famous Kinsey study is *Sexual Behavior in the Human Male,* by Alfred C. Kinsey, Wardell Pomeroy, and Clyde E. Martin (Philadelphia and London: Saunders, 1948).

Institute for Sex Research figures on the ages of men charged with sexual offenses against children are reported in *Sex Offenders,* by Paul H. Gebhard *et al.* (New York: Harper & Row, 1965).

The 1954 study is reported in "Wisconsin's Experience with Psychiatrically-Deviated Sexual Offenders," by M. J. Coogan, in *Proceedings of the 94th Annual Congress of Correction of the American Prison Association* (New York, 1954).

The 1967 study is "The Geriatric Sex Offender," by Frederick E. Whiskin, *Geriatrics,* Vol. 22, 1967, p. 168. Dr. Whiskin is a psychiatrist at Cushing Hospital, Framingham, Massachusetts.

Dr. Joseph T. Freeman is also consultant on geriatrics, Pennsylvania Medical Society and, clearly, my favorite author on this subject. His article "Sexual Aspects of Aging" appears in *The Care of the Geriatric Patient,* edited by E. V. Cowdry and Franz U. Steinberg, 4th ed. (St. Louis, Mo.: Mosby, 1971). The zoo incident is described in Dr. Freeman's article.

Dr. Isadore Rubin is editor of *Sexology* magazine and a fellow of the Society for the Scientific Study of Sex. The quotation is from his chapter "Sex After Forty—and After Seventy," in *An Analysis of Human Sexual Response,* edited by Ruth and Edward Brecher (New York: Signet, 1966).

Dr. Whiskin's article was first presented as a paper at the Second Annual Symposium on Old Age, held at Cushing Hospital in 1963; it later appeared as "On the Meaning and Function of Reading in Later Life," in *New Thoughts on Old Age,* edited by Robert Kastenbaum (New York: Springer, 1964).

The observation about life in nursing homes is cited from an article about Dr. Lichtman, "Nursing Home Elderly Follow Own Life Style," by Eleanor Kalter, New York *Sunday News*, August 27, 1972.

Dr. Berezin is quoted in *Time*, June 4, 1973.

The case studies were selected from a larger number cited by Dr. Freeman in "Sexual Aspects of Aging," *op. cit.*

The Neugarten-Wood-Kraines-Loomis study, "Women's Attitudes Toward the Menopause," is reported in *Vita Humana*, Vol. 6 (Basel and New York: Karger, 1963), and in abridged form in *Middle Age and Aging: A Reader in Social Psychology*, edited by Bernice L. Neugarten (Chicago and London: University of Chicago Press, 1968).

Gustave Newman and Claude R. Nichols are professors of psychiatry, Newman at the College of Medicine, University of Florida, Nichols at the University of Texas Southwestern Medical School at Dallas. Their study, "Sexual Activities and Attitudes in Older Persons," *Journal of the American Medical Association*, Vol. 173 (1960), pp. 33–35, was conducted in the Durham, North Carolina, area and made use of both black and white subjects and included comparisons of sexual activity by race and by socioeconomic status. Blacks were found to be more sexually active than whites; people of lower socioeconomic status more active than those of higher status. Most likely, all this proves is that, again, some of the best things in life are free.

In their study, "Mortality and Survival: Comparison of Eunuchs with Intact Men and Women in a Mentally Retarded Population" (*Journal of Gerontology*, October 1969), James B. Hamilton and Gordon E. Mestler observed institutionalized men who had been orchiectomized (had their testes removed) and women who had been oophorectomized (had their ovaries removed). The authors note that "experience with domestic animals and later with eunuchs apparently encouraged the belief that castrated males tend to be more tractable than intact males." I do not like the terms "orchiectomy" and "oophorectomy," and I had not realized, until reading this article, that the practice is followed in American institutions.

The Kinsey prescription comes from *Sexual Behavior in the Human Male, op. cit.* Dr. Mayer is quoted from his interview by Arthur S. Freese, "Diet and Aging," *Modern Maturity*, April-May 1973.

Doctors Verwoerdt, Pfeiffer, and Wang are associate professors of psychiatry, Duke University Medical Center. Various aspects of their study reported here appear as "Sexual Behavior in Aged Men and Women: I. Observations on 254 Community Volunteers," *Psychiatry*, Vol. 19, 1968, pp. 756–58; "Sexual Behavior in Senescence: II. Patterns of Change in Sexual Activity and Interest of Aging Men and Women," *Geriatrics*, Vol. 24, 1969, pp. 137–54. The first two are also reprinted in *Normal Aging: Reports from the Duke University Longitudinal Study, 1955–1969*, edited by Erdman Palmore (Durham, N.C.: Duke University Press, 1970). Further study of 39 of the original 254 subjects appears as "The Natural History of Sexual Behavior in a Biologically Advantaged Group of Aged Individuals," *Journal of Gerontology,* April 1969. The table "Why Married Couples Stop Intercourse" is based on a sample of 140 subjects and is given in greater detail in *Archives of General Psychiatry,* Vol. 19, 1968, pp. 756–58.

Dr. Jack Botwinick, research psychologist at the National Institute of Mental Health, Bethesda, Maryland, presents an inspired discussion of changes in general responsiveness that occur with age—including sexual responsiveness—in his article "Drives, Expectancies, and Emotions," in *Handbook of Aging and the Individual,* edited by James E. Birren (Chicago and London: University of Chicago Press, 1960).

"The Double Standard of Aging" is the title of an article by Susan Sontag in *Saturday Review,* September 23, 1972.

Dr. Peter C. Pineo, professor of sociology, Carleton University, Ottawa, Canada, is the author of "Disenchantment in the Later Years of Marriage," which appears in *Middle Age and Aging,* edited by Bernice L. Neugarten, *op. cit.*

Retirement Marriage, by Walter C. McKain, is Monograph 3 published in January 1969 by Storrs Agricultural Experiment Station, University of Connecticut, Storrs, Connecticut. The research project was sponsored jointly by the National Institute of Health, the U.S. Public Health Service, and Storrs. Dr. McKain, professor of rural sociology, concludes the monograph with a "Test for a Successful Retirement Marriage," in which elderly couples contemplating marriage may use a point system to rate their prospects for "successful marriage practically assured," "very good chance," "an even chance," "very little chance," and "almost no chance." This test alone makes Dr. McKain's little book —retail cost $1.00—a bargain at any price.

Dr. Victor Kassel's article "Polygamy After 60" appears in *Geriatrics,* April 1966.

CHAPTER 10, RETIREMENT AND LEISURE

Juanita M. Kreps is professor of economics and dean of the Women's College at Duke University. Her remarks appear in *Lifetime Allocation of Work and Income: Essays in the Economics of Aging* (Durham, N.C.: Duke University Press, 1971), which is also the source of the quotation about Abraham Lincoln's aversion to work.

The study of blue-collar workers is reported in *Where Have All the Robots Gone?,* by Harold L. Sheppard and N. Q. Herrick (New York: Free Press-Macmillan, 1972).

The Peter Townsend quotation is from *The Family Life of Old People* (cited in Chapter 8).

Professor A. J. Jaffe is associated with the Bureau of Applied Social Research, Columbia University. His article, "The Middle Years: Neither Too Young nor Too Old," appears in *Industrial Gerontology* (Washington, D.C.: National Institute of Industrial Gerontology, National Council on Aging, 1971).

Leonard Davis's remarks appear in "Tomorrow's Role for Retirees," *Modern Maturity*, August-September 1972.

The United Steelworkers statement is quoted in *The Aging Worker and the Union: Employment and Retirement of Middle-Aged and Older Workers*, by Ewan Clague, Balraj Palli, and Leo Kramer (New York: Praeger, 1971).

William E. Oriel's remark appears in "Congress, Politics, and the Elderly," in *The Future of Aging and the Aged*, edited by George L. Maddox (Atlanta, Ga.: Southern Newspaper Publishers Association Foundation, 1971).

Joseph J. Spengler is James B. Duke professor of economics, Duke University. This quotation comes from his introduction to *Lifetime Allocation of Work and Income, op. cit.*

Alfred Sauvy's remarks appear in "The Passage from Activity to Inactivity," in *First International Course in Social Gerontology* (Paris: International Center of Social Gerontology, 1971). The quotation from Emile Thomas also appears in Professor Sauvy's lecture.

The statements by John W. Gardner and J. Cloyd Miller come from "For Preretirees Only," *NRTA Journal*, July-August 1972.

"Early Retirement Is Coming," by Paul M. Feine, *Dynamic Maturity*, May 1970, is a sound, popular treatment of the subject.

Edward Durell Stone was interviewed by Arthur S. Freese on the occasion of the opening of the Stone-designed Andrus Gerontology Center, University of Southern California ("The Man Who Designed It," *Modern Maturity*, February-March 1973).

"The needs and drives" list of the University of Iowa's Institute of Gerontology (not used in full here) was inspired by Clark Tibbitts, director of training for the Administration on Aging. The list and subsequent comments by Max Kaplan, director of the Arts Center, School of Fine and Applied Arts, Boston University, appear in Dr. Kaplan's chapter, "The Uses of Leisure," in *Handbook of Social Gerontology*, edited by Clark Tibbitts (cited in Chapter 8).

Frances M. Carp reports on her study in the article "Retirement Travel," *The Gerontologist*, Spring 1972.

The table on how older people spend their time is reprinted with permission from Exhibit 22.2 of *Aging and Society*, Vol. 1, by Matilda White Riley (New York: Russell Sage Foundation, 1968), © 1968 by Russell Sage Foundation, New York. (Adapted from Niebanck and Pope, 1965, p. 67.)

"Retirement and the Professional Worker" is the title of an article by Robert J. Havighurst and Ethel Shanas, *Journal of Gerontology*, January 1953.

Dr. Hershel L. Hearn, associate professor of sociology, University of

Missouri, Kansas City, is the author of "Aging and the Artistic Career," *The Gerontologist,* Winter 1972.

The Nation's Stake in the Employment of Middle-aged and Older Persons: A Working Paper was prepared by the staff of the Senior AIDES Program of the National Council of Senior Citizens, Inc., for the Special Committee on Aging, U.S. Senate (Washington, D.C.: U.S. Government Printing Office, 1971).

The case of the cat-food lady is described in *Time,* August 27, 1973.

Bernard Nash's report appears in "Our Work Has Just Begun," *Modern Maturity,* February-March 1972.

Julie Nixon Eisenhower's remark appears in "The Post-Conference Action Year," *Aging,* August 1972.

SERVE is described in *SERVE: Older Volunteers in Community Service—A New Role and a New Resource,* by Janet S. Sainer and Mary L. Zander (New York: Community Service Society of New York, 1971). Other programs are described in "It's Good to Know I'm Still Needed," by Anne K. Reisch, *Lutheran Women,* June 1972; "New Roles and Activities for Retirement," by Gordon F. Streib, *The Future of Aging and the Aged,* edited by George L. Maddox, *op. cit.;* "They're Repairing America the Beautiful," by Robert Dyment, *Modern Maturity,* October-November 1972; "Could You Be a VIP?" by Janet Lowe, *NRTA Journal,* July-August 1972; "Characteristics of Aged Participants and Non-Participants in Age-Segregated Leisure Programs," by Nina Bley, Mortimer Goodman, David Dye, and Bernice Harel, *The Gerontologist,* Winter 1972; and "Leisure Without Guilt," by James A. Peterson, *Modern Maturity,* February-March 1972.

Vol. II of the proceedings of the 1971 White House Conference on Aging appears under the title *Toward a National Policy on Aging* (Washington, D.C.: U.S. Government Printing Office, 1973). Howard Y. McClusky is professor emeritus of educational psychology and adult education, University of Michigan, Ann Arbor.

CHAPTER 11, THE OLD IN THEIR INSTITUTIONS

The Japanese problem is discussed in "Aging Disgracefully," *Time,* June 5, 1972.

The story of Mrs. Z and her babushka appears in "Basic Knowledge for Work with the Aging," by Naomi Brill, *The Gerontologist,* Autumn 1969, Part I.

Margrit Kessi's study is reported in *Aging in Western Societies: A Comparative Survey,* edited by Ernest W. Burgess (Chicago and London: University of Chicago Press, 1969).

The material about the DeWitt Nuring Home is based upon my visit and interviews with Dr. and Mrs. Lichtman as well as the article "With a Parent in a Nursing Home, Offspring Need to Express Their Emotions," by Virginia Lee Warren, *The New York Times,* September 4, 1972.

The case of Mrs. D is discussed in "Follow-up Study of Applicants and Non-Applicants to a Voluntary Nursing Home," by Elaine M. Brody, *The Gerontologist,* Autumn 1969, Part I. Miss Brody is director of social work, Philadelphia Geriatric Center.

The remarks by Dr. Margaret Blenkner, director of research, Benjamin Rose Institute, Cleveland, Ohio, appear in "Environmental Change and the Aging Individual," *The Gerontologist,* June 1967.

The findings of Nancy N. Anderson of the University of Minnesota are described in "Effects of Institutionalization on Self-Esteem," *Journal of Gerontology,* July 1967.

Peter Townsend's bleak view appears in *The Last Refuge: A Survey of Residential Institutions and Homes for the Aged in England and Wales* (London: Routledge & Kegan Paul, 1962).

Professor Morton A. Lieberman, of the Committee of Human Development, University of Chicago, is the author of "Institutionalization of the Aged: Effects on Behavior," *Journal of Gerontology,* July 1969, and of "Psychological Effects of Institutionalization," by Morton A. Lieberman, Valenica N. Prock, and Sheldon S. Tobin, *Journal of Gerontology,* July 1948. The nine personality traits are discussed in "Personality Traits as Predictors of Institutional Adaption Among the Aged," by Barbara F. Turney, Sheldon S. Tobin, and Morton A. Lieberman, *Journal of Gerontology,* January 1972.

Peter Townsend's remarks appear in "The Argument for Gradually Abandoning Communal Homes for the Aged," *International Social Science Journal,* Vol. XV, No. 3, 1963.

Helen Kistin is research associate, Levinson Gerontological Policy Institute, Brandeis University; Dr. Robert Morris is director of the Institute and professor of social planning, Florence Heller Gradute School, Brandeis University. Their article, "Alternatives to Institutional Care for the Elderly and Disabled," appears in *The Gerontologist,* Summer 1972, Part I.

Information about the Sirovich Senior Day Center is based on my visit there, material supplied by Miss Frances King, and the article "An Old-Age Center Where They Know They'll Find Affection," by Nan Ickeringill, *The New York Times,* September 28, 1970. Other centers are discussed in "City Seeks to Double Number of Centers for Elderly," by Peter Kihss, *The New York Times,* September 14, 1972, and in "Day Care Centers for Elderly Offer Many Advantages," by Judy Harrison, *The New York Times,* December 11, 1972.

"Alternatives to Nursing Home Care: Fact or Fiction" are discussed by Jerome Kaplan in *The Gerontologist,* Summer 1972, Part I.

Levindale is described in "A Day Care Program for the Physically and Emotionally Disabled," by Abraham Kostick, *The Gerontologist,* Summer 1972, Part I.

Israeli experiences are described in "Concepts of Old Age Care in a Young State," by I. Margulec, *World Medical Journal,* Vol. 3, 1971, and

"Two Decades of Caring for Aged in Israel," by I. Margulec, in *Depth and Extent of the Geriatric Problem*, edited by Minna Field (Springfield, Ill.: Thomas, 1970). Dr. Margulec is medical director of Malben-Joint Distribution Committee, Israel's main agency for taking care of aged and handicapped new immigrants. At this writing, the Tenth International Congress of Gerontology is scheduled to be held in Tel Aviv in June 1974, under the presidency of Dr. D. Danon, Weismann Institute of Science.

Simone de Beauvoir's remark about Communist countries appears in *Old Age* (London: Deutsch and Weidenfeld & Nicolson, 1972; issued in the United States as *The Coming of Age*, New York: Putnam, 1972).

The lack of architectural foresight in Sheffield is described in *On Our Conscience: The Plight of the Elderly*, by Jack Shaw (Harmondsworth and Baltimore, Md.: Penguin, 1971).

Mobile homes are discussed by Robert C. Reschke in "Mobile Homes: A New Life Style," *Retirement Living*, March 1973.

The story of Hirshen and Partners is told in "Architecture for the Aged," by Ronald Najman, *Saturday Review—The Arts*, May 1973.

Clark Tibbitts, Nathan W. Shock, and Bernice L. Neugarten are quoted in *46 National Leaders Speak Out on Options for Older Americans* (cited in Chapter 1).

Dr. James F. Trela is director of Vocational Guidance and Rehabilitation Services, Cleveland, Ohio. His conclusions appear in "Some Political Consequences of Senior Center and Other Old Age Group Memberships," *The Gerontologist*, Summer 1971, Part I.

The Leisure Haven cartoon appears in *The New Yorker*, January 27, 1973.

The Grenoble plan is studied in greater detail in *Time*, May 7, 1973.

CHAPTER 12, DEATH AND DYING

I have resisted quoting from William Cullen Bryant's "Thanatopsis" in this chapter, which is more than can be said by many other persons who have written about death and dying. Many writers are, indeed, now discussing the subject; and society's conspiracy of silence—which led British anthropologist Geoffrey Gorer to coin the phrase, "the pornography of death"—seems on its way to being broken. There are clubs, seminars, and symposia on the subject; a journal, *Omega*, is devoted solely to the psychological aspects of dying; and various excellent books are now available to the general reader—*Death as a Fact of Life*, by David Hendin (New York: Norton, 1973), and *Last Rights*, by Marya Mannes (New York: Morrow, 1974) are notable recent examples—and to the teenager and younger—such as *Death Is a Noun: A View of the End of Life*, by John Langone (Boston: Little, Brown, 1972). Titles I have found particularly helpful are listed here:

Freud's view of immortality and the description of his dying come from *The Life and Work of Sigmund Freud,* Vol. 3, *The Last Phase, 1919–1939,* by Ernest Jones (New York: Basic Books, 1957), and *Freud: Living and Dying,* by Max Schur (New York: International Universities Press, 1972).

More details about Mrs. Roosevelt appear in *Eleanor: The Years Alone,* by Joseph P. Lash (New York: Norton, 1972).

The opposum's and other imitations of death are described in "Psychological Death," by Robert Kastenbaum, in *Death and Dying: Current Issues in the Treatment of the Dying Person,* edited by Leonard Pearson (Cleveland and London: The Press of Case Western Reserve University, 1969).

Mrs. Roosevelt's view of life after death appears in *This I Believe,* edited by Edward P. Morgan (New York: Simon and Schuster, 1953).

Robert Kastenbaum is quoted from "When a Loved One is Dying . . . ," by James W. Hoffman, *Today's Health,* February 1972. As director of psychological research at Cushing Hospital in Massachusetts, head of Wayne State University's Center for Psychological Studies of Dying, Death, and Lethal Behavior, and now chairman of the psychology department at the University of Massachusetts in Boston, Dr. Kastenbaum has been one of the most prolific and readable writers in the field. He is editor of *New Thoughts on Old Age* (New York: Springer, 1964), co-author of *The Psychology of Death* (New York: Springer, 1972), and author of many articles and research studies. He brings a light touch to a somber field. In describing Charles Darwin's experiments with spiders —and the fact that spiders seem able to feign death when threatened— Dr. Kastenbaum notes that Darwin killed off the spiders with camphor when finished with them. "These little studies gave Darwin new respect for spiders," he says, "and, no doubt, gave spiders new respect for Darwin."

Haldane's humor is explained in *The Obituary Book,* by Alden Whitman (New York: Stein and Day, 1971).

Herman Feifel is clinical professor of psychiatry (psychology) at the University of Southern California School of Medicine. He is the editor of *The Meaning of Death* (New York: McGraw-Hill, 1959, 1965).

Elisabeth Kübler-Ross's book *On Death and Dying: What the Dying Have to Teach Doctors, Nurses, Clergy and Their Own Families* is published by Macmillan, New York, 1969.

Rollo May's *Love and Will* is published by Norton, New York, 1969.

The "bureaucratization" of death is explored in "Death and Social Structure," by Robert Blauner, *Psychiatry: Journal for the Study of Interpersonal Relations,* November 1966. Professor Blauner is a sociologist at the University of California, Berkeley.

Jessica Mitford's *The American Way of Death* (New York: Simon and Schuster, 1963) has become the standard popular work on the mortuary industry.

Robert Slater is professor and director of mortuary science, University of Minnesota, Minneapolis. The discussion of "death and the funeral director" is quoted in *Death Education* (cited in Chapter 1).

Georg Christoph Lichtenberg (1742–99) was a German physicist and satirist. See *The Reflections of Lichtenberg,* edited by Norman Alliston (London: Swan, Sonnenschein, 1908).

The University of California Study was reported by sociologist James Methieu and is cited from "When a Loved One is Dying . . . ," by James W. Hoffman, *op. cit.*

Cicely Saunders is quoted from her article "The Moment of Truth: Care of the Dying Person," in *Death and Dying,* edited by Leonard Pearson, *op. cit.*

The joke is quoted by Donald P. Irish in *Death Education, op. cit.*

The fact that about 80% of U.S. doctors don't believe in telling dying patients the truth appears in "When a Loved One is Dying . . . ," by James W. Hoffman, *op. cit.,* among other places.

Dr. Anselm L. Strauss, professor of sociology at the University of California's San Francisco Medical Center, is quoted from his article "Awareness of Dying," in *Death and Dying, op. cit.*

The American Hospital Association's "bill of rights" is reported by Leonard K. Altman in *The New York Times,* January 9, 1973.

Maurice H. Saffron is cited from "When a Loved One is Dying . . . ," by James W. Hoffman, *op cit.*

The Los Angeles neurologist is a personal acquaintance.

Freud's death is described in *Freud: Living and Dying,* by Max Schur, *op. cit.*

Charles Wertenbaker's death is described in *Death of a Man,* by Lael Tucker Wertenbaker (New York: Random House, 1957).

Harry Truman's final illness is described in *Time,* January 8, 1973.

Dr. Stelmachers's responses are quoted in *Death Education, op. cit.*

Pope Pius XII's pronouncement appears in "Prolongation of Life," *Osservatore Romano,* Vol. 4, 1957, pp. 393–98.

Dr. Robert Veatch is quoted from *Death and Dying,* by Robert Veatch (with Edward Wakin) (Chicago: Claretian Publications, n.d.).

"Death with Dignity" appears in the *AARP News Bulletin,* November 1972.

The study of requests for negative euthanasia is reported in "The Preservation of Life," by N. K. Brown, R. J. Bulger, E. H. Lawes, and D. J. Thompson, *Journal of the American Medical Association,* Vol. 211, 1970, pp. 76–82.

Dr. Robert H. Williams is an endocrinologist, University of Washington School of Medicine, Seattle. His article "Our Role in the Generation, Modification, and Termination of Life" appears in *Archives of Internal Medicine,* Vol. 124, 1969, pp. 215–37.

The British Medical Association panel statement is reported in "Geriatric Medicine," by W. Ferguson Anderson, *The British Encyclopaedia of Medical Practice* (cited in Chapter 5).

Dr. David Cappon's article "Attitudes of and Toward Dying" appears in *Canadian Medical Association Journal,* Vol. 87 (1962), pp. 693–700. Stewart Alsop's remarks appear in his column "All Will Be Well," *Newsweek,* July 31, 1972. See also his book *Stay of Execution: A Sort of Memoir* (Philadelphia: Lippincott, 1973).

Opinions about euthanasia appear in "View of the Aged on the Timing of Death," by Caroline E. Preston and Robert H. Williams, *The Gerontologist,* Winter 1971, Part I.

The quotation from Freud appears in "Thoughts for the Times on War and Death" (1915) in *The Complete Psychological Works of Sigmund Freud,* Standard Edition (London: Hogarth Press, 1961). Tolstoy made the point in another way with his deathbed remark, "I don't understand what I'm supposed to do."

The "sociology of death" is explored in *The Meaning of Death,* edited by Herman Feifel, *op. cit.* A fine review of British and U.S. research on religion and its influence on attitudes toward death appears in *Dying,* by John Hinton (Harmondsworth and Baltimore, Md.: Penguin, 1967). Hinton, a psychiatrist at the Middlesex Hospital Medical School in London, concludes that "a convinced belief in a future life by no means eradicates anxiety over death. . . . Increasingly few, it seems, are protected from the fear of death by the belief that it is not an annihilation, but the beginning of a fuller life."

The relationship of age and attitudes toward death are described in many studies. Pertinent here are *Time for Dying* (Chicago: Aldine, 1968) and "The Social Loss of Dying Patients," *American Journal of Nursing,* Vol. 64, 1964, pp. 119–21, both by Barney G. Glaser and Anselm M. Strauss; "Distance from Death as a Variable in the Study of Aging," by Morton A. Lieberman and Annie Siranne Coplan, *Developmental Psychology,* Vol. 2, No. 1, 1969, and other studies by Dr. Lieberman; and "Effects of Death Upon the Family," by Richard A. Kalish, in *Death and Dying,* edited by Leonard Pearson, *op. cit.*

Dr. Sidney Levin teaches at the Harvard Medical School. His article "Depression in the Aged: The Importance of External Factors" appears in *New Thoughts on Old Age,* edited by Kastenbaum, *op. cit.* The reporter's experience is cited from *Growing Old: The Process of Disengaegment,* by Elaine Cumming and William E. Henry (New York: Basic Books, 1961).

Psychotherapy with geriatric patients in discussed in "The Reluctant Therapist," by Robert Kastenbaum, in *New Thoughts on Old Age, op. cit.*

The "psychological autopsies" are described in "The Mental Life of Dying Geriatric Patients," by Robert Kastenbaum, *The Gerontologist,* June 1967, Part I.

The quotation from Dr. Leale appears in *Abraham Lincoln: The Prairie Years and the War Years,* by Carl Sandburg, one-volume edition (New York: Harcourt Brace, 1954).

CHAPTER 13, AGE AND ACHIEVEMENT

Information about famous persons, including ages at death, comes from various editions of standard biographies, *Encyclopaedia Britannica, Who's Who,* and *The World Almanac,* except when otherwise noted.

Age and Achievement, by Harvey C. Lehman, Volume 33 of the Memoirs of the American Philosophical Society Held at Philadelphia for Promoting Useful Knowledge, was published for the Society by Princeton University Press and in London by Oxford University Press, 1953.

Lehman's 1962 report appeared in *Journal of Gerontology,* October 1962, as "The Creative Production Rates of Present Versus Past Generations of Scientists." A later fact-and-methodology-studded answer to his critics is "The Production of Masterworks Prior to Age 30," *The Gerontologist,* March 1965, Part I, which ends on a reassuring note: "Since life should consist of far more than masterwork productions, this study provides no good reason why anyone should feel at any age level that his usefulness is at an end."

Edward Durell Stone's statement is quoted from an interview with Arthur S. Freese on the occasion of the opening of the Stone-designed Andrus Gerontology Center, University of Southern California: "The Man Who Designed It," *Modern Maturity,* February-March 1973.

Dr. Dennis B. Bromley's remarks appear in his book *The Psychology of Human Ageing* (Harmondsworth and Baltimore, Md.: Penguin, 1966).

The quotation from Lewis M. Terman appears in "Psychological Approaches to the Study of Genius," *Papers on Eugenics,* No. 4, 1947, pp. 3–29.

A fuller account of Winston Churchill's declining years appears in Simone de Beauvoir, *Old Age* (or *The Coming of Age*) (cited in Chapter 8). Mme. de Beauvoir's book is notable for its vivid treatment of the influence of age upon the thoughts, behavior, and creativity of many famous persons, among them Tolstoy, Gide, Renoir, Verdi, Gandhi, Pétain, and Victor Hugo (including a discussion of Hugo's remarkable notebooks, in which he recorded the type and frequency of "amorous performance" he enjoyed until the year of his death at age 83). Among those she studies, Georges Clemenceau perhaps had the most successful old age. His career spanned the years from the time he was war correspondent (1865) with Grant's army in the U.S. Civil War to World War I and after when he was premier of France and head of the French delegation to the Versailles Peace Conference in 1919. Called "The Tiger" because of his looks and attitudes, he was robust and active all his years until, just before his death at 88, he said, "I grow old. I am clinging to life with softened claws."

The suspicion about Stravinsky is expressed in *And Music at the Close: Stravinsky's Last Years,* by Lillian Libman (New York: Norton, 1972).

Lillian Martin is quoted in *How to Help Older People: A Guide for You and Your Family,* by Julietta K. Arthur (Philadelphia: Lippincott, 1954).

CHAPTER 14, THE GOOD LONG LIFE

H. L. Hunt's creeping formula for long life was reported by the Associated Press, September 15, 1972; Jennie Lee MacFadden's more pleasurable notion appears in *Time,* August 14, 1972. The "new passions every seven years" theory is a favorite of psychiatrist Arthur N. Foxe, who believes that an aging person should "search his mind, his heart, and his very bones to find what truly interests him" if he is to stay youthful (*Modern Maturity,* August-September 1972). Brewer's yeast is called "an incredibly nutritive food" and "a gold mine of rare vitamins and minerals to prevent degenerative disease, plus abundant nucleic acids that have been found an effective rejuvenator" (*Prevention—The Magazine for Better Health,* October 1972). In all these and related ideas, a little faith (bolstered by good genes and good nutrition) goes a long way.

For a concise and authoritative review of "Rejuvenation," see the article by David Wakefield Bishop, embryologist at the Carnegie Institution of Washington, in *Encyclopaedia Britannica,* 1967 edition, Vol. 19.

USSR longevity figures used in this chapter come from reports of the Soviet Institute of Gerontology, Kiev; the Novosti Press Agency, Moscow; and the article "Why They Live to be 100, or Even Older, in Abkhasia," by Sula Benet, *The New York Times Magazine,* December 26, 1971. Professor Benet is an anthropologist at Hunter College, New York.

Academician Chebotarev's commentary was published in *Literaturnaya Gazeta,* 39th issue, distributed by the Novosti Press Agency, and appears in abridged form in *The Gerontologist,* Winter 1971, Part I.

Stephen P. Jewett was professor emeritus in the Department of Psychiatry, New York Medical College, and chief consultant and trustee of High Point Hospital, Port Chester, N.Y. He died in 1971 at age 87, "a living example of the longevity syndrome," according to his colleague Dr. Alexander Gralnick of High Point Hospital. Dr. Jewett's article "Longevity and the Longevity Syndrome" appears in *The Gerontologist,* Spring 1973.

A highly scientific study relating smoking and the prediction of the life span appears in *Predicting Longevity: Methodology and Critique,* by Charles L. Rose and Benjamin Bell (Lexington, Mass.: Heath Lexington, 1971).

"Longevity of Prominent Men" is discussed in the Metropolitan Life *Statistical Bulletin,* January 1968.

"Very Old People in the USSR," an article prepared by the Novosti Press Agency, appears in *The Gerontologist,* Summer 1970.

Prediction of Life Span, edited by Erdman Palmore and Frances C. Jeffers, was published by Heath Lexington of Lexington, Mass., 1971.

The information about cigarette smoking and heart disease appears in "Habits and Heart Disease," by William B. Kannel, in *Prediction of Life Span, op. cit.*

The evidence that marriage increases life span is given in *Predicting Longevity,* by Rose and Bell, *op. cit.,* and in *Prediction of Life Span, op. cit.* Earlier findings are usually consistent with theirs. Hardin B. Jones, professor of medical physics and physiology at the University of California, Berkeley, drew up a comparative table of life-span differences which includes, among many factors:

Married status versus single, widowed, divorced ...	+ 5	years
Country versus city dwelling	+ 5	years
Smoking: one pack a day	− 7	years
two packs a day	−12	years
Overweight: by 25%	− 3.6	years
by 45%	− 6.6	years
by 67%	−15.1	years

"A Special Consideration of the Aging Process, Disease and Life Expectancy," by H. B. Jones, in *Advances in Biological and Medical Physics,* edited by J. H. Lawrence and C. A. Tobias (New York: Academic Press, 1956).

APPENDIX 1, EXTRAORDINARY OLD PEOPLE

Quotations from the following persons are excerpted from issues of *Modern Maturity,* copyright by the American Association of Retired Persons and used with permission:

Pearl S. Buck: "Essay on Life," by Pearl S. Buck, October-November 1971.

René Dubos: "Dr. René Dubos Speaks," by Arthur S. Freese, August-September, 1971.

Will Durant: "The Giants of Durant Castle," by Derek Gill, August-September 1972.

Arthur Fiedler: "Indefatigable Fiedler of the Pops," by Mary Sabedra, June-July 1972.

Averell Harriman: "A Visit with Averell Harriman," by Irma Hunt, December 1971-January 1972.

Karl Menninger: "A Conversation with Karl Menninger," by Flora Rheta Schreiber, April-May 1971.

Other sources:

Havergal Brian: "Life Begins at 96," *Newsweek,* August 14, 1972.

Pablo Casals: *Pablo Casals: A Biography,* by H. L. Kirk (New York: Holt, Rinehart & Winston, 1974).

Coco Chanel: *Coco Chanel: Her Life and Her Secrets,* by Marcel Hedrich (Boston: Little, Brown, 1972).

Charles Chaplin: *My Autobiography,* by Charles Chaplin (New York: Simon and Schuster, 1964).

Albert Einstein: "Profiles—The Secrets of the Old One—II," by Jeremy Bernstein, *The New Yorker*, March 17, 1973.

James A. Farley: Quoted in *Growing Old*, by Sister Marie Gaffney, MSBT, and Edward Wakin (Chicago: Claretian Publications, 1972).

Robert Frost: "Robert Frost's Last Adventure," by Stewart L. Udall, *The New York Times Magazine*, June 11, 1972.

Maurice Goudeket: Quoted in *Growing Old, op. cit.*

Helen Hayes: Quoted in *A Brighter Later Life*, by Howard Whitman (Englewood Cliffs, N.J.: Prentice-Hall, 1961).

Karl Jaspers: "An Interview with Dr. Karl Jaspers on Wisdom of Life," by Raymond Harris, *The Gerontologist*, August 1970, Part I.

Margaret Kuhn: Quoted in *International Herald Tribune*, July 24, 1973.

Jacques Lipchitz: Quoted in *The New York Times*, June 6, 1972.

Archibald MacLeish: Quoted in *A Brighter Later Life, op. cit.* Last sentence comes from *The Human Season: Selected Poems, 1926–1972*, by Archibald MacLeish (Boston: Houghton Mifflin, 1972).

André Maurois: Quoted in *The Obituary Book*, by Alden Whitman (New York: Stein and Day, 1971).

Pablo Picasso: "It takes a long time . . ." is quoted in *Tracy and Hepburn: An Intimate Memoir*, by Garson Kanin (New York: Viking, 1971), The Flanner description comes from *Paris Was Yesterday, 1925–1939*, by Janet Flanner (New York: Viking, 1972).

Eleanor Roosevelt: Quoted in *The Road to Change, 1955–59*, Vol. IV of *The Journals of David E. Lilienthal* (New York: Harper & Row, 1969).

Arthur Rubinstein: Quoted in *Tracy and Hepburn, op cit.*

Albert Schweitzer: Conversation with the author in Gabon, July 4, 1960.

Bertrand Russell: Quoted in *A Brighter Later Life, op. cit.*

Gertrude Stein: *The Third Rose: Gertrude Stein and Her World*, by John Malcolm Brinnin (Boston: Little, Brown, 1959).

Baroness Stocks: Quoted in *Age Concern Today* (London), Spring 1972.

Norman Thomas: Quoted in *The Obituary Book, op. cit.*

Dame Sibyl Thorndike: Quoted in *International Herald Tribune*, October 25, 1972.

Arnold Toynbee: *Experiences*, by Arnold J. Toynbee (London: Oxford University Press, 1969).

Edmund Wilson: *Upstate: Records and Recollections of Northern New York*, by Edmund Wilson (New York: Farrar, Straus & Giroux, 1971; London: Macmillan, 1972).

INDEX